STANDARD LOAN

UNLESS RECALLED BY ANOTHER READER
THIS ITEM MAY BE BORROWED FOR

FOUR WEEKS

the last date stamped below

TO RENEW, TELEPHONE:
01243 816 089 (BISHOP OTTER)
01243 816 099 (BOGNOR REGIS)

Educating the Gifted Child

Edited by Robert M. Povey

Harper & Row, Publishers
London

Cambridge
Hagerstown
Philadelphia
New York

San Francisco
Mexico City
Sao Paolo
Sydney

2

CONTENTS

ACKNOWLEDGEMENTS

I wish to thank the authors who have contributed to this book and the staff at Harper and Row, especially Michael Forster and Martin Creese, who have helped the book through its various stages of production. It has been a delight to work with a group of individuals who have approached the task with such interest and enthusiasm.

I am also indebted to those colleagues, authors, and publishers who have agreed to the use of their material in the book – especially in relation to the case study section (Part III). I wish to acknowledge permission to quote extracts from the following books:

Bridges, S.A. (1975) *Gifted Children and the Millfield Experiment*. Pitman. (Case Study 6)

Hitchfield, E.M. (1973) *In search of promise*. Longman. (Case Studies 1, 7, and 9)

Kellmer-Pringle, M.L. (1970) *Able Misfits*. Longman. (Case Study 2)

Ogilvie, E. (1973) *Gifted Children in Primary Schools*. Schools Council Research Studies, Macmillan Education. (Case Studies 5, 11, and 12)

Rowlands, P. (1974) *Gifted Children and Their Problems*. Dent. (Case Study 10)

Finally, I would like to thank my wife for her support and help during the compilation of the book and my daughter for her forbearance during this period.

Robert Povey

NOTES ON THE CONTRIBUTORS

Sydney Bridges
Dr. Bridges taught in schools and trained teachers in Britain, Kenya, Nigeria and Greece. His doctorate was awarded for a study of some 800 African adolescents in western Kenya. He was one of the early pioneers in exploring the problems of the gifted child in the UK and reports of the *Brentwood Experiment* and the subsequent *Millfield Experiment* were published by Pitman in 1969 and 1975, respectively. He served on the Schools Council Working Party on Gifted Children and more recently continued his studies in the USA, South Africa, and Greece where he was Director of Studies at Campion School in Athens. He completed his chapter for this book just a few months before he died.

Ralph Callow
Ralph Callow is Senior Lecturer in Education at Edge Hill College of Higher Education, Ormskirk. He is Tutor to the Advanced Certificate Course on Gifted and Talented Children. Previously he was a primary school teacher and class teacher for the experimental group of gifted children in the enquiry reported by Tempest (1974): *Teaching Clever Children 7–11*.

Henry Collis

Henry Collis was a head master for 28 years, finishing at St. Paul's Preparatory School, London. He has been Chairman of the Incorporated Association of Preparatory Schools and from 1973 to 1979 was Director of the National Association for Gifted Children. He was coordinator of the First World Conference on Gifted Children held in London in 1975 and reported in Gibson and Chennells (1976). He is also a member of the Executive Committee of the World Council for Gifted and Talented Children.

Peter Congdon

Dr. Congdon is an Educational Psychologist with Warwickshire County Council. He has been an advisory remedial teacher and previously taught for twelve years in primary schools and in schools for ESN and partially sighted children. He is director of North Warwickshire Equestrian Centre which organizes riding for the disabled and also of the Gifted Children's Information Centre (address on page 147) which publishes his bookets on various aspects of giftedness. He is also author of *Phonic Skills and their Measurement* (published by Blackwell in 1974).

Joan Freeman

Joan Freeman is Senior Lecturer in Applied Psychology (Education) at Preston Polytechnic. She has been a teacher and school counsellor and is an Associate Member of the British Psychological Society. She has written and lectured extensively on the education of gifted children and was Director of the Gulbenkian Research Project. She is author of *In and Out of School* (Methuen, 1975) and the full report of the Gulbenkian Project – *Gifted children: their identification and development in a social context* – was published in 1979 by Medical Technical Press, Lancaster, and in the USA by University Parks Press, Baltimore.

Michal Hambourg

Michal Hambourg is a concert pianist who started her career at the age of eleven years. She is the daughter of a distinguished pianist, the late Mark Hambourg, and she comes from a musical family with many international links. She is especially interested in the problems of young musicians and is the music counsellor of the National Association for Gifted Children.

Denis Lawrence

Denis Lawrence is a psychology graduate and an Associate Member of the

British Psychological Society. He taught for five years in primary and secondary schools before being appointed Educational Psychologist for the City of Sheffield in 1960. Later he worked in the same capacity for Cornwall County Council before taking up an appointment in Somerset where he is now Chief Educational Psychologist. He is author of *Improved Reading through Counselling* (Ward-Lock, 1973), *Somerset Developmental Check List* (Good Reading Ltd., 1977), and *Counselling Students with Reading Difficulties* (Good Reading Ltd., 1978).

Vernon Mallinson

Vernon Mallinson is Professor Emeritus of Comparative Education in the University of Reading and was created *Officer de L'Ordre de Léopold* for services rendered to Belgium both during and after World War II. He has been Visiting Professor at the Universities of Syracuse (N.Y.), Missouri, and British Columbia. He is also a founder member of the Comparative Education Society in Europe and past President of its British section. He has contributed to several educational journals and among his published works are *The Adolescent at School* (Heinemann, 1949), *Teaching a Modern Language* (Heinemann, 1953), *None Can Be Called Deformed* (Heinemann, 1956), *An Introduction to the Study of Comparative Education* (Heinemann, 1957 – 4th ed. 1975), *Power and Politics in Belgian Education* (Heinemann, 1963), *Modern Belgian Literature* (Heinemann, 1966), and *Belgium* (Benn, 1969).

Eric Ogilvie

Dr. Ogilvie is Director of Nene College, Northampton. He spent twelve years in schools as a teacher and head master, and eight years training teachers. He was Director of the Schools Council project *Gifted Children in Primary Schools* (published by Macmillan for the Schools Council in 1973) and more recently he has been responsible for the *Schools Council Curriculum Enrichment Project*. This project has resulted in the development of a range of teaching materials which are being published by the Schools Council.

Frieda Painter

Formerly a grammar school teacher, Frieda Painter is a part-time counsellor for the Open University and currently seconded teacher for gifted children in Hertfordshire. She is an active member of the National Association for Gifted Children and chairs the Research Subcommittee of the council. Following the publication of her recent research on the attainment and interests of gifted children in the primary school (Painter, 1977), she is currently engaged on another study of gifted children within the comprehensive school setting. This research is being undertaken under the auspices of the NAGC.

Robert Povey

Dr. Povey is Principal Lecturer in Education at Christ Church College, Canterbury, and a Fellow of the British Psychological Society. He was a teacher and educational psychologist before entering the sphere of teacher education and was involved in selecting the experimental group in the early stages of the *Brentwood Experiment* (Bridges, 1969). He is author of *Intellectual Abilities* and *Exceptional Children* (both published by Hodder and Stoughton in 1972). He has published several research papers concerned with the assessment of teaching performance, concept development in young children, and the education of the gifted.

Peter Renshaw

Before becoming head master of the Yehudi Menuhin School in 1975 Peter Renshaw taught in a London comprehensive school, in two colleges of education, and in the University of Leeds Institute of Education. His main areas of research were philosophy of education and the teacher education curriculum. For two years he was editor of the journal *Education for Teaching*. His publications include several journal articles and contributions to the following books: *Dear Lord James. A Critique of Teacher Education* (ed. T. Burgess, Penguin, 1971), *The Future of Teacher Education* (ed. J.W. Tibble, Routledge & Kegan Paul, 1971), *The Education of Teachers in Britain* (ed. D. Lomax, Wiley, 1973), *Curriculum Development in Physical Education* (ed. J.E. Kane, Crosby, Lockwood, Staples, 1976).

Susan Roberts

After graduating in psychology Susan Roberts acted as research assistant to Professor K.J. Connolly at the University of Sheffield, looking into the development of motor skills in children. She then taught as an infant school teacher before qualifying as an Educational Psychologist. Since 1971 she has worked for Essex County Council as Educational Psychologist with particular responsibility for the gifted. She was involved in the formation of the Essex Working Party on Gifted Children in 1971 and is currently Chairman of that group.

Felicity Sieghart
Felicity Sieghart has been Chairman of the Council of Management of the National Association for Gifted Children since 1973 and is coorganizer of the Association's voluntary counselling service. She was also a member of the Executive Council of the UK Association for the International Year of the Child.

Belle Wallace
For ten years Belle Wallace taught biology in a large comprehensive school where she held a senior post of responsibility for pastoral care. As a member of the Essex Working Party on Gifted Children since 1972, she has been closely involved with the development of enrichment materials particularly in the field of biology. She is also conducting research into the role of the World Education Fellowship Movement in the development of progressive education. In September 1978 she took up the post of Advisory Teacher for Gifted Children in Essex.

INTRODUCTION

spec. needs

Who are the children with special educational needs? When educators are considering this question the gifted often remain on the periphery of their deliberations. The 1978 Warnock Report on children with *Special Educational Needs*, for example, specifically excludes the gifted from its terms of reference. Similarly, the views of many teachers can be summarized by the phrase (DES, 1977): 'They can quite well look after themselves'. Unfortunately, in this rather arid educational climate gifted children all too frequently do not look after themselves. Their budding promise fails to blossom and they become, as Suzanne Wiener put it in a *Times Educational Supplement* review article (11 February 1977), 'victims of benign neglect [drifting] rudderless in a sea of conventional teaching'.

It seems appropriate at this time, therefore, to restate the basic fact that each individual child requires the education most suited to his particular needs. Every child has special educational needs and this central pedagogical principle is as relevant to the child who has above-average abilities as to the child in the below-average range. The move towards comprehensive systems of schooling and mixed-ability teaching has given added emphasis to this principle. The challenge posed to teachers and administrators is to find ways of organizing the school system and of developing teaching approaches which will meet the needs of individual children from the brightest to the least able. This book attempts to offer some help in this process. Part I considers research and practice in the education of gifted children at both national and international levels but with an emphasis on developments in Britain. Part II examines some of the techniques and strategies in helping gifted children, and Part III provides some illustrative case studies. By providing a collection of findings and ideas from re-searchers, teachers, psychologists, counsellors, administrators, and parents concerned with the gifted we hope we might help to advance the practical expertise of such groups in handling the gifted child.

One reason for the reluctance of educators to consider the specific needs of the gifted is that the definition of giftedness has remained somewhat woolly and imprecise. In Chapter 1 of the book I have tried to tease out the separate strands of this concept and to provide an overview of research and practice in the education of the gifted. We have concentrated in the remain-der of the book on the intellectually able child, the child who comes in the top 2 to 3 per cent of his age group on intelligence tests. On most recently standardized intelligence tests this will be represented by a score of 130+ and it is salutary to remember that there are as many children in this 'high-IQ' range as in the range of the educationally subnormal (IQ 70 and below). The book also touches occasionally on the education of children gifted in specific areas such as music – the sort of children who are some-times referred to as 'talented' to distinguish them from the 'gifted' or 'high-IQ' child.

In Chapter 2 Frieda Painter discusses the characteristics of gifted children at home and at school, comparing their behaviour and school performance with a bright-average control group. Her findings are based, for the most part, on a questionnaire study of the views of parents, teachers, and primary school pupils. The chapter draws particular attention to the extent to which gifted children are underfunctioning in the classroom. Chapter 3 then looks at the role of the local education authority in the education of the gifted child. In this context Denis Lawrence reports findings from a survey of the views and practices of LEAs in England and Wales. The questionnaire was based on Dr. Ogilvie's (1973) survey of LEAs and we were, therefore, able to make one or two comparisons between the 1973 and 1979 surveys.

The place of special schooling in the education of the gifted is considered by Peter Renshaw in Chapter 4. He argues for a flexible system of educa-tional provision for the gifted and, as head master of the Yehudi Menuhin School, provides a glimpse into the aims and organization of this school for musically talented children. Catering for the musically gifted is also a topic considered by Michal Hambourg in Chapter 5 on the role of the National Association for Gifted Children. This chapter also contains a description by Felicity Sieghart of a counselling service for less specific groups of gifted children and a discussion of the function of the NAGC by its first director, Henry Collis.

In Chapter 6 Joan Freeman discusses the Gulbenkian Research Project on 'gifted children in a social context'. Her findings cast considerable doubt on the notion that 'high-IQ' children are more likely to present behavioural difficulties than other children. 'The wiser the waywarder' (*As You Like It*, Act IV, Scene 1) is undoubtedly applicable in a number of individual instances, but as a general rule the findings from research do not support this view.

Part of the international scene is surveyed in Chapter 7 by Vernon Mallinson. Because of the confines of space we have concentrated in the main on a comparison of the USA and the USSR, and on developments in Western Europe, examining issues from the viewpoint of a comparative educationist. For readers wishing to find descriptions of current practices in countries not covered in this chapter, Section 3 in Gibson and Chennells (1976) may be of interest.

Part II of the book begins with Chapter 8 by Ralph Callow on the recognition of gifted children. As the class teacher of the group of gifted children in the Tempest (1974) experiment he can lay claim to be amongst the most experienced British teachers of the gifted child in the normal classroom and as such he outlines a strategy for identifying the gifted schoolchild. Chapter 9 looks at some considerations relevant to the development of teaching materials for the gifted. In particular it describes some of the ideas and approaches developed by Susan Roberts and Belle Wallace in Essex. Peter Congdon then develops his suggestions for parents in relation to handling the gifted child (Chapter 10). This chapter is based on a paper Dr. Congdon gave to the second International Conference on the Gifted and Talented in San Francisco (1977).

The work of Sydney Bridges is well known even to those who have only a nodding acquaintance with research on the gifted. My first appointment as an educational psychologist was in Essex when George Robb was county psychologist and Sydney Bridges was head of education at the Brentwood College of Education. One of my earliest tasks was to interview some of the children who were being suggested as possible candidates for what became known as the Brentwood Experiment (Bridges, 1969). Since that time Dr.

Bridges has conducted similar experiments at Millfield School (Bridges, 1975) and more recently at Campion School in Athens. Chapter 11 reports some of the work he has been doing at Campion. In Chapter 12, Eric Ogilvie discusses the Schools Council Curriculum Enrichment Project. This enterprise was set up as a direct consequence of Dr. Ogilvie's major Schools Council survey on *Gifted Children in Primary Schools* (Ogilvie, 1973).

In Part III of the book I have compiled a selection of case studies, some original and some from existing texts. Most of the references relate to intellectual giftedness but I have also included one or two cases concerning the emergence of musical talent. Reference is made to these case studies throughout the book and it is hoped that they will help to illuminate some of the main points in the text. The majority of case studies may also serve simply as a useful indicator of the type of child referred to in the text as 'high-IQ' or 'intellectually gifted'.

Whether it is desirable or necessary to identify the children themselves in these terms is another matter, of course, and one about which a number of teachers and research workers are increasingly concerned. It is likely, as Joan Freeman points out in Chapter 6, that the act of labelling the child will have an effect on the child's behaviour and this effect may not always be beneficial. In some cases it might result in a useful rise in self-esteem but in others it can produce priggishness or self-consciousness. Some people prefer to use the term 'bright' rather than 'gifted' when referring to the 'high-IQ' child in an attempt to reduce the 'élitist' flavour of the term, and it may be that the use of such a term would be rather more acceptable to the teaching profession in general. In any case such labels are probably best seen as shorthand classificatory devices for use by professionals in carrying out their teaching and advisory roles. They may well help to draw attention to the presence of such children in the ordinary classroom and thus facilitate adequate identification and provision. The important point, however, is that, whatever terms we use, teachers and parents should recognize and nurture the special abilities of each individual child so that such valuable potential is not retarded but released and realized to the full.

Robert M. Povey

Part I

**Research and Practice in the Education
of Gifted Children**

CHAPTER ONE

EDUCATING THE GIFTED CHILD: AN OVERVIEW
Robert Povey

The problem of definition

Is 'bloafed' as good as 'gifted'?

John White (1970) writes that 'any person is "bloafed" if he is either over six foot tall or over six foot wide or had from an early age some outstandingly large physical feature, e.g., head, foot, thumb, nose or chin.' He constructed this novel concept in order to draw attention to what he maintains is the similarly artificial and arbitrary nature of the concept 'gifted'. White contrasts his definition of 'bloafed' with an example of the type of hotch-potch definition often applied to the term 'gifted': 'a child is labelled "gifted" if either he has a high IQ or he has a very high score on a so-called "creativity" test, or he shows at an early age some specific ability, e.g., in maths, music, painting or social leadership' (c.f. the review of definitions in Shields, 1968, chapter 1).

Such definitions of 'giftedness' clearly do lay themselves open to criticisms that they are contrived and conceptually 'impure'. Educationists appear to be striving to unify under one heading almost as many aspects of high individual achievement as one can imagine. A good example of this tendency is the definition offered in the 57th Year Book of the National

Society for the Study of Education: 'the talented or gifted child is one who shows consistently remarkable performance in any worthwhile line of endeavour. Thus, we shall include not only the intellectually gifted but also those who show promise in music, the graphic arts, creative writing, dramatics, mechanical skills and social leadership' (Havighurst *et al.*, 1958). Despite the obvious attempt to reach a comprehensive and widely acceptable definition of giftedness, however, there is still a strongly arbitrary feel about the definition. Why, for example, should social leadership be included and sport left out? Such definitions in fact appear to carry the concept of 'giftedness' very little further. They have the benefit of a certain 'broadness of definition' but run the risk of achieving an almost never-ending elasticity in order to keep up their comprehensiveness so that at some point they become more of a hinderance than a help.

Operational definitions

In order to introduce greater precision into the definition of 'giftedness' then, perhaps one should turn to some of the 'operational definitions' provided by research workers in this field. This ought to help in clarifying the terminology to some extent and it does so in the context of each individual study. Unfortunately, however, individual studies tend to offer operational definitions at variance with each other (see the review of definitions by Getzels and Dillon, 1973). Thus Terman (1925), in his pioneering longitudinal study of gifted children, took as his main cut-off point the top 1 per cent of the population using an IQ of 140 or above on the Stanford-Binet Intelligence Scale as the criterion score for inclusion in his research group. In the final sample, however, a number of children with lower IQ scores (130 being the lowest) were also included. Several researchers have taken an IQ of 130 as their chosen cut-off point using tests such as the Wechsler Intelligence Scale (see, for example, Tempest, 1974); and some researchers have used still lower cut-off points. For example, in the sample of 'gifted children' studied by Hitchfield (1973) over half the children had IQs below 130 on the WISC. Burt (1975) emphasizes the same point and states in Kellmer-Pringle and Varma (1974) that 'in many post-war enquiries a variety of borderlines are used: thus terms like "bright", "gifted", and their various synonyms may denote the top 5, 10, 20, or even 25 per cent of the school population.'

So one still finds disagreement about the definition of the term 'gifted', even in a restricted sphere of enquiry such as the study of children who perform well on intelligence tests. The IQ cut-off points taken to denote 'giftedness' are chosen in an arbitrary way from study to study. Yet such cut-off points frequently become rigid demarcation lines in the minds of readers with little knowledge of intelligence testing. Student teachers in my experience frequently interpret these arbitrary cut-off points as if they embody absolute truths. Essays begin with dogmatic statements such as 'The gifted child has an IQ of 140 or over' or 'The gifted child has an IQ of 130+.' Usually the essential qualifying statements are lacking (e.g., information about the particular research project involved, which tests were used, and what was the Mean and Standard Deviation of the test). Moreover, some people seem to believe quite genuinely that if a child has an IQ score of 140 (or 130) he is in some God-given way 'gifted', but that if he has a score of only 139 (or 129) then he ceases to be 'gifted'!

In the researcher's terms, of course, the children gaining relatively lower IQ scores might be labelled 'nongifted'. Such definitions of 'giftedness' or 'nongiftedness' constructed in an artificial research context, however, too easily become translated by the teacher into 'rule-of-thumb' judgements which may lead to consequences of considerable practical importance for individual pupils. This points to the dangers of naivety in the interpretation of research data and emphasizes the importance of teachers being able to appreciate the artificial and arbitrary nature of many 'operational definitions' which can take on the appearance of indisputable fact to the uninitiated. It also emphasizes the importance of introducing teachers to some of the basic principles relating to the interpretation of test scores – to such concepts, for example, as the standard error of measurement (see Povey, 1972a).

One is forced then to the conclusion that there is probably little to be gained from the search for an entirely acceptable definition of the term 'gifted' which will embrace all the elements considered by researchers. As Getzels and Dillon (1973) maintain: 'The term "giftedness" is a rubric for several populations of children and for an increasing body of scientific knowledge about them. In doing a study one should specify the definition and the population to which it applies; in examining a study one should take careful note of these specifications; and in comparing the results of several studies one should accommodate their definitions and populations or refrain from comparing them.'

Some common factors

Despite such reservations, however, it is clear that there is a good deal of overlap between many of the studies of gifted children and, without searching for an exhaustive or all-embracing definition, it is possible to suggest some common factors which might help to unify certain aspects of research work on 'giftedness'. To a large degree, in fact, the definition criticized by White (1970) does offer a useful bird's eye view of the areas in which research work has been undertaken, *viz*. (1) work with 'high-IQ' children; (2) work with children who score highly on 'open-ended' tests and (3) work with 'talented' children, i.e., those who show exceptional talent in a specific area such as music or ballet.

For such statements about relevant areas of study to reach a degree of acceptability as 'definitions of giftedness', of course, it would be necessary to consider each of the areas separately and to introduce a much greater degree of specificity and precision into the terminology adopted. Unfortunately the introduction of such precision is only really feasible, at the present stage of research development, in relation to 'high-IQ' research and, as we have already seen, the task is complicated even here by the wide range of high-IQ children studied. It is possible, however, to introduce some precision by ignoring several studies which take an anomalous viewpoint of the most appropriate IQ cut-off point. Thus, in general, one finds that a great many of the most respectable studies of 'high-IQ' children have taken a cut-off point somewhere within the region of the top $2\frac{1}{2}$ per cent of children, or IQ 130+ on an intelligence test with a Mean of 100 and Standard Deviation of 15 points (see, for example, Bridges, 1969; Burt, 1975; Tempest, 1974; Vernon *et al.*, 1977; also Chapter 3). It is possible, therefore, to make fairly meaningful comparisons between studies which take this uniform stance.

As far as the second and third categories are concerned, however, it is much less easy to introduce precision or to make comparisons between studies in these areas of high achievement. Difficulties arise, for example, in the case of open-ended tests because of the wide range of tests employed and in relation to talented children because of a lack of uniformity in the types of skill considered. Similar problems are presented in both cases by the variety of criteria adopted by researchers in selecting their research samples. Another particular difficulty in relation to 'open-ended' tests (such as those used in the very interesting studies of Hudson, 1966, 1968) concerns the poor intercorrelation between such tests. It is claimed (Guilford, 1950, 1967) that open-ended tests assess what is called 'divergent-thinking ability' as opposed to 'convergent thinking' which is assessed in traditional intelligence tests. Yet the intercorrelations between the separate open-ended tests have often been found to be so slim (see e.g., Getzels and Jackson, 1962;

Hudson, 1966) that some doubt is cast upon the 'unity' of the concept of 'divergent thinking'. Similarly, there appears to exist only a tenuous relationship between the tests and what we call 'creativity' in real life, a point I have discussed elsewhere in dealing with the 'convergent/divergent' distinction (Povey, 1972a, paras. 31–34; and 1972b, paras. 59–60; see also Butcher, 1968; Heim, 1970; Lytton, 1971).

In general, therefore, the 'high-IQ' studies appear to offer the most cohesive group of research investigations into gifted children and the only studies which allow anything approaching common yet reasonably precise terms of reference. It is to these studies then that the rest of this book will make most reference and, when discussing 'gifted children', unless stated otherwise (as, for example, in Chapter 4), these will be 'high-IQ' children.

The characteristics of gifted children

The highly intelligent child used to be popularly represented 'as puny, and bespectacled, as precocious in language interests as he is retarded in his emotional development, liable to over-fatigue, difficult to get on with, and so on' (Wall, 1960a). The wide reporting of the work of researchers such as Terman (1925) and Parkyn (1948), however, and the increasing tendency on the part of journalists and the media to espouse the cause of the gifted (see, for example, Branch and Cash, 1966) has effectively dispelled this view. The work of Terman probably provided the main conterbalance to the 'puny, bespectacled' image of the gifted child. Terman and his associates undertook a longitudinal study of gifted children in California, following the group from childhood through adult life. The findings have been reported in five volumes in the series *Genetic Studies of Genius*, the first being produced by Terman in 1925. The fifth volume by Terman and Oden appeared in 1959. Numerous research papers have also reported aspects of the project. Lewis Terman himself died in 1956 but his work was taken over at Stanford University by Robert Sears and the follow-up studies are planned to continue into the 'retirement' phase and also to include studies of the children of the gifted group. Amongst the most recent reports are those concerning the sources of life satisfaction of the Terman men (Sears, 1977) and women (Sears and Barbee, 1977). The data for these reports were collected when the majority of the group were in their sixties.

The experimental group in the Terman study comprised 643 children (352 boys and 291 girls). All had IQs on the Stanford-Binet Intelligence Test of 130 or above and the majority had IQs over 140. The experimental group did not consist of the total population of high-IQ children in Californian schools and cannot be considered entirely representative of this group. It did, however, provide a very substantial group of high-IQ children on which a vast amount of data was amassed over a long period of time. The findings from the research project have also tended to be confirmed by projects of similar but smaller dimensions, such as that of Parkyn (1948) in New Zealand. The initial findings indicated that the children were above average in physical development, social adjustment, and school achievement. The later reports also indicate that the children tended to maintain this above-average level of achievement, thus contradicting the theory of 'early ripe, early rot'. Similarly, the findings offer no support for the widely held belief that high-IQ children are often poorly adjusted; they show that the social adjustment of the gifted group remained above average. (For further discussion of the 'adjustment' issue see Chapter 6.) One interesting finding from the recent study of the gifted men at average age sixty-two (Sears, 1977) challenges another frequently held view that 'middle-class males are obsessed with their work and get most of their life's satisfaction from it'. The group considered work to be important but satisfaction from family life was judged to be rather more important.

As far as family background is concerned, Terman's findings indicate an association between socio-economic background and IQ, the experimental sample including a higher proportion of children from the upper socio-economic groupings than from the lower. It should be stressed, however, that what we are dealing with is the *proportion* of children from any particular socio-economic grouping and not *absolute* numbers, a point often overlooked in discussion of the background features of the gifted. As Vernon (1977) argues: 'the *proportion* of children of professional and business parents who are bright is indeed much higher than the proportion of children of lower-class parents. But the actual number of bright children who come from less privileged families is as large, or even larger, simply because, in the total population there are far more clerical and manual workers than higher-class parents.' This is a point which teachers need to keep firmly in mind since expectations based solely on parental occupation can be quite misleading. It is the *nature* of the home environment rather than its technical rating on an artificial occupational classification which will determine its influence on the child's development. In this respect it is salutary to recall that some of the most able individuals have come from the most humble, manual-working-class backgrounds. Illingworth and Illingworth (1966), for example, describe the backgrounds of a number of highly gifted individuals, some of whom came from very poor home backgrounds. Amongst these are Michael Faraday whose father was a journeyman blacksmith and Carl Gauss, 'the Prince of Mathematicians', whose father, an uncouth bricklayer, tried to resist his son's attempts to acquire an education suited to his abilities and interests. The important lesson to be drawn from such histories is that giftedness can thrive in all kinds of environments. (Contrast Case Studies 7 and 8 in Part III.) The stimulating effect of a good home, whatever the social class, can be a great benefit to the child's development, but poverty and frustration can also act as a spur to achievement in the same way that wealth may sometimes stifle endeavour.

The factors which make for the emergence of high ability and matching achievement are clearly both genetic and environmental with chance and opportunity playing a major role at times. Genetic factors can explain more readily than environmental factors such ancestral quirks as the emergence of high-ability children from low-ability parents and vice versa. (See Part III, Case Study 8.) On the other hand, environmental factors will determine how far inherited potential is realized. 'Heredity deals the cards and environment determines how they are played,' as the saying goes. Terman probably overemphasized the genetic side of these interacting forces, although he recognized that many of his gifted group, despite their high potential, failed to achieve more than moderate success in their chosen spheres of activity, and very few, if any, could be classified in the 'genius' category.

A high IQ may help to equip an individual with the basic requirements for high achievement in a particular field of endeavour, but the realization of that achievement will require the sustenance of a supporting (or sometimes 'provoking') environment. It will also require the intermixing of high or moderately high intelligence with personality factors of various kinds. This intermixing is clearly a very complex process (see, for example, Hudson, 1966, 1968). However, in addition to good general ability, the successful recipe is likely to include both 'catalytic' ingredients such as imagination, open-mindedness, and flexibility and 'basic' ingredients such as persistence, single-mindedness, and application.

Partly as a result of the findings from such large-scale research projects as those of Terman and Parkyn we now seem to have moved from a situation in which the gifted child was seen as an academic wizard but a clumsy weakling to one in which the pendulum has swung rather drunkenly in the opposite direction. Nowadays, for example, one tends to find student teachers using descriptions of gifted children from research reports of the *average tendencies* shown by *groups* of high-IQ children, when compared with children of lower IQ. These descriptions, usually carefully qualified by the authors as average tendencies, are then reported with unqualified gusto by students as unshakeable characteristics of *all* gifted children.

A favourite passage with students is the following from Shields (1968): 'They possess, in addition to their high intelligence, strong drives to do well; they are healthy, energetic, cheerful, sociable, popular and regarded as leaders. They are inventive, possess commonsense, an eye for beauty and a stable temperament; they show a sense of humour and a sense of modesty. The are sympathetic, generous, conscientious and truthful, and also show qualities of prudence and perseverence.' The fact that in their own experience many of these students have come across *individual* pupils who are highly intelligent, wear glasses, are rather puny and useless at mechanical pursuits, etc. does not, however, deter them from expecting the average findings from groups of children to apply to each individual case of high intelligence. It is probably apposite to state, therefore, at this stage in the development of research into giftedness that the image of children of 'pure gold' conveyed by the glowing descriptions of authors of books on gifted children is as fictitious when applied to individual cases as were the earlier descriptions of the puny and bespectacled child. It is also important to bear in mind the qualifications made by Wall (1960a) that although the able child tends to be superior to the average in a number of ways, not only in performance on intelligence tests, 'the degree of superiority to the average is not the same in all fields and is greatest in those most closely related to what we understand by intelligence – originality, intellectual interests, achievement test results.' It is also clear that when the gifted group is looked at as a collection of individuals, then one finds 'the same infinite variety of patterns as in any other group, and examples can be found of personality defect, social maladjustment, behaviour problems and physical handicaps of various kinds' (see also Illingworth and Illingworth, 1966; Kellmer-Pringle, 1970; and Part III, Case Studies 2 and 10).

The handicap of brilliance

George Robb has discussed some of the problems facing gifted children in terms of the 'handicap' of brilliance (see chapter 9 in Branch and Cash, 1966; also Robb, 1974). This interesting juxtaposition of terms which are more likely to be found in opposition highlights the fact that children who are intellectually gifted may nevertheless sometimes be handicapped in their home or school environments. At home the gifted child may sometimes appear as a 'fish out of water', a child with abilities and interests quite outside the experience of his parents and brothers and sisters. (See Part III, Case Study 8.) This can, of course, bring great pleasure and a wealth of rewarding experiences to both the child and his family, but it can also impose considerable strain upon their relationships (Rowlands, 1974). Similarly, intellectual maturity can offer no clear guarantee against poor emotional and social adjustment and the gifted child may experience considerable frustration as a result of his comparative immaturity in such spheres (Kellmer-Pringle, 1970).

At school one of the main handicaps is the tendency of teachers to provide gifted children with learning programmes geared towards the 'average child'. (See Part III, Case Study 5.) Learning programmes of this type are insufficiently challenging for children of well-above-average capabilities who are, therefore, likely to waste much of their time in schools which provide such inappropriate teaching. According to an estimate by Hollingsworth (1942), writing about the American child in an ordinary elementary school situation, 'children of IQ 140 waste half their time. Those above IQ 170 waste practically all of their time.' A gifted child may thus tend to become bored and may 'opt out' of such a situation by engaging in pursuits of his own making. These may have some educational benefit on occasions but they may also simply serve to disrupt the class and antagonize teacher/pupil relationships.

A gifted child may also tend to 'coast along' at school doing what is required to achieve commendation by the teacher but no more and by no means sufficient to realize the potential in educational achievement of which he is capable. As Tempest (1974) says: 'Children soon learn to meet expectations and if a gifted child can easily and quickly do what is required of him and, in so doing, win the approval of teacher and parent, why should he do more?' Having been conditioned by the school context to do exactly what is required of him and no more, the child settles for doing what Bridges (1969) describes as 'the stint'. In discussing some of the work carried out with groups of gifted children who were brought together for special classes one afternoon a week at the Brentwood College of Education, Bridges observes that the standard of written work was somewhat disappointing. 'The tendency was for the work to be churned out with the least possible manifestation of interest or of response to a challenge.' He postulates that this behaviour might be related to school situations in which children appear to be conditioned into a satisfactory acceptance of limited, rather 'convergent', and unadventurous written work.

Another 'handicap' which is sometimes discussed (see, for example, Bridges, 1969, chapter 3) relates to the fact that these highly intelligent children are usually educated within their chronological age group which means that they lack the stimulation of contact with individuals who are their 'intellectual peers'. Similarly, the fact that the prevailing standards of achievement in the child's class are generally rather below the sort of standards he is capable of reaching may occasionally result in the child 'playing down' his capabilities and conforming to these standards in order to avoid the danger of becoming isolated from his friends (Bridges, 1969; DES, 1978). The more likely handicap which such a child might suffer, however, would be the lack of a sufficiently perceptive teacher to recognize his abilities since many teachers appear to give reward and recognition to children showing assiduous and conforming behaviour rather than behaviour indicative of high intelligence.

There is some disagreement amongst researchers, however, about the extent to which teachers fail to identify children of high intelligence. Hitchfield (1973), for example, concludes that the results of her study 'indicate that criticisms of the failure of teachers to identify and provide for the most able children are probably being made on a few extreme cases since the majority of such children were found to be known and catered for satisfactorily.' Other researchers, however, starting with Terman (1925) and including more recently Pegnato and Birch (1959), Tempest (1974), and Painter (1976), report evidence to show that teachers often seem to have a very limited ability to pick out 'high-IQ' children. As far as British studies are concerned, the evidence reported by Hitchfield seems rather less convincing than that of Tempest on this point.

Hitchfield's research utilizes some of the data collected by the National Children's Bureau as part of its longitudinal study of children born in England, Scotland, and Wales during one week in March, 1958 (see also Chapter 10). She selected a group of these children for study as gifted children and her book contains some most illuminating examples of individual cases (see Part III, Case Studies 1, 7, and 9). The criteria used in the selection of this group of eleven-year-old children, however, do not comply with the criteria most usually adopted for the selection of 'high-IQ' children of the type studied by Tempest and others (viz., children in the top $2\frac{1}{2}$ per cent of the IQ range). They were selected on the evidence obtained when the children were seven years old and on such criteria as above-average performance on the Goodenough Draw-a-Man Test, teachers' estimates of children's above-average attainment in reading and number work, and on parents' recommendation. No intelligence test data were utilized since the children had not been given any such tests at the seven-year age level. On the other hand, when the children were studied at the age of eleven they were given the shortened form of the WISC and this revealed that 42 per cent of the boys and 64 per cent of the girls had IQs of less than 130. To draw conclusions about gifted 'high-IQ' children from such a sample seems to require a return to a rather unacceptable degree of elasticity of definition.

Hitchfield attempts to argue that the gifted children as a group were being identified by their teachers as above average at the age of eleven. She takes the term 'above average', however, to denote 'the top 6–30 per cent of their age group', a definition which would place a good number of the children in the 'average' range on the most usually accepted interpretation of percentage ratings (see Povey, 1972a, appendix 2). Yet, even if one ignores such odd use of terms, the evidence hardly seems to support the argument. For example, 60 per cent of the gifted children were not regarded by their teachers as 'exceptionally good' in any of the areas selected for study at eleven, e.g., use of books, maths, oral ability, general knowledge (Hitch-field, 1973, chapter 5), and nearly half (45 per cent) of the children with IQs of 140 plus, including 4 with IQs of 150+, were not rated by their teachers as in the top 5 per cent in any of these areas (chapter 15). Similarly, 21 per cent of the children in the sample with IQs over 130 would not have been included if the data relating to teacher's estimates of ability only had been considered – these children emerged in response to a request for parents to write to the bureau if they had a 'gifted' child born in the sample week.

This evidence seems, at the very least, therefore, equivocal, and much of it might well be taken to support the argument that teachers are not good at identifying children with high intellectual ability. Taken in conjunction with the other evidence available – for example Tempest's (1974) study which showed that out of 72 children nominated by their infant school teachers as gifted, more than half had IQs below 127 on Young's Non-Readers Intelligence Test (Young, 1964) – the more reasonable interpretation of Hitchfield's findings would seem to be that it points to teachers' poor recognition of high intelligence in their pupils. (For further discussion of this point see Chapter 8.)

Although it is clear, therefore, that gifted children can be regarded as 'handicapped' in certain ways, it would be foolish to suggest that they suffer a handicap in the same sort of way that one might talk about the handicap of educational subnormality. Since they represent opposing ends of the 'normal distribution curve' in relation to IQ scores, it is tempting to argue, of course, that each requires similar provision, so that if it is right to provide special schooling for the ESN it is also right to provide special schooling for the gifted. Indeed the use of the term 'severely gifted' has recently been employed to highlight the handicaps which some gifted children suffer as a consequence of their exceptional talent. Anyone who has had any contact with severely subnormal children, however, would be quick to dispel the view that the two types of 'handicap' can be considered in quite the same light. For even when a gifted child may make less than full use of his potential capabilities and is ill-served by his school or home environment, his educational horizons are boundless when compared with the horizons of the very low-IQ child whose progress even towards the acquisition of intelligible speech may be almost entirely dependent upon the presence of dedicated parents and teachers. It is important, therefore, to view the gifted child in his own right and to examine the efficacy of various educational approaches.

What educational provision do the gifted require?

The arguments concerning possible methods of dealing with gifted pupils in schools are well established (see, for example, the excellent discussion in Wall, 1960b). The main approaches are those of segregation, acceleration, and enrichment (see Povey, 1972b).

Segregation

Arguments concerning the merits of segregating gifted children into special schools tend to founder on the rocks of 'élitism'. As Lord James of Rusholme has argued in Bereday and Lauwerys (1961): 'Vague democratic sentiments have made us reluctant to admit wide divergences of intellectual ability', and yet we must recognize such differences if we are to identify and nourish talents which are amongst a nation's most valuable natural resources. Even if such recognition is given, however, it is still by no means clear that the most satisfactory way of caring for the intellectually gifted is to cream them off into special schools for gifted children. The unfair effects of rigid selection are well established (see, for example, Barker-Lunn, 1970; Douglas, 1964). Such studies show that pupils of similar ability may nevertheless have uneven chances of gaining selection to 'A' streams or grammar schools according to their socio-economic background, children from upper socio-economic groups having a better chance of selection than children from lower socio-economic backgrounds. Similarly, once pupils have been allocated to a stream, a calcifying process tends to set in, whereby the pupils generally tend to take on the characteristics of the stream in which they have been placed (Hargreaves, 1967) and often remain in those streams irrespective of future progress or lack of it. The teachers' expectations will also tend to follow the initial labelling process (Nash, 1976). What then happens is that pupils of the same initial level of measured ability will tend to improve, or deteriorate, in accordance with their initial placement, children placed in the upper streams tending to improve and children in the lower streams to deteriorate in their scholastic performance. This phenomenon is often referred to as the 'self-fulfilling prophecy' and it offers a self-justifying mechanism for selective systems. Since pupils tend to take on the stereotyped performance and behaviour of the class or school to which they have been allocated, this allows the selectors to claim that the selection procedure is manifestly seen to be accurate.

It is clear, therefore, that any system which involves an element of selection has awkward built-in problems. Thus it is virtually impossible to establish adequate selection and review procedures which are able to operate the system on grounds of ability alone without the intrusion of such 'nonintellectual' factors as the effects of socio-economic background. Similarly, any selection procedure, even one using the most reliable and valid tests, has a built-in 'error zone' (see Povey, 1972a, appendix 2 on SEm). Such problems, accentuated by the effects of the 'self-fulfilling prophecy', give rise to circumstances in which error-prone selection procedures determine to a large extent and in a rather arbitrary manner the future achievements of many of the children passing through them. Furthermore, under a system of segregated education for the gifted the selection barrier would come to assume a crucial significance in the eyes of many parents and schools and this would inevitably lead to the worst type of abuses (IQ coaching, timetabled test periods, and the like) which beset children's education in the days of widespread '11+ fever'.

If, on the other hand, research evidence were to show quite unequivocally that gifted children were disadvantaged in normal schools when judged in terms of the quality of their academic accomplishment, then the drawbacks of selective arrangements would have to be weighed very carefully against the merits of special schooling. In the present state of research, however, there seems to be little firm evidence to support the view that gifted children require special schooling in order to flourish. Indeed, as I have argued elsewhere (Povey, 1975), even in the spheres of music and ballet, for which pupils are often assumed to require special education (see, for example, Burt in Kellmer-Pingle and Varma, 1974), the evidence is far from conclusive. When the views of top professional artistes were examined (Povey, 1975) little consistent support emerged for the provision of separate education for the gifted, except in the sphere of ballet; and in the case of future professional singers the views of a substantial number of top British singers showed a highly consistent opposition to any idea of segregated education for schoolchildren. In this climate of opinion the arguments in articles about gifted children have, therefore, tended to concentrate upon possible ways of providing adequate educational facilities for the gifted within the normal school setting (see Hopkinson, 1978). The merits of special schools for some children, however, should not be overlooked and Peter Renshaw gives a lively defence of the place of such schools in a flexible system of educational provision (Chapter 4).

Acceleration

One approach which is sometimes adopted is that of accelerating children ahead of their chronological age group, so that a seven-year-old pupil, for example, might be placed in a class a year or more higher, or a preschool child may start school early. (See Part III, Case Study 3.) This approach has the advantage of placing the child with his intellectual peers, but it sometimes has the parallel disadvantage of removing him beyond the orbit of his more average level of emotional development (see Robb, 1974). This may create difficulties for the child in making satisfactory social relationships within the classroom. The teaching programme may be a closer match to his intellectual level but the mismatch between his social maturity and that of his classmates can result in much personal unhappiness for the child.

On the other hand, there is a good deal of evidence to suggest that the problems of acceleration have been exaggerated (see Vernon et al., 1977). Indeed it is possible that more harm may result from a situation in which a gifted child is subjected to a rigidly prescribed curriculum well below his level of ability than from the situation in which he is accelerated. Worcester (1956) suggests, for example, that high-IQ children held back with their own age group are less well adjusted than those who are accelerated, and on the basis of such research Vernon (1977) argues that we should be more ready to consider this approach in individual cases. This argument seems to hold weight, however, only in the context of a very formal and rigidly enforced curriculum and is at best, as Vernon acknowledges, only a partial palliative. In a more flexible teaching environment one should be able to find rather less fixed solutions (e.g., by utilizing 'setting' or 'withdrawal' arrangements for particular pupils and in relation to specific subjects). Such possibilities then bring us to a consideration of the next general approach.

Enrichment

On the whole this seems to offer the most satisfactory approach to the education of the gifted since it offers a way of coping with the children's requirements within the normal school by enriching the basic curriculum. This is often interpreted in a misguided way as the provision of more and more work of the same nature (e.g., 'ten extra maths' or 'ten extra comprehension questions', cf. Kerry, 1978). Although such tasks can sometimes be of value, 'enrichment' programmes should be seen as something rather more radical. Thus the gifted child might be provided with activities and facilities rather different from those usually arranged for the pupils (e.g., the opportunity for a gifted mathematician or scientist to engage in an extended mathematical or scientific project perhaps involving cooperation with pupils or staff from higher classes or from other schools). The work of Bridges (1969; 1975) and Tempest (1974) has aimed at helping to provide suitable enrichment programmes for gifted children in the normal school setting. The book by Bridges (1969) which reports the 'Brentwood Experiment' describes clearly the background to the venture and the learning programmes developed for use with the groups of children who came once a week to the Brentwood College of Education in Essex for their 'enrichment sessions'. The tutors and students who engaged in this work obviously became deeply immersed in the problems of teaching gifted children and the book offers to teachers and students some insightful observations and suggestions about teaching gifted children. (For recent developments in Essex see Chapter 9 and for discussion of a similar experiment in Bristol see Hoyle and Wilks, 1974.) More recently Dr. Bridges reported similar work at Millfield School (Bridges, 1975) and his research at Campion School in Athens is described in Chapter 11.

The book by Tempest (1974) also sets out details of the teaching activities employed with the group of fifteen children involved in his project (all with IQs above 130 on the Young, 1964, test). The children were selected when they were in the final term of the infant school and spent the next four years together as a class of gifted children taught by Ralph Callow, author of

Chapter 8 in Part II of this book. The explicit idea behind the project, however, was not the wish to promote the development of special schools but the hope that 'the experience of observing and teaching a group of clever children for four years in a primary school would furnish suggestions for the enrichment of the curriculum and examples of methods of work and general attitudes which would be helpful to teachers who have one or two children of this ability in their classes and to those who are preparing to teach.' The specific examples of projects and assignments which form a large part of this book will undoubtedly prove of considerable value to class teachers who find themselves struggling to keep up with one or two children who are intellectually very advanced. Similarly, the follow-up study of the 'Tempest children' through their secondary school careers (to be published shortly) should offer some illuminating longitudinal data on the development of gifted children at the adolescent stage. Some of the original Tempest projects are discussed in more detail later on by Susan Roberts and Belle Wallace (Chapter 9), and the recently developed Schools Council Enrichment Projects (Scceps) are described by Dr. Ogilvie in Chapter 12.

Some concluding thoughts

There is a growing amount of evidence to suggest that the predominant view amongst educationists in Britain is towards the continued integration of the gifted within the normal school system, but with an increased provision of some form of 'enrichment' programme for such pupils. The report by a team of H.M. Inspectors on approaches to teaching the gifted child in middle and comprehensive secondary schools (DES, 1977) dismisses the provision of special schools for 'gifted all-rounders' as unnecessary. The inspectors placed great emphasis on the provision of a broad and balanced curriculum for all pupils at least until the age of sixteen. They argue that such a curriculum should contain provision for the development of specific talents but not to the exclusion of other important areas of the curriculum. Similarly, the Schools Council survey of educational opinion into the teaching of gifted children of primary age (Ogilvie, 1973) reported that the majority of teachers included in the survey were opposed to fulltime classes for gifted children. Fifty-five per cent of teachers also disapproved of Day Release classes for five–eight year olds, although 58 per cent approved such classes for nine–thirteen year olds. A large majority of teachers (60–80 per cent), on the other hand, would accept the idea of 'periodic specialization'. The actual provision of 'enrichment classes' by local education authorities, however, somewhat lags behind such statements of approval. Only about 5 per cent of the authorities surveyed had any such provision (Ogilvie, 1973, chapter 6) and Denis Lawrence's recent LEA survey (reported in Chapter 3) shows very little change in this position.

Two of the key factors in the improvement of provision for such children are probably, first, a more systematic attempt to identify highly intelligent children and so demonstrate the need for some 'enrichment provision' and, second, a greater degree of individualization in the approach to teaching and learning in primary and secondary schools (see Ogilvie, 1973, chapter 5). In relation to the identification of gifted children there is certainly a strong case for an increasing adoption of 'screening procedures' at all levels of schooling (see DES, 1977). At the middle and secondary school level the inspectorate suggest in their report that 'a sound indentification procedure for gifted children should be a part of a programme of monitoring individual differences throughout the school' (DES, 1977). They discuss certain practices which might help in this process, including the use of school records and tests. On the use of records they argue that these should be cross-checked more consistently between 'feeding' and 'receiving' schools so that children identified as gifted at an earlier stage of schooling are adequately followed up in the later stages. They also offer in the second part of the report some ideas about the distinguishing features of giftedness in specific areas of the curriculum.

Whilst one can readily agree with the report's comment that 'it is the teacher who is in the front line when it comes to identification', it is equally important to take issue with its statement that the identification of gifted children 'owes little to school or LEA testing'. In the light of evidence already discussed in this chapter it is clear that testing acts as a supplement and support to the teacher's judgement and must form an essential part of any systematic diagnostic process. (For further discussion of this point see Chapter 8.) In the early stages of schooling the process of identifying children at the gifted end of the IQ scale as well as at the slow learning end would be greatly assisted if more schools adopted a systematic testing programme, particularly with pupils in the seven to eight-year age group. It is important to remember the point made by Ogilvie (1973), however, that such tests should have a sufficiently high ceiling for gifted children to be able to show their 'giftedness'. Amongst the most useful tests at this stage would be an orally presented test, as advocated by Vernon et al. (1977). One such test designed for use with top infants or first-year juniors is the Non-Readers Intelligence Test (Young, 1964), though with juniors the ceiling is a little restricted. A parallel test with more 'head room' is the Oral Verbal Intelligence Test by the same author (Young, 1973). As far as reading is concerned, group tests such as Spooncer's Group Reading Assessment (Spooncer, 1972) offer a useful screening device for first-year juniors, but for estimates of reading ability allowing greater head room it would be necessary to turn to some of the reading tests devised for individual administration (see Spooncer, 1976). Jackson (1971) also provides a comprehensive list of the tests available for use by teachers together with an excellent discussion of testing generally.

The second point about the individualization of learning is dealt with fully in Part II of this book. It concerns the attempt to provide each individual child with learning programmes suited to his level of ability and rate of working rather than to that of a hypothetical average level of ability of a class of pupils. Such an approach (which clearly involves a skilful use of grouping, assignments, work cards, etc.) would help even more directly towards meeting the needs of the gifted. Carried to its farthest extreme, of course, individualized learning programmes for every child would obviate much of the need for extra enrichment sessions. In the harsh reality of the classroom, however, in which teachers with varying degrees of ability and resources are required to 'educate' thirty to forty children at a time, this can present an almost insuperable task. Nevertheless, this should be the target towards which the teacher aims and the closer he approaches the target the more adequate will be the provision for not only the gifted but for each individual pupil of whatever level of ability.

CHAPTER TWO

GIFTED CHILDREN AT HOME AND SCHOOL
Frieda Painter

Ogilvie (1973) has shown that primary school teachers have a variety of attitudes towards gifted children. A majority of the teachers in that survey, however, did express agreement with the following statements:

1 as much attention should be given to the gifted as to 'disadvantaged' children;
2 the gifted are disadvantaged in not being allowed to progress according to their ability; and
3 failure to recognize potential giftedness was likely to be harmful to its development.

Despite such avowed interest in gifted children, it is nevertheless a matter for serious concern that (a) over half the teachers felt there was 'anti-intellectualism in the schools' and that (b) as many as 80 per cent of the answers referred to the low expectations of teachers and parents acting as a brake on the children's progress. These replies were given when the respondents were asked what conditions they considered to be important in preventing the development of a child's optimum rate of learning. From this it may be seen that a dominant view was that a good deal more should be asked of very able children than was currently the case. Dr. Ogilvie comments that these findings showed that the teachers envisaged a number of restrictions in the schools operating to retard the progress of individual children. He discusses these restrictions further in Chapter 12 of the present book.

Many of the findings from the Schools Council inquiry have been paralleled and substantiated in the discussion document 'Gifted Children in Middle and Comprehensive Secondary Schools' published by the Department of Education and Science (1977). This document reports the outcome of an investigation carried out by a team of HM Inspectors. The definition of giftedness which was adopted in this report covered those children aged eight to eighteen years:

a who are 'generally recognized by their schools as being of superior all-round intellectual ability, confirmed where possible by a reliable individual intelligence test giving an IQ of 130 or more; or

b who exhibit a markedly superior developmental level of performance and achievement which has been reasonably consistent from earlier years; or

c of whom fairly confident predictions are being made as to continual rapid progress towards outstanding achievement, either in academic areas or in music, sport, dance or art; and whose abilities are not primarily attributable to purely physical development.'

Between them the team made visits to 130 schools, half of which had previously been identified as places likely to make provision for gifted pupils. The inspectors observed lessons, talked to staff and pupils, examined the children's school work and the school records.

As in the case of the Schools Council inquiry, the inspectors discovered confusion and differences of opinion among teachers regarding the concept of giftedness – was it to be considered the possession by a child of high general ability, or the expression of a more specific attribute as in the case of musical talent?

The team found major differences in the attitudes held by teachers towards 'giftedness'. In one establishment the staff refused to attempt to identify giftedness as they claimed it was wrong to recognize a special category of pupil, although they recognized a remedial category which was segregated for special treatment. In some schools the inspectors perceived indifference rather than hostility, but in most places it was merely that the existence of 'gifted' children as such had not even been considered. In some other schools where it was claimed that provision was made for the gifted the inspectors were doubtful as to the efficiency of the methods of identification used. Contributory factors here were the absence of a clear definition of the meaning of the term 'gifted' and the fact that some gifted pupils might pass unnoticed because they were working below capacity either due to lack of challenge in the demands made upon them or from the children's personal choice. This tendency for able children to remain 'unstretched' by the demands placed upon them in the classroom was also noted in the inspectorate's primary school survey (DES, 1978).

These views accord with the findings made in the 'Brentwood Experiment' (Bridges, 1969) where it was shown that teacher and parent expectations of gifted pupils were too low and that the children had developed a 'stint' technique whereby they produced work just sufficient in quality and quantity to satisfy the adults. (See also Chapter 11.) By contrast, slow learners are usually unable to conceal their differences from the main pupil body.

Besides the usual methods of identifying gifted pupils through teacher observation and test results, the inspectors suggest that it may also be helpful to look at the children's activities outside school and to take into consideration their parents' views.

The inspectors' report has made an invaluable contribution to the debate on the education of gifted children. It has drawn attention to the serious deficiencies which currently exist in relation to the concept and occurrence of giftedness, and has helped to clarify the issues involved in the associated problems of identifying and providing for the needs of exceptionally able pupils.

Characteristics of gifted primary school pupils

The gifted sample

Against the background of the disturbing situation in British schools revealed by the studies discussed above, it is appropriate to reexamine the findings made regarding gifted pupils in a third study (Painter, 1977). This was an enquiry into the school progress and characteristics of 73 intellectually gifted (IQ 140 and over, mean 159) British primary school children, about two-thirds of whom were boys, in comparison with 64 bright-average pupils (IQ 80–130, mean 115). The gifted group (age range five to twelve years) was matched for sex, school class, socio-economic background, and age with the control children. All the children were tested individually on the Stanford-Binet Intelligence Scale and with NFER attainment tests in mathematics and English. Questionnaires were completed for the individuals in each group by their teacher, parents, and the children themselves. These covered the children's attitudes to and performance in school, the age of their friends, how popular the gifted were with other children, and the way they preferred to spend their time both at school and at home.

Part played by schools

The schools cooperated willingly in a project aimed at providing additional useful information about the children in their classes. Without their unstinted help, the inquiry could not have been undertaken in its present form.

The teachers assisted the study by nominating a number of candidates for the 'gifted' sample, and other children in the same school classes with whom they could be compared; they approached the parents of the suggested children to obtain permission for their children's participation, and the parents' agreement to complete a questionnaire. Almost universally the attitude of the teachers was that they wanted to do the best they could for all their pupils, whether or not they were termed 'gifted'. A measure of the help which the teachers rendered is given by the fact that the teachers' questionnaires were completed and returned for every child in the study, without exception. The forms were filled up by either the class or head teachers, or sometimes by both together.

The parents

With few exceptions those parents asked gave their permission for their children to participate in the study. Nearly all completed questionnaires as requested, so contributing to a pool of information about gifted children.

Scope of the questionnaires

Complementary questionnaires, divided into five parts, were directed towards the teachers, parents, and the children themselves. In each case the information sought was:

1 factual relating to physical circumstances;
2 concerned with the children's attitudes to, and performance in, school work;
3 the children's social relationships;
4 out-of-school occupations and home activities;
5 any additional comments.

Most of the questions were presented in a 'closed', forced-choice format but a number of 'open' items were also included in which the respondents were invited to give their own comments. The following discussion examines the answers given by the teachers and parents and cross-reference is made to the contents of the children's questionnaires for comparison purposes.

Physical circumstances

The teachers reported over half of the gifted children as being about the same age as the average in the school classes of which the pupils were members. Another 12 per cent of the gifted were about six months older than this and 18 per cent approximately six months younger. Seven of the gifted but only one of the control children were a year or more below the class average (i.e., they had been 'accelerated'. See Part III, Case Studies 3 to 7).

The teachers were asked to estimate the heights of the sample children compared to the average for their school classes to see whether, if it became the usual practice to accelerate gifted children into a more senior class, they would be handicapped with respect to their size. The teachers' replies showed that the gifted as a group tended to be the same height as their age group, so it seems they might be at a disadvantage among children a year older than themselves. However, this generalization should be seen against the wide variation in height between individual gifted children.

As to the children's physical health, the teachers reported this as being 'good' or 'very good' and only two of the gifted were shown to have had 'poor' or 'very poor' health. The school-attendance levels, too, were high for the majority of the children. Here, a point of interest is the difference between the two groups of pupils: for the gifted, twice the percentage as compared with those in the bright-average group were shown as having had a full school-attendance record during the previous twelve months. From this it follows that only exceptionally could absence from school be judged to be the cause of a relatively limited scholastic attainment level. This question, too, serves to indicate the care and accuracy with which the questionnaires were completed by teachers and parents, since there was a remarkable coincidence between the replies from the two sources.

On the first part of their questionnaire the parents were asked about their child's birth position in the family. It was found that about half of the gifted compared with one-third of the bright-average group were first-born children. The present results in this respect fit in with the evidence from previous research studies which show that good intellectual performance tends to be associated with high birth position and low family size (see, for example, Davie *et al.*, 1972).

Attitudes towards school

The great majority of the sample children were shown by the responses on the forms to like school, the children's responses in this respect matching those of the parents. The findings showed, however, that the parents of the gifted overestimated their offsprings' favourable feelings and underrated their negative reactions towards school; the converse was the case with the bright-average pupils' parents. Although a proportion of the gifted children's parents were able to gauge apparently correctly the levels of their children's intellectual capacity, they were less correct in their estimate of their children's liking for school.

The school day

The replies from the parents showed almost one-third of the gifted group but only one-quarter of the bright-average children, liking the classroom periods most when considering the total time spent at school. The proportions were almost reversed for 'play time', with one-third of the controls but not quite one-quarter of the gifted group's parents giving first place to this option. When the children's own answers are considered, there is reason to doubt whether the numbers of children preferring 'classroom' to 'play time' activities is as great as the parents believed. The highest proportion of children in both groups replied that 'play time' was the part of the school day most preferred. Even so, the difference between the two sets of children remains, with more of the exceptionally able than 'bright-average' pupils choosing 'being in the classroom' as an option. This finding is perhaps not entirely surprising since the gifted group were selected upon the basis of intellectual ability and it is in the classroom that such aptitudes can most easily be applied.

School work

The main emphasis in the teachers' questionnaire was on various aspects of the children's school work. The responses were examined under the following headings:

　　classroom organization and the modes in which the pupils were taught;

　　degree of attentiveness in class;

average levels of the children's achievements in classroom work, and variation in standards according to the subject matter;

classroom activities in which the pupils performed 'best' and 'poorest';

standards of achievement at games and swimming.

The teachers' replies indicated that classroom seating was arranged in such a way that over half the gifted studied on their own, a significantly larger proportion than the 30 per cent of the bright-average children who studied in this way. The pupils' work was so organized that the majority of the bright-average group worked at a table with four or five others but only two-fifths of the gifted worked in this type of group setting. This was probably in part a result of the teacher's methods of ability grouping within the classroom. The traditional approach with the teacher taking the class as a single unit was not widely favoured by schools in this research and only a small percentage of either group of children experienced such classroom arrangements. The seating arrangements also reflected the children's preferences, 42.5 per cent of the gifted group preferring working on their own compared with 30 per cent of the bright-average children. (See also Chapter 8.)

Next, the teachers were asked about how attentive the children were in class, using a scale from 'very attentive in class' through 'average attentiveness' to 'inattentive' or 'disciplinary problem'. Their replies showed the gifted group to be significantly more attentive than the control children, almost two-thirds of the gifted but less than a third of the bright-average being rated as 'very attentive'. Only 2 out of the 73 gifted children were said to be either inattentive or a disciplinary problem, while eight of the bright-average came into these categories. When the 'very attentive' category is compared with the remaining categories combined the association between gifted/high attentiveness and bright-average/average-low attentiveness is significant at the $P < 0.001$ level on a chi-squared 2×2 test ($\chi^2 = 16.34$).

The teachers added special comments about the school work for 31 per cent of the gifted pupils. The work of eleven of these was said to be markedly superior to that of their peers, the terms 'excellent', 'exceptional', and 'enthusiastic' being used. Two of the eleven were also said to be original thinkers and one to have been particularly interested in problem solving. The standards of work of another six of the gifted were reported as 'good' or 'very good' and the children were said to have had a mature vocabulary, a broad general knowledge background, etc. A further three were recorded as having an interest or ability in 'music', 'drama', and/or 'sport'.

Dissatisfaction was expressed by the teachers with only two of the gifted individuals, one of whom was described as an 'under-achiever' and the second as 'lazy, making a minimum amount of effort'. In another case the teacher seemed critical of a boy about whom he remarked that he had to be really interested in the subject before he would 'put a lot into his school work'. The teacher of a gifted girl, who said that her pupil was 'average but worked hard in class', had apparently failed to appreciate the level of the child's ability. (See Part III, Case Study 9 for a similar illustration.)

The teachers did not indicate any of the control group children as 'brilliant', but two of the pupils were considered to be 'creative', one in project work and the other in 'writing stories'. Two other children were thought to have been 'good all-rounders' and one boy was described as 'good at needlework'.

The teachers' comments suggested some dissatisfaction with six of the bright-average pupils, the children being described as 'inattentive', 'careless', 'making insufficient effort with school work', etc. Disapproval of another boy seemed implied by the remark 'he prefers football to academic work'.

The school work of over 90 per cent of the whole gifted group was described as above average and, at first glance, this might be considered adequate. On closer examination this conclusion is seen to be unjustified. Less than one-third of the gifted group were performing one year or beyond the average for their age group, while for 8 per cent the standard of work produced was average, or below average, for their school class. This shortfall existed in spite of the fact that the pupils included in the gifted group were those who had been able to score on an intelligence test within the top 1 per cent of their age group. For the 73 gifted whose chronological ages ranged from five to twelve years with a mean of eight years, eight months, the average mental age was fourteen. The large difference of five years, four months above the value for the chronological age indicated the high level of mental development which had been reached by the gifted children but was by no means reflected in the teachers' assessments nor by their attainment test scores (Painter, 1977).

When a subgroup of 31 very high-IQ individuals (160 and over) is taken separately, the difference between the mean chronological and mental age is greater still – six years, eight months. For these 31 exceptionally gifted children only eleven are rated as having an attainment level in their school work of a year or more above the classroom average, while three are shown as being only average, or below average, in their school attainment levels.

The teachers' approval – even enthusiasm – of what they describe as a high level of performance by the gifted pupils must, unfortunately, be viewed with concern rather than with satisfaction. It is a measure of the low standard of the work being demanded from children of outstanding mental ability and the consequent understimulation such pupils receive due to the (for them) low expectations of their teachers. This failing, discussed in Chapter 1, was perceived by Bridges (1969) and is recognized, too, by many teachers (Ogilvie, 1973).

An effort was made to discover which were the strongest and weakest areas of the children's classroom work and whether or not there was a marked variation between the gifted and bright-average children in this respect.

The teachers were asked to indicate the type of work at which each child was 'best' and 'poorest'. Their replies are shown in Figure 2.1 (a) and (b). As may be seen, reading and mathematics/science are named by the teachers as being the best performed by the largest proportions of the gifted group; an intermediate position is taken by creative writing and project; and the most rarely named are painting, pottery/craft, and music and movement.

Mathematics is also the best-performed class work for almost one-quarter of the bright-average pupils. This proportion was lower than for the gifted children but not significantly so. The percentages of the bright-average considered to attain best in creative writing and reading were similar to those for painting and pottery/craft. The range of 'best' performances as judged by the pupils' teachers was thus much wider for the bright-average than for the gifted group. There was, too, a tendency for the bright-average pupils to have a stronger leaning towards that part of the curriculum concerned with arts and crafts than was the case with the gifted group. This finding is also reflected in the children's subject preferences. The mathematics, creative writing, and reading preferences were combined to form a '3 Rs' group. When the preferences of the pupils were examined on this basis, significantly more pupils in the bright-average group were shown to prefer painting and craft work to the '3 Rs' in comparison with the gifted group (P <0.05). Similarly, when the teachers' estimates of classroom performance are considered, there is a statistically significant difference between the proportions of gifted and bright-average children achieving 'best' ratings in the '3 Rs'. Seventy-six per cent of the gifted were rated as 'best' at the '3 Rs' compared with 41.5 per cent of the bright-average.

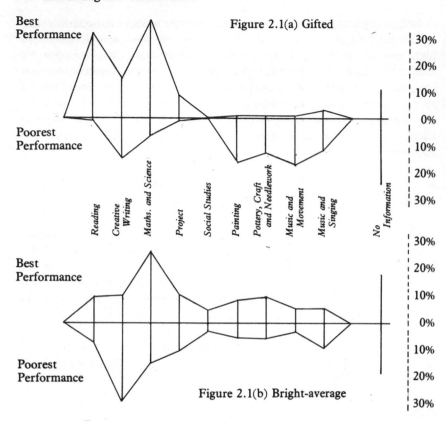

Best Performance

Figure 2.1(a) Gifted

Poorest Performance

Reading

Creative Writing

Maths. and Science

Project

Social Studies

Painting

Pottery, Craft and Needlework

Music and Movement

Music and Singing

No Information

Best Performance

Poorest Performance

Figure 2.1(b) Bright-average

In almost one-quarter of the cases of gifted children the teacher omitted to name an area of classroom work in which the child was weakest (compared with under one-fifth of such omissions for the bright-average group). Conversations with some teachers suggested that the omissions were due to the gifted pupils producing work of a good quality over most areas of the curriculum. Music and movement, painting, and creative writing were, however, the three subject areas, in diminishing order of frequency, for which the teachers showed the gifted group to be weakest.

Over one-quarter of the bright-average group were shown by the teachers to be 'poorest' in creative writing, and nearly half of the group were said to be weakest in one of the '3 Rs'. This is significantly higher than the 21 per cent of gifted children given 'poorest' performance ratings in this curriculum area. The teachers were also asked to rate the children as 'very good', 'average', or 'poor' at 'games and swimming'. Excluding four of the gifted group for whom no information was obtained on this topic the following results emerged: 30 per cent of the bright-average group were rated as 'very good', 63 per cent 'average' and 7 per cent 'poor' compared with parallel figures of 20 per cent, 52 per cent and 28 per cent for the gifted group. There is thus a distinct tendency for the bright-average to be given higher ratings than the gifted in these areas of achievement. On a chi-squared 2 × 2 test in which the 'poor' ratings are compared with the combined 'average' and 'very good' ratings this association is significant at the P <0.01 level ($\chi^2 = 7.45$).

Play

The parents' replies about their children's play have been divided into six categories. These are set out in Table 2.1.

The parents' replies show the very wide variety of types of play that the sample children enjoy. Although many of the activities are common to both the gifted and the bright-average, there are important differences. When the gifted play the usual children's games, they often do so in a way which is more complex and more mature in its conduct.

The gifted, too, spend some of their time on more adult pursuits; scientific, technical, and debating activities are only referred to in their case. The difference may be illustrated by the comments of two of the parents. One wrote that her son spent very little time playing as he preferred to concentrate on thinking about the book he would like to write. Another parent replied to the question by writing: 'Reading, studying, and thinking on his current pet subject.'

Out-of-school activities

In another question the parents were asked on which of a list of occupations their children chose to spend much of their free time. (The children were also asked to identify their preferred home occupations.) Most of the replies referred to reading, 'making something', 'watching TV', and 'outdoor games and sport'.

There was, however, an important difference between the two groups of pupils in the degree of popularity of these options. According to the parents, the percentage of the gifted who were avid readers was more than twice that for the bright-average and it was almost double for 'making something'. (These findings were supported by the results from the chil-

Table 2.1 Parents' replies: Types of play (aged five–twelve years)

Imaginary	**Play by gifted and other children** Dressing-up, making plays – historical, schools, shops, spies and space, playing with dolls and toy soldiers.
Environment	Nature study – fossils, streams, insects, fishing, bird watching, walking and exploring, care of pets.
Classification	Stamp collecting, road signs, flowers, identification of animals, birds, insects, bones.
Music	Playing records, singing.
Indoor games	Lego, monopoly, jig-saws, painting, drawing, gymnastics, table-tennis, badminton.
Outdoor activities	Football, tree climbing, adventure playgrounds, Scouts, Guides, tennis, swimming, horse riding, camping, building camps and dens.
Technical/Scientific	**Play by gifted group only** Dynamic performance of paper darts, making electrical gadgets, designing elaborate road systems, construction, photography.
Board games	Draughts, chess, playing cards.
Intellectual pursuits	Reading in general – reading history, reconstructing Second World War battle scenes, discussion group, Debating Society.

dren's own questionnaire.) 'Outdoor games and sport' (37 per cent) was the most important category for the control group. 'Watching TV' was named for 20 per cent of the bright-average but only 14.5 per cent of the gifted. (The children themselves, on the other hand, gave rather higher responses: 23.4 per cent and 21.2 per cent respectively.)

A marked difference was evident between the replies of the two groups of parents in relation to their children's interest in puzzles and mathematical quizzes. Whereas eight children in the gifted group were said to be keen on these activities, only one of the control children was placed in this category, a finding which was mirrored by the children's responses. The proportions of parental choices were fairly equally distributed in the two groups for 'looking after pets' and 'creative writing'. For 'drawing and painting' the groups were fairly evenly balanced in the parents' estimation but almost three times as many control children as gifted said they preferred 'drawing and painting'. 'Listening to music' was rather more popular with the bright-average pupils in the parental assessments. This may have been a reflection of the modern habit of playing pop records or it may have been a reflection of differing parental views of such an activity since the two groups of children themselves gave very similar response patterns.

Over-all, the gifted had a wider spread of out-of-school interests and tended to engage in a larger number of different activities than was usual among the bright-average group. This result might have been expected since the intellectually gifted children had been selected on the basis of mental ability, and many of the games and hobbies on which they spent their time required various special skills and the application of thought. (For further discussion on this point see Chapters 6 and 10.)

Social relations

Asked about their children's social relationships, the parents' replies showed that about 60 per cent of both groups were one of a set of friends and in each case over one-quarter of the children had a particular friend, generally someone who was at school with them. A few children were shown as being friendless (7.5 per cent of the gifted group compared with 3 per cent of the bright-average children). In the children's own replies the discrepancy between the two groups increases further. Six of the gifted believed they had no special friends among children, compared with only one of the control children (9 per cent and 1.6 per cent respectively). That as large a proportion of the gifted as this saw themselves as being without friends is a matter for concern.

Teachers are in a good position to observe the popularity of the children in their classes and their replies gave the same picture as the parents – except that they show rather more of the gifted to be less popular amongst their classmates than the bright-average children. The teachers' ratings are set out in Table 2.2 (p. 38). It will be seen that the gifted children tended to be less popular than the bright-average. When the 'not very popular' and 'isolate' categories are combined to give a 'low popularity' group and the 'average' and 'very popular' categories to form a 'popular' group, the association between 'giftedness'/low popularity and 'bright-average'/popularity is statistically significant on a chi-squared 2 × 2 test (χ^2 = 5.22, P <0.05). In their general remarks the teachers commented specifically upon the popularity of only six of the gifted group with their school peers. Of these, one child was described as 'sociable', two as having few friends, while the remaining three appeared to have been without friends.

Table 2.2 Teachers' ratings of sample children's popularity

Group	Very popular	Average popularity	Not very popular	An isolate
Gifted	23%	60%	14%	3%
Bright-average	27%	70%	3%	—

The parents' replies showed that under one-third of the gifted group preferred companions of their own age and almost as many were said to like being with children a year or more older than themselves; another one-quarter were very variable. This contrasted with the replies given for the bright-average children, of whom over half of the total group preferred children of their own age, and only 13 per cent chose children older than themselves – a proportion which was less than half that reported for the gifted children.

Although it is not an unusual occurrence (see Part III, Case Study 6) it is perhaps surprising to find in this study that almost as many gifted children chose the friendship of those older than themselves as of their own age since the great majority were in school classes with pupils nearly the same age as themselves. They would, therefore, have had less opportunity of mixing with older children. The indications here seem to be that, given the opportunity, intellectually gifted children will tend to make friends with those chronologically older than themselves. Should this be the case, then there is little reason with regard to social relationships why gifted children should not be accelerated to an older class at school. (See Chapter 1; also Part III, Case Studies 3 to 7.)

Personality traits and adjustment

Gifted children show a wide range of personality characteristics. Although assessments of personality and adjustment were not obtained in any precise way in this research the parents' open-ended comments showed that amongst the children were both highly extrovert and introverted individuals. For other traits, too, great variation was found. Some individuals are described as being excitable, agile, and demanding; another is said to be quiet and serious. One child was described as someone who enjoyed organizing people and another had an enquiring disposition and enjoyed 'research'. Others were described as 'very sociable with all ages', another 'as liking conversation', a third as enjoying most things and being very helpful at home, a fourth as being enthusiastic about everything undertaken, and a fifth as always occupied and reliable. Among those gifted children who did prefer their own company, some were also able to get on with people of all ages and were flexible in their social relationships. There are found, too, the easily bored gifted children and the ones with no close friends.

The 'puny, bespectacled' stereotype of the gifted child described in Chapter 1 is sometimes found amongst the gifted group but, as Dr. Povey argues in that chapter, the range of characteristics is very wide. Gifted children show highly developed mental powers far beyond those found in normal children of their own age. Nevertheless they *are* children and show the usual childish characteristics. Herein lies the essential problem of gifted youngsters: they belong fully to neither the world of children nor to that of adults.

It is impossible to make any general statement about the specific characteristics found among gifted children except to say that they appear to show a far greater range of behaviour than is found with average children. In their reading, at ages around eight, nine, and ten, for example, gifted children will alternate between the avid consumption of comics and the appreciation of literature, biographies, histories, the writings of authors such as Jane Austen and Rudyard Kipling, or technical books on electronics and computer science.

Conclusions

Despite the limitations of questionnaire techniques the present findings offer some interesting observations concerning the behaviour of one group of gifted children at home and school. The response rate was unusually high for a questionnaire study and there are consistent trends in the views expressed by the parents, teachers, and children which serve to counteract the subjective nature of the individual responses. Many of the findings are also consonant with the results of other research studies and this suggests that several of the characteristics observed in the present study are likely to be representative of gifted children more generally.

Significant differences between the behaviour and characteristics of the intellectually gifted and bright-average children in the present sample are shown in one or both of the following:

a   the possession by the gifted of similar features to those seen in other children but these occurring to a significantly higher degree;
b   the existence of unusual aptitudes and interests.

The personality characteristics found in gifted children seem to cover the same range of combinations found in others; they also have a wide range of interests and engage in a larger number of activities than the bright-average. The gifted have a strong liking for intellectual pursuits – an interest in discussing and debating current affairs – not found among the 'bright-average' children. There is a great love of reading and pleasure in classroom work – behaviour patterns which probably contribute to the gifted child's more limited degree of popularity with his peers.

It is probable that almost the whole gifted group are not extended in their school work and that 10 per cent are suffering adverse effects from their environment due to limited friendships with their peers, poor relationships with teachers, boredom and frustration through lack of the opportunity at school to pursue the study of their special interests to a higher level. The findings in this study support those in the other investigations already mentioned and again point to the pressing need for appropriate educational provision to be made for gifted pupils.

CHAPTER THREE

THE ROLE OF THE LOCAL EDUCATION AUTHORITY

Denis Lawrence

Although half a century has passed since the start of the famous longitudinal investigation into the characteristics of 1,000 gifted children in the USA (Terman, 1925), interest in this group has been slow to develop. It took fifty years before the first World Conference on the needs of gifted children took place (1975). The first ever National Conference on the subject in this country, officially organized by the DES, took place two years later and it seems that there is suddenly a renewed interest in the gifted child. Today more LEAs than ever before are seen to be showing interest in the identification and treatment of gifted children, as shown by the survey discussed in this chapter.

Although the schools in the UK have a fine tradition of catering for the needs of the handicapped, they have yet to display the same enthusiasm for the needs of those at the other end of the continuum. Despite the awakening of interest in the needs of the gifted, the situation is still very confused and policies largely uncoordinated. The lack of an agreed definition of what constitutes giftedness does not ease the confusion. Some authorities define the gifted in terms of an IQ cut-off point varying between 130 and 140. There are others who prefer to extend the definition to cover children showing outstanding talents in all fields, including music, drama, and sport as well as intellect. A further view commonly expressed is that, since unusually talented children 'differ as much amongst themselves as children of ordinary ability . . . there is no such thing as a typical gifted child' (Hildreth, 1966). Even where there is agreement on definition, confusion still remains with regard to the proper treatment of this particular group. There are those who recommend an enrichment programme as opposed to a policy of acceleration by placement in an older age group. There are those who prefer to recommend segregation. The DES-sponsored survey by Hoyle and Wilks (1974) has helped to clarify the position, recommending first a widening of the definition of giftedness and secondly pointing out that as far as the gifted are concerned there is little evidence that one form of organization is any more helpful than another.

Despite this, the arguments still rage and it is ironic that much of the renewed interest in the needs of the gifted child has arisen out of the rise of the comprehensive system of education. Before the comprehensive schools the grammar schools aimed at catering for those children who were above average in ability. This would include the intellectually gifted but such children were not usually identified in any special way except perhaps as the 'high flyers' in the 'A' stream class. Varying percentages of the school population would gain selection in different parts of the country according to the actual number of selective places available (Douglas, 1964). In general, however, a standardized score of 115+ would often be required for selection to a grammar school and on a test with a Mean of 100 and Standard Deviation of 15 points this would represent the top 15 to 16 per cent or so of the school population. The intellectually gifted, on the other hand, are more usually identified somewhere above IQ 130, i.e., within the top $2\frac{1}{2}$ per cent of the population, the precise location depending upon the particular 'threshold level' selected (see Chapter 1). Thus a threshold level placed at IQ 130+ would take in about $2\frac{1}{2}$ per cent of the pupil population whereas one placed at a higher figure would encompass a narrower range. In my own authority we have tended to adopt a cut-off point at the 1 per cent level in our projects on the intellectually gifted.

As argued in Chapter 1, the general consensus today, however, seems to be that all children, including the gifted, should continue to receive a broad education, at least until the age of sixteen years, and those with special talents should be helped through programmes of enrichment rather than segregation. However, unless teachers are instructed in methods of identifying those with unusual talents there is the possiblity that these children can so easily be overlooked, especially those who tend to underachieve. This need not arise, of course, where the teacher is able to use individualized programmes of instruction. Unfortunately, the size of classes tends to mitigate against this and small group teaching is usually the best that can be achieved in the majority of cases.

Judging from the recent increased interest referred to above, it should not be long before there are agreed definitions and eventually proper provision. Even then, however, there still remains the important question of priorities. A typical LEA readily giving financial support to the handicapped where necessary has yet to be convinced that similar help should be available for those with unusual talents even when the selection is limited, say, to the top 1 per cent of the ability range. The signs, however, are that parents are going to be applying to their LEAs in greater numbers for this help as they are being encouraged to take a more positive role in their children's education. This should be no cause for concern, bearing in mind the relatively small numbers involved at such high cut-off points as the 1 per cent level. But it is clear from the survey reported in this chapter that very few LEAs do offer financial help. Moreover, no amount of inspired optimism from those interested in the gifted will have the desired effect until the general public at large give their support. It is the lay committees in the county halls who need to be persuaded, and at the moment the needs of the gifted child are still viewed as low down in the general list of priorities in educational spending.

LEA survey

In December, 1978, a questionnaire was sent to all LEAs in England and Wales in an attempt to investigate the extent of this awakening of interest in the gifted child. The questionnaire (which is shown on pp. 50-51) was based on that devised by Dr. Ogilvie for his 1973 Schools Council Survey. Although only 49 out of 105 LEAs replied, this is quite a high return for a postal questionnaire (see Lovell and Lawson, 1970). It is clearly important to exercise caution in interpreting the results, but a response rate of 47 per cent is sufficient to allow us to draw some tentative conclusions and form some comparisons. As most of the LEAs in the survey requested that their information should remain confidential it was decided to keep all the results anonymous. This would avoid the likelihood of unfair comparisons being drawn between authorities. The results are discussed in relation to the separate sections in the questionnaire.

Q.1. *Has the LEA a policy for identification and treatment of gifted or exceptionally able children?*

It is intriguing that only 16 per cent state they have a definite policy although 80 per cent are involved in some way with the needs of the gifted. It seems that in these authorities there is a great deal being done which has often not quite reached the stage of a formal LEA policy. Typical of the replies under this heading is that of the authority which stated 'We are currently re-examining the whole area of provision for children who might come under the gifted category.' Other authorities indicated that working parties and pilot activities are currently being organized and 33 per cent kindly took the trouble to write an accompanying letter referring to their active consideration.

There was one strongly dissenting voice amongst the generally positive responses and the arguments presented against having a policy are worthy of serious consideration. The authority in question has given the matter some considerable thought and concludes as follows: 'This Authority has no plans to devote attention to the gifted . . . giftedness is an ambiguous term and in itself does not constitute a problem.' This conclusion was arrived at following a survey which revealed that bright children in the authority were above average in most respects, including social and emotional adjustment. It was felt that the gifted select themselves. This conclusion is in line with the famous Terman study showing that gifted people produce a smaller proportion of psychological upsets than is found in the general population (see also Chapter 6).

Although most authorities would agree that the gifted child is usually better adjusted than his fellows, one important reason given for devoting attention to this gifted group is that they are often relatively isolated from their peers and so tend to underperform and be overlooked. This isolation is a real geographical isolation in schools situated in sparsely populated areas of the typical rural county.

Q.2 *Which methods of identification of 'gifted' children are used?*

It seems that the most common practice is to rely on teachers' opinions (47 per cent), usually supplemented with standardized tests. Only two authorities used teachers' opinions as the sole method of identification, the others using teachers' opinions supplemented by the use of guidelines. Typical of these guidelines are those devised by Laycock for use in the Toronto schools. (These guidelines are set out on pp. 51-52.) A survey in my own authority has shown that teachers using an adaptation of these guidelines managed to select children on the whole who had scores above IQ 130 on the Verbal Scale of the Wechsler Intelligence Scale for Children. The WISC testing was carried out after the teachers had selected the children and revealed that only three from a sample of forty-three had been overestimated by teachers.

Use of intelligence tests has tended to go out of favour as the sole method of selection, particularly since the discredited 11+ examination has disappeared. Only one authority used an intelligence test as the only method of screening. Where other authorities used an intelligence test this was supplemented by attainment tests. These results suggest that educationists may not not be quite as hooked on the 'IQ approach' as they appeared to be in many respects in 1973 (see Chapter 12). They are in line with Dr. Ogilvie's conclusions in the 1973 survey, however, emphasizing the importance of using other forms of evidence to supplement the IQ data in the identification of the gifted. Such evidence might be sought, for example, from vocabulary, creative writing, and other attainments.

It is not surprising to discover that personality assessments are used rather less frequently, but interesting to note that where they are used (in seven authorities) attainment tests are also used. Some psychologists hold the view that the predictive value of attainment testing could be increased considerably by the addition of personality testing. However, the relative unreliability of personality tests has hindered their popularity. It is evident that despite this they are tending to be used more often, so it is hoped that where this is the case they are interpreted and administered by qualified personnel.

The use of 'creativity' tests has not gained favour. This is perhaps not surprising considering the evidence reported in Chapter 1 about their doubtful validity. The research project by Hitchfield (1973) also concludes that 'there is no support to the idea that intelligence and creativity are separate factors.' One LEA reported a pilot study incorporating the use of the Torrance Test of Creativity, but gave no further information.

Q.3. *Does your advisory staff give any special guidance or training to teachers to help them recognize and provide for the needs of gifted children?*

Dr. Ogilvie's 1973 survey showed that only about 18 per cent of LEAs gave any clear guidance to teachers about recognition of giftedness. It seems that there may have been some improvements in this respect. An encouraging 50 per cent of replies under this heading indicated that something positive was being done. It seems that a considerable effort is being made in many authorities to provide in-service training and discussion groups. (Chapter 9 by Susan Roberts and Belle Wallace describes a particularly interesting example of such efforts in one LEA.) Several of the authorities had sent teachers on a DES one-week residential course on the gifted. It is also of note in this context that some initial teacher training courses include seminars on the needs of the gifted. Clearly there is much more to be done in this area. The school psychological services in some authorities compiled admirably useful booklets for teachers, outlining the existing methods of identifying gifted children and giving suggestions with regard to treatment.

Some authorities are experimenting with peripatetic advisers who provide the busy classteacher with specific learning programmes for the gifted. As I have argued elsewhere (Lawrence, 1978), it is also feasible to see this type of task as one which an extended remedial teaching service might take on as part of its provision for children with exceptional needs. In general, however, it seems that the educational psychologist is left to take the initiative, otherwise nothing is done; and it is significant that most authorities find themselves understaffed in their psychology departments. Although half of the sample who replied to the questionnaire are concerned that teachers should be helped to recognize gifted children, several authorities made a point of stating that this approach was an alternative to the adoption of a deliberate policy. In these particular authorities it was felt that 'gifted children by and large tend to present themselves naturally'. Encouragement is given to teachers to identify them on a purely informal basis.

Q.4. *Are heads encouraged to seek professional advice from (say) an adviser or educational psychologist if they know or suspect that a child is gifted in one or more areas of activity – i.e. is there an established system of 'referral' as perhaps with backward children?*

Sixty per cent of the replies actively encourage this kind of intervention and it seems likely that this finding indicates something of a change of attitude on the part of LEAs since the earlier survey in which only 26 per cent of the authorities reported such provision. Most of the LEAs in the present survey used a formal system as part of their general referral policy. It is significant, however, that most of their replies were qualified with comments such as 'the referral system is not used merely to identify the gifted'. In other words, although these authorities appear to be well aware of the need to identify and provide for the gifted (perhaps more aware than they were in 1973), there is still a distinct reluctance to set up machinery specifically for this purpose. No doubt many are concerned that there are dangers in screening specifically to identify a gifted group. There is a genuine concern over the return to a similar system which existed in the days of the 11+ selection procedure. Whilst this feeling is understandable, and no doubt those children with exceptional talents would, in effect, 'refer themselves', they would only do so under this system if they came to the notice of the teacher by presenting particular problems. The understaffed psychology service naturally give priorities to those with the most serious problems. This means that the gifted group, unless showing these additional signs, are likely to be overlooked.

Q.5.(a)(c) *Does the LEA help gifted children by running special Saturday morning classes or by supporting enrichment classes during normal school time?*

These two questions are discussed here together as their replies indicated that these were the least favoured methods used to help the gifted. Only 18 per cent organized Saturday morning classes and only 8 per cent supported enrichment classes during normal school time. It seems likely that the extent of provision in this form is very similar to that existing in 1973 when the corresponding percentage figures were 25 per cent and 5 per cent respectively. It appears that where there is help available it is preferred that this should be given in the ordinary class situation. Two authorities are experimenting with visiting teachers who provide individual enrichment programmes for selected children. One of these authorities is also appointing extra psychologists for the purpose of identifying such children and supporting the teachers. The subjects covered in this scheme include the whole range, e.g., mathematics, English, modern languages, science, music, history, geography. This is an ambitious project with a cost amounting to £200,000 and is concerned with 4,000 children in all parts of the county.

One authority among the 8 per cent supporting enrichment classes outside school has been running such classes for eight years. These are organized in the local university school of education. It is evident that a policy of enrichment is preferred by LEAs to one of either segregation or acceleration. The Ogilvie (1973) findings also emphasized the value of the 'enrichment method'.

Q.5.(b)(e) *Does the LEA help by providing scholarships to outside institutions or by early transfer to secondary schools?*

Just over half of those LEAs (52 per cent) who actively seek to identify the gifted prefer to help through the award of scholarships to specialized institutions such as colleges of music or ballet, etc. As these institutions exist for those already identified as particularly talented, this kind of help provided by LEAs is not really part of any policy of their own. Even so, this seems a large proportion in view of the fact that, since the 1976 Education Act, offers of places at independent schools (except in cases of dancing and music) have to be approved by the DES.

Just under half (46 per cent) prefer to deal with the problem through early transfer to secondary school. Roughly half of the sample appear to do tests, which presumably means that where 'giftedness' is interpreted as being of superior intellectual ability the early transfer would be recommended. These authorities rightly warned of the dangers of assuming that because a child was seen to be intellectually superior this automatically meant he was emotionally and socially superior. Where the 'giftedness' is seen to be the possession of an unusual aptitude such as music then a scholarship to another institution may be awarded. Again, the replies to these questions are broadly parallel to those in the 1973 survey when about half the LEAs stated that they made provision by 'scholarship' or 'early transfer'.

Q.5.(d)(f) *Does the LEA help by encouraging private training or by providing loans or increased capitation or special materials in some other way?*

About half the LEAs encourage children to register with private organizations for training (e.g. in sport) but just under half of LEAs (42 per cent) are prepared to assist the gifted in a concrete way. The general tone of their qualified replies conveys the impression that the responsibility for how the money is spent rests firmly on the shoulders of the classteacher. Only one authority has a definite budget for loans or materials.

Q.5.(g) *Does the LEA help by other means?*

One-quarter of the sample indicated that help was provided in other ways not covered by the questionnaire. One LEA in particular has already experimented with two residential courses at selected centres outside the schools for children aged ten–thirteen and thirteen–sixteen respectively. They have been organized on the themes of creative drama, speech and writing, and logical processes of thought. It is planned in future that they should become more subject orientated. It is further planned by this authority to extend the policy to the primary sector on a nonresidential basis.

Q.6. *Do methods of identification and provision differ at primary and secondary level?*

Rather surprisingly, only 14 per cent indicated a difference in approach between primary and secondary levels. Notably these were also the LEAs who preferred to help the gifted through early transfer to secondary school.

Counselling of parents to help the gifted

Although this was not a separate heading, provision was made under 'other methods' and only one LEA referred to the need to counsel. This is an area which requires further examination, particularly in view of the considerable evidence of the effects of parental attitudes on children's attainments (see Chapter 10). On a different level, it can be a burden for some parents to be informed that they have gifted children when they themselves are, like most of us, perhaps average people.

Conclusions

It is clear from this survey that the majority of LEAs in the UK are still without a policy for the gifted. The attention paid to other exceptional groups such as the retarded or the emotionally maladjusted stands in marked contrast to this neglect. When we consider that the problems posed by the gifted rarely impinge on teachers in an unpleasant way or to the same extent as the problems presented by the handicapped, this attitude becomes more understandable. It is not easy to persuade the average LEA that an ambiguously defined group, variously referred to as gifted or unusually talented, should receive a share of the budget when there are other more easily identifiable groups demanding more attention. Moreover, to suggest that money should be allocated for the needs of so-called gifted children is interpreted in some quarters as pouring extra riches on an already privileged group. This is an emotional argument but no less powerful for that. The word 'gifted' tends to provoke an emotional reaction. This could perhaps be overcome to some extent by following the lead given in the Warnock Report (1978) recommending the abolition of labelling handicapped children. Could we not begin to talk of children with 'exceptional needs' rather than the gifted? The accusation that by providing for the gifted group we are favouring a policy of élitism can only be countered by research evidence showing the benefits of a policy for the gifted. There is, perhaps, need for a national study. It is quite ridiculous that LEAs interested in providing a policy have to plough through tedious hours trying to arrive at some consensus of opinion not only with regard to definitions but also with regard to the best method of helping these children. It is hoped that this book might help in the search for greater clarity in the definition of terms and provide a source of ideas and approaches to teaching the 'gifted'.

Finally, to neglect the unusually talented in our schools is to neglect an opportunity to influence the future leaders in our society. A moment's reflection on the current moral and political chaos which exists throughout the world today is surely a sound argument for the need to identify those in our midst who possess superior talents and to help nurture them to the full.

Local Authority Survey into the provision for 'gifted' or 'exceptionally able' children

1. This LEA has a policy for the identification and treatment of 'gifted' or 'exceptionally able' children.

        YES   NO
(Please encircle as appropriate)

If the answer to question (1) is YES it would be helpful to receive any relevant reports or pamphlets which are available.

2. Which of the following methods of identification of 'gifted' children are used? Please encircle appropriate letter(s) *A* to *F*.

A Intelligence tests.   D Teachers' opinions.
B Attainment tests.   E Check list criteria.
C Personality tests.   F Other methods (please specify):

Questions (3) to (5) were included in an earlier Schools Council survey on 'gifted' children. Please add brief details or comments where these might be of interest.

Comments

3. Does your advisory staff give any special guidance or training to teachers to help them recognize and provide for the needs of gifted children?   YES NO

4. Are heads encouraged to seek professional advice from (say) an adviser or educational psychologist if they know or suspect that a child is gifted in one or more

areas of activity – i.e., is there an established system of 'referral' as perhaps
with backward children?   YES   NO

5. Does the LEA help gifted children:

(a) by running special Saturday morning
classes or by providing home tuition by
peripatetic teachers?   YES   NO
(b) by awarding scholarships or exhi-
bitions to outside institutions (e.g., Colleges of Music, Royal Ballet School, etc.)
for Saturday morning or full-time instruc-
tion.   YES   NO
(c) by supporting or organizing enrich-
ment classes during normal school hours
(e.g., at a College of Education)?   YES   NO
(d) by encouraging children to register
with private organizations for training
(e.g., sports clubs, etc)?   YES   NO
(e) by arranging admission to secondary
education before the normal age of trans-
fer?   YES   NO
(f) by the provision of or loan of special
materials or an increase in capitation
allowances?   YES   NO
(g) by other means?   YES   NO

6. Do your methods of identification and
provision differ at primary and secondary
level?   YES   NO

If you wish the information to remain anonymous please pace a tick in this box

GIFTED CHILDREN : A TEACHER'S CHECKLIST

(From Laycock, 1957)

Exceptionally able children are likely to show the following characteristics:

1. Possess superior powers of reasoning, of dealing with abstractions, of
   generalizing from specific facts, of understanding meanings, and of
   seeing into relationships.
2. Have great intellectual curiosity.

3. Learn easily and readily.*
4. Have a wide range of interests.
5. Have a broad attention span that enables them to concentrate on, and persevere in, solving problems and pursuing interests.
6. Are superior in the quantity and quality of vocabulary as compared with children of their own age.
7. Have ability to do effective work independently.
8. Have learned to read early (often well before school age).
9. Exhibit powers of observation.
10. Show initiative and originality in intellectual work.
11. Show alertness and quick response to new ideas.
12. Are able to memorize quickly.
13. Have great interest in the nature of man and the universe (problems of origin and destiny, etc.)
14. Possess unusual imagination.
15. Follow complex directions easily.
16. Are rapid readers.*
17. Have several hobbies.
18. Have reading interests which cover a wide range of subjects.*
19. Make frequent and effective use of the library.*
20. Are superior in mathematics, particularly in problem solving.*

---

* A child showing most characteristics on the checklist, but not those starred, is likely to be a gifted child who is underachieving educationally.

CHAPTER FOUR

THE PLACE OF SPECIAL SCHOOLING IN THE EDUCATION OF GIFTED CHILDREN

Peter Renshaw

'Equality of opportunity for all'

A commonly accepted aim underlying the educational system of this country is that each child should be given equal opportunity to realize his or her potential to the full. Perhaps a less palatable formulation of the same principle is that each child should be given equal opportunity to become unequal. Apart from the fact that people are equal by virtue of their common humanity, it is fairly obvious that we are all demonstrably unequal in any other descriptive sense of the term. What matters in any just system of educational provision is that individual differences between children are identified and then catered for in a manner appropriate to the particular need or talent. In a society purporting to be egalitarian in character, the emphasis in recent years has been on trying to meet the special needs of those children with some form of educational, social, or physical handicap. This admirable aim has been underlined by the move towards comprehensive education, the end of selection at 11+, and the widespread introduction of mixed-ability group teaching. Without doubt, certain individual children have benefited enormously from some of the changes that have occurred in the last decade, but it is also increasingly important to acknowledge the validity of the claims made by some of the critics of the present system.

One of the most sensitive areas of criticism, and one which cannot be ignored by any government, is the growing failure of the educational system (especially at school level) to foster quality and excellence. To many so-called egalitarian teachers such values, quite misguidedly, bear the stamp of 'élitism', with the result that many schools are becoming particularly effective at maximizing mediocrity. This is a sad indictment of the kind of world we are living in and it would be hoped that educationists would have the will, the flexibility of mind, and the resourcefulness to meet the very special needs of the 'talented' and 'gifted' children in our schools. Admittedly, there are very real problems connected with the definition of 'giftedness', but no educator of any worth can fail to recognize that there is a qualitative difference between the abilities of children which any nation neglects at its peril. On moral, psychological, and economic grounds it is imperative that specific talents are identified and developed to the full under optimum conditions. It is a fallacy to assume that 'the gifted can look after themselves'.

The need for a flexible system of educational provision

In order to allow all children to realize their potential it is necessary to promote a flexible system of educational provision. Unfortunately, at present this ideal is often bedevilled by such constraints as economic expediency, political ideology, and conflicting vested interests. Perhaps saddest of all, only too frequently some teachers feel threatened by children who are decidedly more able than themselves and thus fail to do full justice to such pupils under their care. At its worst this state of affairs can lead to indifference or even hostility to the whole idea of giftedness. This point is made very clearly in a recent discussion paper written by a working party of Her Majesty's Inspectorate (DES, 1977, p.8).

> Some schools had little wish to consider giftedness. In one school teachers refused to identify giftedness on the grounds that in a school which purported to be comprehensive, it was wrong to recognise a special category of pupils for whom some unusual provision might be made. The only school in which this extreme view was encountered was one where strong egalitarian views were held by staff. Paradoxically, the staff were not averse to the recognition of a remedial category which was segregated out for special treatment, nor to the thesis that individual needs should be identified and provided for. Although outright refusal was encountered only once, strong reluctance to identify giftedness was not uncommon.

Another problem arises when teachers who are prepared to accept that some children are far more gifted than others find themselves unable to identify and meet certain specific individual needs. The willingness is there but the expertise, even at a diagnostic level, is lacking. In the area of music, for example, it is often recognized that children with considerable musical potential ought to receive some kind of specialized training from an early age. Early skill training is usually considered to be especially important for performers of stringed instruments (as it is also in the area of ballet). But how can an unmusical, nonspecialist class teacher in a first school be expected to identify the talented young musician with any degree of skill? In the Gulbenkian Report (1978) on 'The Training of Professional Musicians' an attempt is made to provide a list of criteria that might help the non-specialist teacher to spot a musically gifted child. These criteria are based on a series of tests designed by Chetham School of Music to reveal a child's musical resourcefulness and creative responses. Essentially they are looking for 'an acute ear and an unwavering sense of pitch, an instinctive musical understanding, a concern for the sheer quality of sound, a lively sense of rhythm and a good memory for tunes, kinetic skill, motor-visual co-ordination and an ability to handle classroom instruments or a recorder in a way that seems "professional" or to the manner born and, perhaps most important of all, motivation' (p.34). Such a list of qualities might be identified by the highly skilled staff of a specialist music school like Chetham's but it is highly doubtful whether the ordinary class teacher would be able to perceive the subtlety of response of the highly talented musical child.

Similarly, at a wider level, some local education authorities and certain national bodies do recognize the acute needs of those children with exceptional gifts. However, they then fail to provide the quality of experience necessary to sustain and develop specific talent to the highest possible standard of excellence. Certainly in music the opportunity for young people to engage in a wide range of activities, both in and out of school, has increased enormously in the last decade. All LEAs employ teams of peripatetic music teachers, whilst the more enterprising authorities run flourishing music centres, youth orchestras, and youth choirs. (See Part III, Case Study 12.) Also one authority, ILEA, has taken the initiative to establish a specialist music wing within a comprehensive school, thereby enabling young musicians to develop their particular talents within the ambiance of a normal school. In addition some pupils prefer to receive their instrumental instruction privately, sometimes receiving a grant from their

LEA, whilst others are fortunate enough to be awarded a junior exhibition at one of the colleges of music. Many of the most advanced young performers aspire to a place in the National Youth Orchestra, which provides a high quality musical and orchestral training from some of the country's leading musicians. Nevertheless, despite this vast reservoir of opportunities, it is still questionable whether the quality of provision, in general, is adequate to meet the needs of the outstanding young artist. Of course, there are pockets of excellence in different parts of the country, often centred on one inspiring and able teacher, but for the most part there is much mediocrity resulting in wasted talent. It is partly for this reason that several specialist music schools have been set up and it is to be hoped that in the course of time they will play an increasing part in raising the quality of the musical life of the country.

One problem arising from this discussion of musical provision is that of possible jealousy and territorial threat. Most teachers, heads, and advisers enjoy building up their own power base and, not surprisingly, highly talented young artists can pose a threat to the established order. Too many educationalists in positions of influence are encapsulated in their own preconceived notions and only too frequently demonstrate a total lack of flexibility and sensitivity towards the gifted musician. For example, some head teachers see their own timetable and curriculum as sacrosanct and therefore would never consider providing an individual programme for a pupil, allowing for instrumental instruction and practice time, perhaps off the school campus, during school hours (see Part III, Case Study 11). Such an action might create a precedent which would possibly disturb the seemingly rational organization of the school. Some instrumental teachers, thankfully not all, tend to be very possessive and are thus often reluctant to recommend their most able students to pursue more advanced work with a more appropriate teacher if and when necessary. Many uninformed parents are dependent on the advice of such teachers and consequently fail to give their children the quality of instruction they deserve. Some advisers, too, are not as cooperative as they might be. In some authorities the music adviser is keen to foster local talent and might even be prepared to provide bursaries for particularly gifted children to study with teachers of national standing. But in quite a few cases this financial support is given only on condition that the student fulfils such obligations as playing regularly in the local youth orchestra. Not only might this be an inappropriate experience at a certain stage of a child's musical development, but it might also prevent him from pursuing such fruitful avenues as the National Youth Orchestra and the International Musicians' Seminar at Prussia Cove, Cornwall, both of which offer opportunities for work at a higher level than could be provided by a local authority. In other words, there are occasions when a form of economic blackmail operates which effectively denies certain talented children access to specific forms of high-quality experience. Nevertheless, it is understandable that authorities expect some return on their investment.

Different forms of provision

Although most of the examples discussed so far have been taken from the area of music, the general point being made is that it is of paramount importance to eliminate all the petty constraints militating against the flexibility which is necessary if the special needs of individual gifted children are to be met. Imagination and flexibility of attitude are vital if the DES and LEAs between them intend to take positive steps to rectify the present disastrous situation. Sometimes financial restraints are held up as an insuperable problem, but more often than not intransigent attitudes and fear of upsetting the status quo too frequently lead to inertia and lack of fruitful change.

To be fair, some enterprising developments have taken place in certain areas in the last few years. For example, both the Royal Ballet School and the Yehudi Menuhin School have been accorded a special status as centres of education for the performing arts, with grants made direct from the DES. The financial security gained from this direct grant is invaluable to the integrity of purpose of each institution. The four other specialist music schools (i.e., Chetham School of Music, Manchester; Purcell School, Harrow; Wells Cathedral School; St. Mary's School, Edinburgh) are less fortunate financially as they are dependent on private endowments and on the goodwill of those LEAs interested in supporting these schools for some of their talented musicians. Within the public sector itself different forms of provision for the education of gifted children are being explored by some authorities. In general there is little support, on either social or educational grounds, for the setting up of specialist schools in subjects like mathematics, science, and foreign languages although schools of this type have been established in some countries (see Chapter 7). Therefore most of the current provision takes one or more of the following forms.

a   The child with a particular gift remains in the normal classroom but the teacher receives consultative support from an outside agency.

b The normal classroom remains the instructional base, but the gifted child receives additional teaching which might involve promotion, withdrawal from the class for certain specific activities, or pursuing an accelerated programme in the particular area of interest.

c Some children have the opportunity to attend special classes and enrichment courses, both during and after school and also during vacations. Often these are organized in relation to the needs of children within a limited geographical area and they might be centred on the university, polytechnic, or research establishment of the region.

d In some conurbations it is sometimes prudent for a child to be transferred to another comprehensive school which has developed a strong department with exceptional facilities and expertise in a particular activity. It would seem highly desirable to extend this idea further and to encourage authorities to develop specialist wings of high quality in a number of carefully selected comprehensive schools.

e A form of provision that might be explored further is that of the specialist day school. (This exists in the private sector with the example of the Purcell School for young musicians and several dance schools in different parts of the country.) Ideally such a school would constitute a centre of excellence in a specific area of the curriculum (e.g., the humanities, visual arts, languages, mathematics, or science), supported by a wide-ranging general education. Quite rightly, most educationists feel that all children up to the age of sixteen should be initiated into the 'language' and 'literature' of the central forms of human experience. In fact it is of vital importance for a child to be able to place his or her specialism in a broad conceptual frame. But this desire to foster a general education should not prevent some schools from developing into centres of excellence with a sharply distinctive focus. As long as a balance is maintained in the curriculum, such schools should be encouraged to pursue their specialism to the highest possible standard of achievement. The main advantages of a specialist school can be stated briefly as follows:

1 Unity of purpose. Both the staff and the students are bound together by shared values and a community of interest.

2 The opportunity for children with similar talents and depth of commitment to work together provides the stimulus of competition and example.

3 An environment which is designed to understand the special needs of a specific group of children can deal supportively with possible

emotional and psychological problems. It is not unknown for gifted children in ordinary schools to be misunderstood by their parents, teachers and peers. At its worst this can lead to different forms of social handicap, emotional disturbance, and intellectual impoverishment.

4   One of the strongest features of any centre of excellence is the concentration of resources in a single institution. This would include human expertise at a high level (not necessarily just teachers), appropriate curricular material, special facilities, and multi-media support. Perhaps the biggest asset of a specialist school lies in the quality of the teaching staff. Ideally any gifted child needs to have his conceptual horizons extended by a teacher who is capable of operating at the frontiers of his particular discipline.

5   In a school characterized by its unity of interest there is a much greater chance of establishing a degree of coherence in the programme of studies for each child.

6   The timetable can be planned to allow the maximum flexibility,

The Yehudi Menuhin School – an example of a specialist music school

Yehudi Menuhin founded his school in 1963 with the intention of creating the ideal conditions in which musically talented children might realize their potential to the full. The school comprises 45 highly committed boys and girls, ranging from about eight to eighteen years of age. About five new places are available each year and in the selection process the emphasis, especially in the case of the youngest children, is on musical potential rather than achievement. Such a potential cannot be identified and evaluated through a battery of objective tests. Rather it is sensed by a panel of highly experienced musicians using their informed intuition and sensitive insight. The main quality being looked for is the ability of the child to move the listener. This is often accompanied by an uncanny authenticity of response in which the young person puts his own distinctive stamp on the music. In other words, the talented musician is not necessarily the well-taught pupil whose motivation stems from his parents. Far more important are the qualities of openness and receptivity to the music, together with the ability to listen in a highly concentrated manner. These can often lead to a child giving a unique performance in which is displayed considerable maturity of insight. Once a pupil is accepted by the school, such qualities and talents need to be nurtured with understanding, care, and respect. This demands great patience from the staff because most of the children are extremely autonomous individuals with strong, alert personalities, who enjoy leading a rich emotional life.

In character the Yehudi Menuhin School is residential, cosmopolitan, interracial, and interreligious. At its heart it recognizes the importance of human relationships and thus it tries to foster a relaxed, open, family atmosphere which is flexible and supportive enough to satisfy individual needs. The school is conceived as a learning community in which a myriad of experiences is initiated and explored by young and old alike. At the root of this joint endeavour lies a shared form of authority and responsibility based on trust. This sense of sharing extends to the relationship between home and school which is viewed as a partnership whereby parent, teacher, and child are encouraged to work together in the hope of fulfilling individual aspirations. Thus it is not surprising that the quality of the psychological and moral climate is regarded as vital to the general and musical development of each child. This constitutes the basis of a shared form of life in which commitment, quality, and relationships are of the very essence.

Although the school is characterized by its distinctive commitment to musical performance, the primary goal is the all-round, educated artist rather than the narrow technician. Great care is taken to provide a balanced curriculum which can do full justice to the musical and general education of each student. The school day is structured to enable music and academic studies to alternate in four blocks of time for each child. This results in a complex timetable in which each pupil is given virtually an individual programme. Compared with an ordinary school, lack of time places certain constraints on the nature and number of courses that can be offered. Basic areas of study are English language and literature, foreign languages (French, German, and Italian), mathematics and the physical and human sciences; these are supported by environmental studies, history, philosophy, social studies, child development, art, crafts, and drama. Results in GCE examinations at Ordinary and Advanced levels have been encouraging in a wide range of subjects. For example, in 1978 there was a 100 per cent pass rate in the 'A' level examinations with seven passes in two subject areas, whilst at 'O' level there was an 83 per cent pass rate, with thirty-five passes in seven subject areas. Moreover, in the last two years two students have gained entry to Cambridge University, one being awarded an exhibition to King's College. Therefore, despite the overriding purpose of the school, the academic work is taken seriously by most of the students and staff. One interesting spin-off from the disciplined pattern of learning acquired in their music training is that the pupils expect a structured style of teaching in their academic work. On the whole this leads to an alert response, lively motivation, and a desire to learn.

The instruments taught at the school are violin, viola, 'cello, and piano. Each child has two hours of instrumental lessons a week, together with some additional supervised practice. The children regularly sing together and there are weekly classes in such general music activities as composition, aural training, harmony, and analysis. In addition to playing in the orchestra, most of the string players receive weekly tuition in chamber music and on the piano, whilst the pianists are coached in the accompaniments they provide for all the school concerts as well as in sonatas with string players. Considerable emphasis, then, is placed on the acquisition of broadly based musical experience and skill, learnt in such a way as to develop the pupils' analytical and reflective powers. The qualities fostered by the music staff include an acute sense of listening, a spontaneity of response to the music, artistic sensibility, an understanding of the heart and not just of the mind, and, perhaps most important of all, the ability to reach the 'soul' of the music being performed.

About half of each day is devoted to music. The children receive intensive weekly tuition from their regular teacher. Yehudi Menuhin comes to the school as often as possible and gives lessons to all the violinists and violists, whilst the 'cellists and pianists have monthly instruction from William Pleeth and Louis Kentner respectively. In addition to this the children have the opportunity of working with celebrated musicians from different parts of the world. Finally, in order to broaden their musical experience further, senior students are encouraged to attend orchestral courses, chamber music courses, and master classes during the vacations.

Instead of internal music examinations, concerts and recitals are given by the pupils at music societies, festivals, schools, colleges, and universities throughout the country. Several international competitions have been won by students whilst still at school and those who have completed their studies have an impressive record of scholarships to music colleges, conservatoires, and universities, both in this country and abroad: in New York, Philadelphia, Moscow, Brussels, Paris, Rome, Salzburg, Cologne, and Hamburg. Many of these past pupils have subsequently embarked on successful careers as soloists, chamber music players, and teachers.

There is no doubt that the staff and students at the Yehudi Menuhin

School feel most privileged to be engaged in a way of life in which the human spirit as well as the intellect is cared for; a world in which imagination, inspiration, and dedication are the norm; a world which is striving towards excellence, allied to an informed sensibility. Central to this way of life is the quality of the human beings working within the community, the quality of the human stimuli from outside the school, and the quality of its uniquely facilitating environment, which is designed to foster certain attitudes and a certain way of perceiving and responding to the world.

Critics of this conception of a specialist school might point out that such a way of life has the possible danger of cutting the children off from the tough realities of the outside world. They might quite legitimately question whether a talented young musician could become a great artist if cocooned from the strains and stresses of the social world. This is an important question and one which both staff and students of the school view with concern. At one level attempts have been made to extend the pupils' social horizons by organizing informal concerts in old people's homes, in schools for physically handicapped children, in those for educationally subnormal children, in homes for the blind, in a borstal, a rehabilitation centre, a mental hospital, a hospice for terminal cancer patients, and in a coal-mining village in Yorkshire (the morning after the concert the students went down the mine to the coalface). Links have also been established with a primary school in Tower Hamlets, East London, with a boys' comprehensive school in Southeast London, and with a girls' comprehensive school in Leeds. In these last three instances the schools brought their own form of music making to the Menuhin School (i.e., a Carl Orff workshop, a brass band, and a folk group respectively) and the visiting children spent a night at the school. A most helpful working relationship has also grown up with a local First school where several older students spend an afternoon each week teaching some of the young children in a variety of activities. In addition to these more direct experiences regular talks are given to the pupils on social and political questions, particularly by people who have been intimately connected with such problem areas as Rhodesia, South Africa, Chile, and China. The question of human rights is kept alive by contacts with Amnesty and through the large number of visitors from Israel who have left the Soviet Union in the last few years. Courses in social studies and child development also form a normal part of the curriculum for all older students. Therefore the school does not try to escape from matters of fundamental human concern.

Admittedly, it could be argued that these experiences might not impinge very deeply into a child's consciousness and that they are unlikely to lead to social action later in life unless they are felt directly at a gut level. Moreover, the giving of concerts as a form of social service could be viewed as an empty moral gesture which alleviates the conscience of the talented minority (or of the staff), and does little towards enhancing the lives of those in acute social, mental, and physical need. But perhaps the same criticism could be levelled at the idea of community service in schools generally. This does not seem a good reason for ceasing to engage in these kinds of activities. Whatever the sceptics might say, there is plenty of evidence to show that if young people share their gifts with others in an open, generous, and unassuming way, much positive good can be done and much pleasure given, as well as gained.

Central to the philosophy of the Menuhin School, then, is the belief in the need to enrich the lives of both the children and staff with the widest possible range of human experiences. This is regarded as fundamental to the education of the developing artist. But perhaps this conviction that artistic insight is partly dependent on the depth of a person's social awareness should not be overstressed. For instance, each individual, however young, has his own dilemmas and problems – he has experienced joy and pain, happiness and fear, anxiety and anguish. In other words, a child's own limited, but nonetheless human, situation provides a repertoire of experiences which can influence the quality of a musical performance. Moreover, and perhaps most importantly for a specialist music school, there is no doubt that artistic understanding feeds heavily on listening, looking, seeing, feeling – that is, it draws on other artistic experiences, not necessarily on loosely related social experiences.

Conclusion

In conclusion, it must be stressed that this chapter is not suggesting that all children with specific talents and gifts should be educated in specialist schools. This would seem to be one fruitful avenue for some children depending on the need and the nature of the circumstances. By concentrating on the example of the Yehudi Menuhin School, I hope to have shown that it is possible for a child to receive a high-level, quality education, and training in his own special field of interest, without detriment to the breadth of experience and understanding so fundamental to being an educated person.

CHAPTER FIVE

THE ROLE OF THE NATIONAL ASSOCIATION FOR GIFTED CHILDREN

*The National Association for Gifted Children**
Henry Collis

In 1965 a conference on the education of gifted children under the chairmanship of Sir George Trevelyan revealed that not enough was being done for these children and that a specialist organization was urgently needed. The next year the National Association for Gifted Children was launched and soon became a registered charity.

As soon as the association came to be known, letters started arriving from parents in need. The number of enquiries has grown steadily and can confront the small headquarters with quite a problem of keeping up to date. Here are examples of two received in 1978. The first mother was referred to us by the family doctor and writes: 'With my four-year-old boy any answer to a question only leads to another question. My husband and I are both teachers but are completely worn out. We have tried him with tranquillisers and the doctor has tried psychiatry. All to no avail. Today he has had the tantrum of all tantrums because I was not able to tell him why he could not see the wind. Do *please* help us to help him, instead of shouting and getting cross.' The other mother was referred by a health visitor: 'We have had

*NAGC, 1 South Audley Street, London W1Y 5DQ

thirteen years of worry over John who is now thirteen. The last six months have been sheer hell. I know there must be an answer somewhere and I pray that it is your association. Is it?'

It is not for me to say whether the NAGC is the answer or not, but it certainly was in part for parents and children like this that the association was formed in 1966. Many parents join us when distraught because of their exceptionally demanding and restless children, and are very relieved to meet other parents and not to feel so alone. Our membership, which includes a special rate for students, stays constant at about 4,000 families and others professionally interested (e.g., doctors, teachers, educational psychologists, health visitors). Why with a constant stream of new members does the total not grow? Because when the children are about fifteen or so our job is largely done and families drift away. The new intake of, say, 1,500 families a year brings new life and new problems and keeps us involved with some 7,000 gifted and talented children. Incidentally, I wish that in Britain we had not stuck to the portmanteau word 'gifted' instead of adopting the custom of other countries. They refer to 'gifted' as meaning intellectual, and 'talented' as covering excellence in such areas as the expressive and visual arts, manual dexterity, physical prowess, personal relationships. There is no doubt that there has been far less sympathy with and understanding of the top 2 per cent in the intellectual ability range and the 15 per cent or so creatively endowed, because of the queasy reaction some people have to the simple word 'gifted'. They forget how literally correct the word is. I fancy that if we had started using 'gifted and talented' long ago this description would have been accepted as common parlance, and children and parents affected would have found life easier.

Certainly the name 'National Association for Gifted Children' has caused many difficulties, especially in fund raising, which has been one of my main commitments as director. Very, very rarely has anything worthwhile come just as the result of a letter on our notepaper, however persuasively worded and fully documented. Every effort has had to be made to meet a trustee or the director or secretary of the foundation. Their surprise that gifted children are not automatically the luckiest things on two legs has been considerable. When they begin to realize how much more of a handicap it can be in a deprived area to be three years ahead than one year behind, they start making notes. When they hear of poor homes being turned head over heels by these restless demanding children, they begin to see why the NAGC exists. When one refers to the few who are well on the road to becoming expert criminals with consummate evasive action, they are usually showing signs of accepting the word 'gifted' in a different light. Prejudice, born out of ignorance of the real facts, recedes and a lively interest takes its place.

The NAGC is fortunate in receiving at the moment (1979) grants from the DES, the DHSS, and the Scottish Education Department. They are far from large but help to make the association accepted nationally, just as a small annual grant by the local education authority to some of our forty-five branches gives them a feeling of local respectability. All these branches are run by volunteers, mostly parents.

How do people become members? Most parents who join us are in the middle and lower income brackets, and for those with very low incomes we are always ready to waive the subscription. Many are recommended to come to us by an educational psychologist or head teacher. The more disadvantaged a family, the more resistant they are to accepting that they have an exceptionally intelligent child. To be talented is different; it is prestigious. Otherwise they thrive on conformity and sometimes even urge poor work performance at school. We ask for no proof of giftedness in the child because to do so would be to smack of élitism and might well exclude the very families who need our help most – those in very underprivileged areas where, for environmental reasons, children may only achieve moderate scores on intelligence tests. Such children may, however, possess a latent potential well within the gifted category, a potential which is only waiting an opportunity to show itself.

The principal object locally is for the parents and other members to meet and exchange views and to talk, perhaps for the first time, quite freely about their children. Hitherto it may well have been an embarrassing subject. Then we hope they will run weekend activities for the children (whom we call directly 'Explorers Unlimited'). In London there are three clubs which operate on Saturdays except during school holidays. Some 300 children attend and there are always waiting lists. Some children as young as three (but of course with a much higher mental age) are catered for. The main group, aged six to fourteen, are split up into small units and taught as wide a variety of skills as the expertise of the parents makes possible, eg., drama, computers, electronics, art, craft (including candle making, basket making, balsa modelling, jewellery, woodworking) mineralogy, chess, ecology, pottery, music making, science, astronomy, anatomy, ornithology, French, and Italian. Care is taken to avoid direct conflict with school curricula, or we should only exacerbate the situation by making the children further ahead still. One branch includes esperanto and another Chinese calligraphy –

neither taught very frequently in school. Other examples of NAGC activities can be found in Pickard (1976).

What is the object behind all this effort? Primarily it is so that like minds may challenge each other. This can mean that children unique in their school classes (perhaps even in their school) come to realize that just to be very clever is not enough. They have got to become well motivated or they will be overtaken in life by others less able than they are. In these activities and in their discussions with other Explorers they may encounter an experience quite new for them – that of not being on top and *not* winning every argument. How salutary this can be and what a valuable lesson for life where we have to meet success *and* failure and still survive.

Frustration at school and mishandling at home may have made the children self-centred, withdrawn, or aggressive. Three hours with their intellectual or creative peers can begin to make them better adjusted and less antisocial. We are lucky here in that the great majority of our members' children are delightful, well balanced, enthusiastic, and blessed with that special sparkle which indicates real giftedness. In their company the isolate makes friends, the manipulator finds that somehow he has been gently coerced into doing what he never intended to do, and the 'centre of attraction *wherever* he goes', as his fond mother says, rather enjoys being ordinary for a change. One thing we regard as very important – so as not to split families, the brothers and sisters are usually welcome, however ungifted, and can also become useful members of the 'Explorers Club', working together in their own groups.

An increasing number of educational authorities are giving practical help in the way of free premises and teacher help. Residential courses are run during the summer on all sorts of subjects. A week is usually as long as the instructor can survive . The sort of courses which might feature in one year are: science/outdoor activities in South Wales; field studies in Northern Ireland; art in Devonshire; practical chemistry in Leeds; an orchestral course in Kent; film production in Northampton, and theatre and drama in London.

A very important development over the years has been the employment of part-time regional officers, only possible when special grants for the purpose have been made by various charitable trusts. The first appointment was made for the South and West and there is no doubt that several branches, mainly Devon, have found this professional support of the greatest help.

Two new projects could be very significant. One regional officer, employed as the result of a grant from the chairman of a large firm on a trading estate, has gone into all the local primary schools and helped to identify children of exceptional ability who could well be gifted. With the cooperation of the area education officer, heads of schools, and parents, these children have now formed an 'Explorers Club' which can meet in the excellent welfare premises of the firm which gave the original help.

Another regional officer is hard at work in an inner-city district where there are many immigrants. He is bringing together very bright children from five ethnic groups and enabling them to have challenging activities with the NAGC Explorers of the local branch. One hopes that finance will be forthcoming for a further steady penetration into these deprived areas where gifted children can be discovered and helped to lead worthwhile lives.

There is also a schools' liaison officer who travels widely, talking at educational seminars, meeting school staffs in teachers' centres, calling on LEAs and other official bodies. She spends a great deal of time trying to soothe troubled parents without interfering with schools directly. Often it is just a matter of persuading the mother to seek an appointment at school and ask for advice about her child who is so frustrated at home. Any head worth his or her salt will recognize symptoms which are arising from boredom at school and try to arrange some sort of enriched curriculum or even see the child personally for a short daily conversation. Parents of gifted children are much more vulnerable than teachers usually realize. Like their children they can conceal their feelings more than most people and this is why they are often misunderstood. I have found them very eager to cooperate with the school without interfering, but where the head is unsympathetic they feel that they walk a tightrope between being considered overproud mums who are trying to pressurize the school, or mums who have no interest in their children once they go through the school gate.

The need for our voluntary counselling service which Mrs. Sieghart describes in the next section has arisen to a large extent through gifted children being ignored by teachers who regard them as a threat and feel they can perfectly well look after themselves. Then there is tension at home. I realize only too well the strain of taking a large class of average and below-average children and then finding one child with an intellectual ability three years ahead of the rest. However, the dedicated, sensitive, patient teacher can manage somehow to create a rapport with a child like this and keep him sparkling.

It is a valuable complement to the counselling scheme that there is an element in the DHSS grant for the holding of seminars in different parts of the country to help child specialists, paediatricians, health visitors, and teachers of the youngest classes to recognize and understand gifted children. The incidence is so small that the medical profession and allied disciplines cannot devote much training time to learning about children who may be handicapped by isolation through being too bright. What a shock it is to the five-year-old who taught herself to read fluently at three and a half to find a totally blank response when she asks the child in the next chair how she enjoyed this or that book. Suddenly there is a barrier which hurts and can cause aggression.

For members who have children with musical gifts there is the opportunity to take them to Michal Hambourg, our music counsellor and a concert pianist herself. She writes of her work in the last section of this chapter.

Over the last five years NAGC has been involved in three special projects – research on gifted children in a social context (Calouste Gulbenkian Foundation, described in Chapter 6), a follow-up study to Professor Tempest's Southport Enquiry (Leverhulme Trust Fund), and in 1978 research about gifted children in comprehensive schools, for which there is financial assistance from the Department of Education and Science.

Taking stock, there are still many NAGC aspirations unfulfilled, but on the credit side the association now enjoys much closer links with the DES and LEAs, where most of the chief education officers have named contacts on their staff for our headquarters or the local branch to approach. Explorers' Clubs are better organized and have proved themselves, and an encouraging number of families feel that membership has been beneficial. In a few cases there have been dramatic rescue operations and it is rewarding to see these boys and girls going on to further education far better equipped and far more socially at ease than ever seemed possible a few years ago.

What has been the most exciting event so far? Undoubtedly the first World Conference on Gifted Children which the NAGC held in London at the beginning of September 1975. There were many Jonahs who felt we had overstretched ourselves and might regret such an ambitious idea. In the event there were over 500 participants from 51 countries, including a number of official delegations, a government reception at Lancaster House, and the final euphoria which resulted in the formation of the World Council for Gifted and Talented Children. A report of the proceedings was published in Gibson and Chennells (1976). The second World Conference took place in San Francisco in 1977. Jerusalem was the setting for the third conference in July 1979.

Finally, following the lead of the International Year of the Child (1979), let us think very specially about the rights of every boy and girl, however slow or however bright. The London conference left nobody in any doubt about our obligations to children of high potential and particularly to those children who are not reaching their potential. Mrs. Sieghart, the national chairman, gave this message in her closing address:

> Our responsibility to this whole generation, and in particular to the gifted, is so great that many of us feel it to be positively frightening. Our children may tell us that we are to blame for the state of the world, and we have left them a terrible legacy. Perhaps they are right, but we too inherited a world which we thought had been poorly fashioned by our parents, and so on. But the least we can do, perhaps, is to say to those who will succeed us, our children, very well, you will find the world as we have left it, blame us if you must but we have done one thing for you while we had the power: we have given you that which we had in our own gift, and we have done all that we could to enable you to develop those gifts with which you yourself are endowed so that you may use them as you wish, for good or ill, and pass them on in your turn. I do not think that we can rightly be asked to do more than that, and that is a good deal (in Gibson and Chennells, 1977).

Families under Stress
Felicity Sieghart

In common with most other children, the gifted child is part of a family setting. There seem to be many examples of families containing a gifted child in which the whole family experience considerable stresses. It seems to me immaterial whether the stress comes directly from the gifts or whether it is the result of the parents' anxieties about the unusualness of their child. The result is the same and there seem to be many factors that contribute to it. I have interviewed a large number of mothers of gifted children over the last ten years and have been amazed to find that most of them do not want to have a very gifted child. Some fear the responsibility it puts upon them; others feel inadequate since they are not so intelligent themselves; and another category, who were perhaps frustrated gifted children in their own childhood, anticipate the difficulties their own offspring might have and are fearful for them. All of them would like to have had successful, intelligent, but normal children. Some have spoken to me in terms of depression and anxiety, almost as if they were speaking of a handicapped child, and several have asked me in all sincerity if there was anything I or anyone else could do in order to change their child into a more ordinary one.

Undoubtedly, there are various pressures which parents can find difficulty in coping with. The problems often begin very early in life since so many parents have reported to us that their child from the start needed so much less sleep than the average baby (see Part III, Case Study 6). Five or six hours of sleep a night seems to be the required amount for many gifted toddlers, a situation which leaves their parents exhausted and unready to face the next day. Speech develops early in most gifted children and, with an insatiable curiosity for knowledge and the answer to the world's problems, they bombard their parents with an incessant barrage of questions. Many are quite profound. For instance 'Who will be God, when God dies?' 'Who was I before I was born?', and many others. Often this 'demandingness' can be more than a parent can tolerate. It is at this point that a mother can telephone the association's offices and announce her fears that she will soon become a child batterer. Sometimes one parent can cope much more successfully than the other, causing tension between husband and wife.

Another problem that can occur within families is that a very able child can so overshadow his siblings that an otherwise bright child cannot survive the competition and becomes a total under-achiever at school. We have on occasions advised parents to have a relatively less able sibling of a gifted child assessed by an educational psychologist and they have often been amazed to find that the child is really quite bright. The parents' estimate of the child's abilities had been distorted by the constant comparison with his highly gifted brother or sister. Different stresses arise when adoptive parents of normal intelligence find that they have to bring up a child with an intelligence far beyond their own and feel that they do not have the resources to provide it with all the intellectual feeding it will need. Similarly, single mothers feel an inadequacy to play the roles of mother and father to a specially gifted child.

Over the past two years, our association has devised a new method of bringing help to the families of gifted children who feel that the problems they face are bringing real stress into their family lives. We have tried to understand the problems of the mother of a preschooler who asserted 'you cannot *make* people do anything' and of another mother who commented 'the child appeared so rational so early that I expected rational behaviour.' We appreciate that the families who join NAGC probably do not represent a true cross-section of the families of gifted children (see Chapter 6). Often they turn to us for support because they are encountering problems. Some of the families show their need in their initial letter applying for membership and, of these, quite a number can be helped from head office by a letter which answers a specific enquiry about schools or some other specialist service. More often, it is only when the new member has been attached to a local branch of the association and been welcomed into the group of other volunteer members that the reason they joined the association really becomes clear.

Our new method of help has been to organize a voluntary counselling service. With 45 branches spread over the UK it has been essential for us to regionalize the help we can offer to families. We have always had untrained listening ears. Many of these people are parents of gifted children themselves and what they lack in professionalism, they make up for in the first-hand experience they have gained. They have survived the ordeal themselves and have lived through the sleepless nights and the insatiable demands. However, the receipt of a three-year grant from the DHSS for counselling work inspired us to set up a more formal, trained service. As laymen, we felt ourselves inadequate to the task of training and we set out to investigate other bodies who trained counsellors. Our budget was small and we realized that the amount of training we could afford to give would have to be limited. Of the agencies we consulted, the National Marriage Guidance Council seemed to us to have the most suitable programme which could be tailored to suit our needs. We now have 20 voluntary counsellors at work in the UK with sufficient training to accept their own limitations. They refer to professionals locally when this is necessary and, for their own support and for discussion of their case problems, they rely on meetings with tutors from the NMGC. We are constantly learning in setting up such a scheme but, once again, the fact that all these counsellors have been parents of gifted children has caused their clients to feel a greater confidence in them than otherwise would have been the case.

The counselling service we provide needs to be a very elastic one and one which can be adapted to the needs and circumstances of a particular family. The sort of problem described by a mother at an activity day of the association might well ostensibly be a school problem, perhaps that her gifted child has come to dislike school through lack of challenge. In the course of this, or perhaps a subsequent talk, it can easily emerge that the father is very ambitious for his son and it is he who is in fact unhappy that the child is appearing to underachieve. In this way he is projecting all his anxieties onto the child. Because of the geographical spread of our membership, some of the counselling has to be done on the telephone. This is obviously a different technique from a face-to-face interview and our counsellors have to learn it during their training. A few of the members come for weekly sessions of counselling; many more have an initial session and then return for more help whenever particular difficulties seem to arise in their family. To be directive and to resort to the giving of well-intentioned advice, however good, would not help the families to sort out their problems and so, however sporadic the interviews, the counselling stays essentially nondirective in character. Some clients are immensely grateful if their problems resolve; others conveniently forget what life was like before they asked for help – an experience common to all those in the helping professions.

To illustrate the variety of cases we deal with, I would like to mention two of the cases that have come my way over the years. To have given concrete advice to both families would have been quite unfruitful, since, in the early stages, they were unready to accept their problems for what they really were. The acceptance was gradual and only achieved by a considerable degree of change and growth on the part of both sets of parents.

The first boy, John, was an adopted child living in the West Country. His adoptive parents only succeeded in giving birth to a son of their own when John was three. They noticed early on that he was very bright and an early talker but only fully became aware of the situation when they compared the progress of their younger child (who turned out to be slightly mentally retarded) with the milestones of their elder child, John. When they first contacted me, John was six. A number of problems had arisen already. John was very bored at school, made no friends of his own age, and badgered his parents all day to play chess with him. These were the outward and obvious problems. Apart from this, the family was torn apart by deeper emotional problems. Both parents found it hard to accept that it should be the adoptive child rather than their own son who showed such talents. There were a lot of hidden hostile feelings to John and they gave me the impression that they felt great resentment that they should have this double affliction – the handicap of retardation and the handicap of brilliance.

As John moved from school to school, underchallenged and unpopular, I had considerable contact with this family. Sometimes they came to see me; sometimes when life was particularly difficult, they telephoned me. It was obvious that no one had very much sympathy and they needed to talk about their feelings to a willing listener who was not emotionally involved with them. John's apparent handicap was very poor coordination. Other children did not like him because he was so quick to reply in class, but they also jeered at him because he was so hopeless on the football field and could easily be pushed over by boys even smaller than he was. It occurred to the parents that there might be something physically wrong, but there was nothing that their local GP could diagnose.

Some time later, the distraught mother contacted me again. After developing acute headaches, John had been seen by a specialist who had found that he was suffering from a brain tumour. He was operated on unsuccessfully, was partially paralysed as a result, and the prognosis was very poor indeed. This situation was beyond the scope of an NAGC counsellor and I referred the case to a suitable professional who was able to talk to the boy and his parents about impending death and the feelings of fear, impotence, and anger that accompany such a knowledge.

The second case concerned a boy, Alan, living with his family in the North of England. Alan had a younger sister, a father who was an academic, a doting mother, and a grandfather who lived with the family. Alan could best be described as an isolated child, remote from the world, very interested in scientific subjects, but with no friends in any age group. It was only established after two years at school that he had a hearing defect which probably contributed to his isolation. Though interested in his school work, he hated school and dreaded play time where he was subjected to bullying and all kinds of indignities. Although almost as bright as her brother, the younger sister behaved very differently. She chose to play down her giftedness, achieve sufficiently to remain somewhere in the middle of the class, and few would have suspected from her overall performance that her potential was considerable. None of these difficulties could be discussed by the adults in the family when I first started to see the mother. The fact that the parents had no visitors did not seem strange to them, but they were very worried about their son who seemed so lonely. The boy only seemed happy when he came on NAGC activities where the other children at least tolerated him and respected his intelligence. In this company, he could even make attempts to play, something which had never been encouraged at home. At first, the parents were anxious for a solution to their children's problems, but very reluctant to bring themselves into the picture. I think they were helped by seeing their son accepted into an NAGC group and, through this, made to feel more acceptable people themselves.

This boy, Alan, will probably never have a very satisfying social life, but I think that contacts between NAGC and his family have enabled all members of the family to relax and, as a result, be more able to fulfil their individual potentials.

Undoubtedly, there are more complications arising from the upbringing of any child who is appreciably different from other children. Parents sometimes need help in understanding their task. We hope in NAGC that, in providing a service which it would be difficult to obtain from any official agency, we are contributing to the happiness and fulfilment of an ever-growing number of parents and their gifted children.

The Musical Problems of Talented and Gifted Children
Michal Hambourg

A great many of the problems of gifted and talented children arise from a sense of apartness, an awareness of living in an extra creative dimension which is difficult to communicate to the world at large, and in which they are totally involved. As a musician with an inherited talent, who has a lifelong preoccupation with the meaning of musical experience, I felt that I might be able to share problems and insights with musically gifted children. My aim would be, therefore, to help to alleviate some of the pressures and tensions which arise from unusual qualities such as the possession of musical giftedness.

Music is often a great source of sustenance to gifted academics whose structured disciplines are rigorous. The personal pleasure of learning a chosen instrument and acquiring technical skill exacts a self-imposed discipline which involves the whole personality.

Children come to my home to talk, to listen, and to play music. It is in the sharing of these experiences with me that shy and withdrawn children can begin to realize the 'bond of sound' and to find out that we can exchange musical ideas. We make music together and often they ask me if I know a specific work; when I play it, they express intense interest and pleasure. This is my first step in bringing them to the realization of the enjoyment that they can give by sharing their own gifts of interpretation with other people.

In the same spirit, playing in duets, ensembles, and orchestras, experiencing music together, is a great help in establishing much needed friendships.

Involvement, interest, and affection are keystones in this aspect of my work which lies mainly in the realm of the soul and of the imagination. We talk about our concepts of sounds, shapes, and forms, about colours in music, and about our feelings as we listen, and gradually the nervous and preoccupied children who visit me begin to realize that music is an intensely living part of our world, and that it is an area where they can contact many others; again this is a step towards overcoming their sense of isolation.

It is important that wherever possible music should be a part of the family interests; it is lonely for a young child to practise without guidance, and clearly musical training should be supervised. When parents are not musical, they can still keep a tactful watch, and should ask the teacher as to the best way of doing this. One of the most delicate advisory areas is the fitting of music into a curriculum already loaded with other work; often a child is learning two instruments and taking part in the orchestra and the choir, as well as preparing homework. This means that not enough time can be given to the real substance of music. The gradual development of an important critical faculty, listening to oneself as one plays, learning in so doing to control the emotions and thereby to consider the meaning of the composition, can be inhibited by superficial work periods where the best that can be achieved is a form of technical proficiency. This is where my teenagers get caught. Some of them have worked in this musical pattern for five or six years, and because of its limitations they will suddenly rebel, get bored, and decide to give up. It is here that the music counsellor fulfils a therapeutic function; in a one-to-one situation where personal interest and concern plus musical knowledge are offered, it is possible to ' :lp these young people through the impasse by reassuring them and encouraging their valid musical insight. A practical asset here is a personal demonstration of the powerful aid that an accomplished technique provides in assisting the art of interpretation.

The specialist musician has different problems from those of the gifted academic with musical skills. Owing to their extreme preoccupation with the inner world of sound, young specialist musicians often have trouble in giving their full attention to matters outside their music. It is difficult to explain the nature and effect of this constant inner stream of music to people who do not experience it; nevertheless it is important to do so. From birth the musician will be aware of the ever-present nature of rhythm and sound and is powerfully affected by them. Very loud noises, constant exposure to television, radio, and stereo, the background accompaniments blaring forth from stores and railway stations are extremely exhausting to children with highly sensitive hearing. Many of my talks with parents involve explaining this to them, and also, because every child responds differently, it is necessary to discuss particular needs and sensitive methods of recognizing and ministering to them. The families of these children need support and information about seemingly unpredictable behaviour, and also practical advice concerning every aspect of life from public performance to sleepless nights. The daily life of the young artist, lived on a deep emotional level with outbursts of furious temper and a host of petty demands masking feelings of insecurity, requires much loving tolerance from the long-suffering family who need their counsellor as a listening and sympathetic safety valve.

Today in the musical world there are manifold opportunities for young players; excellent courses in music, competitions for aspiring performers, well-designed school music programmes, television and radio concerts. Before embarking on these, careful stock must be taken of the child's potential; some very talented players have not the nervous stamina to sustain competition work. I advise that the utmost cooperation between families and teachers *must* exist in order to select a course suitable to the musical nature of the child. It is too often forgotten that the life of the musician begins at an early age, and that the question of retirement does not exist. Given the right help and early training, musical insights become deeper and more fruitful as time goes on. When this dimension is ignored, many talented musicians find that their source of creativity suddenly dries up in the early thirties and they experience painful problems trying to find the path again.

Tentative guidelines for the education of the young musician must be laid with the utmost care, taking into account all aspects of the personality, and planning step by step with the teacher's specialist skill and advice (see also Chapter 4). To musically gifted performers, playing in public is an intense effort of musical concentration. All available resources must be used in order to communicate the composer's ideas to the public; the performer is the living link between composer and listener. I cannot stress too strongly the difference between using an instrument as a form of gymnastic exhibition in finger skill, and the gradual harnessing of this skill into performance in depth, which is the true role of the interpreter. Public performance for the very young musician is tiring and overstimulating. In early adolescence when serious study and careful relaxation are needed, it can be destructive to musical development. On the other hand, the excellent concerts devised by responsible teachers in which young musicians have the chance to show family friends and distinguished guests what has been achieved during the term are very much to be encouraged, as are opportunities to play to groups of fellow pupils or musical gatherings at home or in friends' houses.

Mozart was undoubtedly one of the world's most gifted musical children. From musical history we know much about the great musical pressures exerted upon him by his overambitious father, Leopold. We know how adversely these affected his health and growth during adolescence. The terrible pressure of his perpetual exposure to the public, at an age when he needed peace and quiet in which to work, undoubtedly helped to contribute to his delicate physique and early death.

I urge parents to talk with teachers; often unmusical families feel they have nothing to offer, not realizing that their interest and knowledge of their child can make a vital difference when assessing the situation as a whole. Where home life is concerned, for all my families, I recommend the provision of a 'place to be quiet'. In busy overcrowded family life, children are hard pressed to find a space where they can work, listen to music, and be alone in order to think about their musical responses. Sometimes the school can help by making a practice room free when only the communal living room is available at home. It is my hope gradually to find local friends sympathetic to music and its aims who will be supportive to young musicians and their specific need for practice rooms, musical talk, and a sense of belonging to their neighbourhood.

I hope I have said enough to make it clear that my function as music counsellor is primarily an interpretative one. We can lay down certain facts gained by our own experience and that of others, offering them for consideration. But in the last analysis, where art is concerned, every gifted and talented child has a specific area of need and it is in the exchange of musical understanding that I can sometimes reach the heart of the problem and thus dissipate tension and frustration.

CHAPTER SIX

GIFTEDNESS IN A SOCIAL CONTEXT
Joan Freeman

The definition of excellence is always relative and the concept of 'giftedness' varies across time and across cultures. A quality seen in one society and at one time as valuable may be regarded as worthless in another context. Children are also seen as gifted at different levels of achievement, even within the parameters of their own society. For instance, a highly selective school may describe one boy as of poor ability in relation to his fellow students yet the same child could be described as truly 'gifted' in another school.

It is also true that teachers are often very uncertain about what constitutes 'giftedness'. A national investigation by Her Majesty's Inspectorate in Britain (DES, 1977) reported: 'The plain fact was that "giftedness" as a concept had not been thought about.' On the whole, teachers in Britain are not in favour of recognizing giftedness as a problem. Where a child is seen as both gifted and in difficulty, teachers usually see the problems in individual terms rather than as an example of a specific category of children (Ogilvie, 1973; DES, 1977). Perhaps in the present state of confusion and paucity of evidence, this is the safest approach.

Nevertheless some children are identified as 'clever' or 'gifted' and the identification and labelling of a child as 'gifted' constitute part of the process of socialization: that is, the development of attitudes and behaviour through interaction with others, according to the standards of an individual's group. A child learns to behave in the context of other people, i.e., society. It is by this means that the human young grow up and adjust to their societies, so that they may continue to live in them in psychological comfort, the process going on both in families and in schools. A child is not called 'gifted' out of the blue, nor can the terminology be without effect on the child's self-image.

Labelling a child as gifted and thereby 'different' is a positive action. The motivation for placing such a label on a child will have some relationship to what happens afterwards. It is important to know why identification is considered to be necessary, whether it would be of help to the child or others, and whether the label is indeed justified. The question about the effects produced by labelling a child 'gifted' is one of the questions examined in this chapter.

Another question to be examined concerns the backgrounds of the children identified as gifted. The double effect of both the home and the school on children's behaviour has been studied in depth by only a few researchers in Britain, notably the Newsons in Nottingham (Newson and Newson, 1977). Their investigations have always included visits to the child's home, which is, after all, where the child spends most of his life.

I first discovered the importance of this for myself when I was investigating the effects of home and school on aesthetic talent in children (Freeman, 1977). I found that both home and school were able to initiate interest in the arts, but it was only where the home was entirely supportive that the child could achieve sufficiently well to be categorized as 'aesthetically talented'. Where research into children's development does not include visits to the children's homes, then a large slice of the influence on their lives must have been missed out.

The final question to be examined concerns the behavioural adjustment of gifted children. Definitions of giftedness are often descriptive and may include such comments as 'the gifted child needs little sleep' or 'is generally difficult to handle'. But these signs may or may not be directly related to giftedness. Many are linked to other behaviours which are not seen as problematic and this emphasizes the importance of seeing each child as an individual, thus avoiding the dangerous generalized viewpoint described in Chapter 1.

Setting up the Gulbenkian Project

This project was made possible by the National Association for Gifted

Children (UK). I was given free access to their records, but in no way did they seek to influence the process of the research. It was named after the Gulbenkian Foundation, which provided financial support. As already indicated, the primary aims of the research were to find answers to the following questions:

1   Are children who are identified as gifted by their parents different from other children who are not so identified?
2   Are the home backgrounds of children identified as gifted by their parents different from those of other children who are not so identified?
3   Do gifted children, however identified, suffer from emotional problems when receiving nonspecialist education?

The National Association for Gifted Children (NAGC) had been in existence for eight years at the beginning of the project. All the correspondence, from the time of its inception, was examined – 6,500 sets referring to about 4,500 children. It was from this material that the target sample of children emerged. Their parents had all joined the association on their behalf within a period of four years; they lived in the Northwest of England and were aged between five and sixteen.

Two control groups were identified by screening all the members of the target child's class, using the Raven's Progressive Matrices (Raven, 1965). This was used as a nonverbal and fairly culture-free test of general intellectual ability. The first control child (C_1) was selected as having a Raven's raw score very close to that of the target child. The second control child (C_2) was taken from the class at random in terms of ability. Both control groups were matched with the target children for age, sex, and educational experience, i.e., they were from the same school class. None of the control group parents were members of NAGC. The final sample consisted of three groups of 70 children each – the target and two matched control groups. There were thus 210 children in all, 210 families and 61 schools. Their homes were spread fairly evenly over the Northwest of England.

Procedure

All the homes and schools were visited at least once. During the home visit, the children were given the Stanford-Binet Intelligence Test (Terman and Merrill, 1960) and the parents steered through a long questionnaire. Ratings were made of the home and neighbourhood. For the most part the ratings and questionnaires used in this research followed a 'structured' rather than 'open' format.

In the schools, the class teachers filled in the Bristol Social Adjustment Guide Day School Edition (Scott, 1976). This provides a systematic measure of a child's behaviour in school, with particular regard to adjustment. Head teachers answered a questionnaire. The children were also given a personality test and a music-ability test, as well as having a questionnaire to complete.

Eventually, 217 pieces of information were collected for each of the 210 children. The head teachers provided 47 pieces of information each about how their 61 schools were run. All the data were analysed factorially, by analysis of variance (using orthogonal comparisons), by regression coefficients, and by nonparametric methods.

Differences between children

This section discusses the findings in relation to the differences between the children identified by their parents as gifted and those not so identified. The findings are presented under the following headings: intelligence, behaviour at home, behaviour at school, other differences.

Intelligence

The target and first control children had been accurately matched for intellectual development on the Raven's Matrices Test. But when their Stanford-Binet scores were compared, they were found to be significantly different.

Table 6.1(a) Raven's Matrices Scores of the Target and Control Children

IQ	T	C_1	C_2
Mean	34.53	34.60	28.76
S.D.	12.85	11.45	11.58

Table 6.1(b) The Stanford-Binet IQs of the target and control groups

IQ	T	C_1	C_2
Mean	147.1	134.343	119.200
S.D.	17.413	17.133	16.094

The relative differences between the results of the two tests are considered to be due to a combination of the following factors:

1   The Raven' Matrices is nonverbal and 'probably the most culture-free test of general intelligence yet devised by psychologists' (Jensen, 1973). The Stanford-Binet does emphasize learned ability, especially at the upper levels. In fact the target group had actually had more out-of-school tuition of various kinds than the first control group.

2   There are always differences between tests given to a group, as in the screening procedure using the Raven's, and a one-to-one interview type test, such as the Stanford-Binet.

3   Nearly two-thirds of the sample children scored in the top 5 per cent of possible scores in the Raven's test. This is the recognized ceiling effect, where children of varying degrees of brightness cluster at the top of the scale and the test does not provide sufficient headroom for the most able to show their paces. The Stanford-Binet provides a more precise measure of the higher ranges of academic ability and is a particularly suitable test for use with gifted children.

4   Two tests used on the same sample will inevitably produce somewhat different results since scores are always particular to the test used.

The Stanford-Binet test results clearly indicate, however, that the target children, when assessed on an individual IQ test, have a significantly higher mean IQ than their controls. It seems likely that their parents had recognized their children's intellectual giftedness and had sought membership of the NAGC as a consequence of this awareness. It is also possible, however, that other reasons were involved in their search for outside help. These are discussed later in the chapter in relation to question 3.

Behaviour at home

The target children were twice as frequently found to be first-born or only children than either of the control groups. As such, they would probably come in for twice as much parental anxiety. They were described by their parents as being considerably more alert at birth than the other children and as walking and talking earlier, but not reading earlier.

The parents of the target children described them as being 'difficult' to bring up over three times as often as either of the control groups. More specifically, they were seen as particularly sensitive, very emotional, and having had difficulty with sleep. They were seen as very independent children, who felt themselves to be different from others. These children were blessed with extraordinarily good memories and made excellent school progress. They were said to prefer educational-type television and to read widely. Unfortunately, they had very few friends, compared with the other groups, and those which they did have tended to be older than themselves.

The behavioural characteristics described by the target parents were significantly different from control parents' descriptions of their children. Nearly five times as many target parents as controls described their children as very emotional and twice as many described them as particularly sensitive. But the target parents described their children as feeling different nearly seventeen times as often as parents of the control groups. This, of course, was the parent's description of the child's feelings, not the child's self-description. Maybe some thought that, under the circumstances, that was how they *should* feel.

When asked about themselves, however, the children did not validate these parental descriptions. Nearly all were very happy at school, but the target children played much less competitive sport than the controls. Perhaps they were indoors practising their music or engaged in their out-of-school lessons.

The target children did appear to be more sensitive than the control children but certainly did not feel more liked or disliked by others, in spite of their designated 'giftedness'. No child described him or herself as feeling different.

Behaviour at school

There was not one single significant difference between the control groups when their scores on the British Social Adjustment Guides were compared. But all the variables listed below showed significant differences ($p < 0.01$) between the target and control groups, in relation to the proportion of children gaining scores of one or more. They are given in percentages of 70 (the number in each group).

The terms 'Underreaction' and 'Overreaction' indicate the general type of behaviour involved. Sometimes this can be specified as a clear syndrome. Underreaction, for example, includes unforthcoming behaviour, withdrawal, and depression. Overreaction includes inconsequence (in which the child tends to act impulsively without an advance mental rehearsal of the consequences), hostility, and peer maladaptiveness (or behaviour which results in bad relations with other children of the same age). Some of the items on the test are not specifically related to such syndromes and where this occurs the results are grouped under headings such as 'Nonspecific underreaction'.

Table 6.2 Children's social adjustment in school

BSAG scores of 1+ in percentages of 70	T	C$_1$	C$_2$
Underreaction			
Withdrawal	23	10	10
Nonspecific underreaction	37	24	21
Overreaction			
Inconsequence	50	26	34
Hostility	39	17	13
Peer Maladaptiveness	29	14	9
Total overreaction	63	54	30

These figures represent the class teacher's observations on each of the three sample children in her class. The percentages overlap because many of the children were assigned to several categories of maladjustment. Any one child would not be expected to show all the signs indicated by the teacher all the time, or all at once.

The high level of inconsequence and hostility observed in the target children would be a considerable handicap to making good relationships. Both parents and teachers agreed that the target children were poor at making friends.

The target group scored particularly highly in the overreaction category. When examined further in terms of the guides, the target children were found to be at least twice as likely to incline towards the following behaviour than their controls. They were hyperactive, showing off, being moody, sullen, provocative, and very aggressive.

These comparisons provide a highly dramatic picture of the target and control children's behaviour in school. As pupils, the target children could be easily distinguished from the rest of the class by their difficult behaviour.

Other differences

This was material taken from remarks by the parents, children, or teachers when they were being interviewed. The health of the children was particularly noteworthy. Some aspect of physical ill-health, such as stomach complaints, respiratory complaints, speech problems, poor eyesight, and poor coordination were described for 42 per cent of the target children. Of the first control group, 16 per cent had some problems, as had 22 per cent of the second control group. Twice as many target children thus showed symptoms of what could be interpreted as anxiety.

Differences in home backgrounds

The family backgrounds of the target children were also very different from those of the controls. Where the home background was unusual, in that there was a remarriage, a one-parent family, an adopted child, or siblings over six years older, the target children were way ahead. Twenty per cent of target parents reported some of these conditions, compared to 9 per cent of the first control group and 6 per cent of the second control group. One-parent families were actually found seven times as frequently in the target group as in the controls.

When the parents of the target group children were compared with those of either of the control group parents, they were found to give very different answers to the questionnaire designed for them. The mothers of the sample children were particularly intriguing. Although they had all received a good education, the mothers of the target children had attended university more often. Yet in spite of this (or perhaps because of it) they showed a distinct and significant element of dissatisfaction with their own education. Fourteen per cent of the target mothers described themselves as bitter about it, compared with 4 per cent of the first control group and none of the second control group.

These feelings of disappointment about their education were even more surprising when related to their work. Over half (53 per cent) of the target mothers were engaged in professional or top managerial work, compared with 33 per cent of the first control mothers and 30 per cent of second control mothers.

It was a significant feature of the target families that mother took a far higher share of responsibility for the children's education. In 13 per cent of families, she was solely responsible, compared to none in the first control group and 6 per cent in the second control group. The target parents seemed to fall very much into the pattern described by the Rapoports in their descriptions of two-career families (Rapoport and Rapoport, 1971 and 1977). The husbands appeared to have become considerably occupied in their careers, while the wives seemed to cope with more than their fair share of responsibilities.

The target mothers were also more active in their general and reading interests than either of the control group mothers. They were a group of particularly lively and interesting women.

No less than 69 per cent of the target fathers were in professional and top managerial positions. The first control fathers were not far behind at 60 per cent, but the second control fathers were less elevated, having only 49 per cent in those occupational positions. This may be compared to about 3 per cent of the general population. The differences between the education interests and outlooks of the fathers were not of very high significance ($p < 0.05$) between the three groups although the fathers of the target group were also moderately less satisfied with their education than either of the two control groups.

The parents of the target children, as couples, appeared to have been more successful in their career achievements than those of either of the control groups. Both had improved considerably on their parents' career statuses, although even a generation ago, there had been a difference in occupational status between the target and control grandparents. Are the target children, then, to carry on the family tradition of increasing prosperity? Only another survey will provide the answer.

Educational attitudes were very varied between the parents of the three groups. The target parents were nearly four times as keen on the inclusion of music and art in their children's education as parents of either of the control groups. They also provided a much greater amount of extra scholastic help for their children and were much less happy with their child's school than the control parents whose children attended the same class.

The target parents' attitudes to education were more positive in terms of what they had provided and in their expectations of the children. But they did exert more pressure to achieve on them, judged by remarks such as:

'John [a target child] is a brilliant boy and of course one of us sits with him every night while he does his homework. Oh yes [in response to questioning], we have a daughter too, but she's such a silly girl'.
'Of course he [a target child] will go to boarding school when he's seven. I can't bear the thought of it, but he has to have the extra tuition which he will get there, to get on in the world. The local school is just ordinary.'

The homes of the target children were far richer culturally than those of the control children, but not in respect of housing standards. They were very much more concerned with both practice and listening to music. The target homes contained many more books and musical equipment than the control homes.

Emotional problems and the gifted

Such extreme differences in behaviour and life style between the target and control groups had not been expected. It would have been relatively easy at this point to have assumed that the target group, with their significantly higher IQs, were behaving in the way they did because of problems brought about by their high intelligence. But there were, after all, children in both control groups of very high intelligence. In order to compare the children of very high IQ with the other children, therefore, the children were regrouped according to IQ level. Taking a working figure of IQ 141 or more as representative of 'high IQ', the re-formed groups emerged as shown in Table 6.3.

Table 6.3 Children in the high- and moderate-IQ groups

Group	Number	Mean IQ	Standard deviation
High	82	155.012	9.903
Moderate	128	119.797	11.589

Comparisons were then made between the high- and moderate-IQ groups on all the data.

It was clear from the results that those features which had distinguished the target group from its controls were rarely those which distinguished the high-IQ from the moderate-IQ children. Signs of unhappiness in the children reported by parents, such as difficulty with sleep or a paucity of friends, did not feature in the list of significant child behaviours which could be identified with high IQ. Many of the parents, however, clearly considered that such difficulties were related to giftedness, frequently explaining to me, for example, that their children only behaved badly because they were gifted. As for the teachers, they did not see any difficulty in the behaviour of the high-IQ group when they were compared with the moderate-IQ group.

Thus the problems experienced by the target group parents may not have been related to their children's giftedness in any very direct sense. It is also possible that their reasons for joining the NAGC had as much to do with their children's behavioural difficulties as with their intellectual giftedness, though of the 70 sets of parents, 64 gave that as the basis. (Only six parents gave their children's 'musical giftedness' as the reason for joining the

NAGC). As with all voluntary organizations, the covert reasons why people join together in it are at least as important at the overt ones, but rather more difficult to expose. Parent members of the NAGC can join whether their children are gifted or not (and many of them in my experience are not), but it is probably safe to assume that such parents entertain the belief that their offspring are gifted. In addition to an awareness of real or imagined giftedness, however, it may sometimes be the adult's inability to manage their children to their own satisfaction which motivates joining such an organization (see also Chapter 5). From the evidence reviewed in this section it seems most likely that behaviour difficulties with gifted children are related more directly to such matters as parental expectation and handling than to intellectual giftedness *per se*.

Conclusions

The three questions asked at the beginning of this chapter have to a large extent been answered through this research.

1   Children who are labelled as gifted by their parents (i.e., the 'target' group) are undoubtedly different from their peers. They are difficult to bring up and show maladjusted behaviour at school. They also have more physical ill-health. Doubtless they are more unhappy.
2   Their parents are likely to have achieved more success in their own careers and expect more from their children in achievement. Mothers are particularly dissatisfied with their own education. They provide a culturally livelier home background than other parents, but tend to have a more 'unusual' family structure.
3   When intellectually gifted children (drawn from the control as well as the target group) are compared with 'moderate-IQ' children in normal, nonspecial education they do not seem to have a greater preponderance of emotional problems. They are described as doing well at school and are not seen as any more unhappy than less gifted children. Whether they reach the levels of achievement that they might otherwise do is another matter.

Unhappy behaviour in children may be brought about by either environmental or constitutional factors or, more likely, a combination of the two. For its possessors, giftedness is often said to bring unhappiness and problems in its wake. There is no evidence from the present research that this is necessarily so.

Some marked differences were found in the research, however, between high-IQ and moderate-IQ children. Primarily, the highly intelligent child is said to 'feel different', and although the child herself often denies this absolutely, we adults are inclined to take the parents' word for it. High-IQ children have outstanding memories and the ability to concentrate for great lengths of time; their leisure activities tend to be of an intellectually more involving nature. Such children delight in television and comics, but in a chosen, rather than a passive manner. Gifted children are clear in their decisions, and the higher their ability, the greater their clarity of mind.

These marks of distinction are not problems; the gifted children seemed to thrive in a normal educational atmosphere in England. The problems which do exist, though, seemed to be helped along by adults. Petty school rules, such as a five-year-old not being allowed access to the older children's library, or a fluent reader obliged to go at the class pace are frustrating to gifted children. (See Part III, Case Studies 5 and 11.) Such clashes between giftedness and a rigid educational system must occur, but whereas an emotionally balanced child can surmount them, the insecure child may go under.

Virtually all the gifted children and their parents in this sample were happy with their school. But a significantly higher proportion of target (NAGC) parents were not happy about it, when compared to their control groups. Dissatisfaction with the school was not a function of giftedness *per se* in this sample, but appeared to be related to the expectations and ambitions of the parents.

The evidence outlined in this chapter does not support the idea that problem-bound gifted children should be segregated for their own good from normal children. Those gifted children who were found to have problems were also found to have a cluster of disturbing environmental effects. That *some* gifted children have problems is certain, but there is no reason to generalize from them to all such children. Fortunately, an association exists for those who feel they need it, but whether a more stretching education would increase the children's happiness or future welfare is unproved.

Both Terman (1925) and myself, separated by 6,000 miles and fifty years, have found gifted children to be emotionally and physically superior to other children. We also agree that their success in life must be very dependent on their social contexts.

CHAPTER SEVEN

EDUCATING THE GIFTED CHILD: A COMPARATIVE VIEW
Vernon Mallinson

Speak, Lord; for thy servant heareth . . . And all Israel from Dan even to Beer-Sheba knew that Samuel was established to be a prophet of the Lord.

I Samuel, 3, ix and xx.

It is not always readily remembered that the problems of how best to meet the requirements of the gifted child has been with us from all time; that once a social group has been formed some kind of élite must always emerge; and that civilized societies have found inescapable the task of both searching out and encouraging talent (or genius, or giftedness) of all kinds. In Biblical times it was a relatively easy matter. There were signs and premonitions in plenty. As 'giftedness' asserted itself, so was the Lord's will seen to be working itself out; and God's chosen people, were they wise, would heed the wisdom of His prophets and obey the dictates of His chosen leaders. But neither prophet nor leader was invulnerable. He also could fall into error and merit just retribution – a timely reminder that, whilst the exceptionally gifted should be an asset to the community they have the privilege of serving, it does not necessarily follow that this will be so.

The marrying of the sophistication of Greek thought with the equal sophistication of the main tenets of Christianity led to complications which are still in the process of being resolved. Plato forcibly argued that if the ideal state were ever to be achieved, then this could only come about through carefully seeking out the gifted and providing for them an education to stretch their abilities to the full and separate them from the masses who were to be the governed. He postulated that a small number of individuals were endowed with innate or inherited powers, but that these needed properly nursing and tending in order to come to full fruition. In other words, he opted for a strictly selective form of education in which the 'children of gold' were to be distinguished from those of 'silver' or 'iron and brass'. By the time of the Renaissance and Reformation, formal school systems mainly under the tutelage of the Church had become commonplace throughout Western Europe, and promising scholars from the poorest and most humble backgrounds were often given the opportunity to attain some of the highest positions available to proven ability. Such a scholar was Erasmus, and he along with many *confrères* scattered throughout Europe zealously advanced the cause of the new learning introduced by the renaissance of interest in Greek and Latin studies. He argued persuasively that Greek and Latin studies were central to the education of the truly civilized man, and worked on the premise that in any social group there can never at any time be other than a small civilized nucleus – though the bigger that nucleus, of course, the better for civilization in general.

So was the pattern set for Western Europe as a whole which, in basic essentials, has remained unchanged down to the present. It has meant that school systems have evolved partly as nurseries for the cultivation of individual talents, partly as sieves for sorting out and stretching to the full those of *academic* promise. There was no problem over deciding who were the gifted, for they would of themselves emerge by a kind of process of natural selection. It was repeatedly noted that the academically gifted child (particularly in his earliest formative years) tended to be equally good at all subjects, possessing an overall curiosity, and displaying above-average ability in generalizing or reasoning and in dealing with the abstract. It was in obedience to such clearly held beliefs that such stiff academic hurdles as the *baccalauréat* or the *Abitur* were originally devised.

Meantime, the search for a national identity was gaining momentum, and as each separate nation state asserted its right to be different so did it evolve its own concepts of excellence based naturally on its own peculiar cultural heritage and background. This meant in effect that, whilst there was still general agreement over the methods to be used in allowing the gifted to emerge, there could be no real consensus of opinion as to what constitutes 'giftedness' or even genius, except when dealing with the visual arts, music, or dancing. For such promising children special schools were soon devised and have now come to be internationally accepted. In its consideration of the academically gifted, however, each nation has evolved its own peculiar philosophical approach. England and Wales, for example, originally inspired by the success of St. Paul's School (opened in London in 1512 by John Colet, Dean of St. Paul's, in pursuit of the Erasmian ideal), have sought to produce that liberally educated 'gentleman' whose talents, at whatever level, could be of service to the State. Genius as such has tended to be distrusted. The French, on the other hand, are wedded to Cartesian thought, foster genius, have a strong intellectual tradition, insist on the importance of *une culture générale*, and place the emphasis everywhere on training in the art of rational objective thinking and expression. The Belgians (as a 'new' nation dating only from 1830) extol the virtues of that kind of liberal bourgeois democracy which gave them their revolution and kingdom, and hold firmly to the view that every healthy social group needs outstanding men and women at all levels. They argue that, whilst false conceptions over equality of opportunity can dangerously lower standards both of intellectual attainment and of national vitality, this is no reason why recruitment to key positions should be restricted to only one social group. The Americans, as de Tocqueville once pointed out, have always been more interested in equality than in liberty and have embraced a kind of individualistic egalitarian ideal stemming from Jefferson's belief that the common man would think and act rationally if allowed to do so. And this has led to a dramatization of the individual at all stages of his development, to a worship of success, and ultimately to the cult of the average man which means conformity to the standards set by the current majority.

Thus, whilst ideas might differ as to what constituted 'excellence', the nations of the Western world had no real problems to face over the education of the gifted until unprecedented scientific and technological changes began to occur in the mid-twentieth century. These made it clear that the form of humanistic education which had been so well suited to an essentially unchanging and settled way of life must now be replaced by a new approach seen in terms of the rapid shifts, changes, and vicissitudes of modern existence. We now need a society in which all men, whilst still united by a common culture, have ever-increasing opportunities for their own individual advancement. We can no longer afford the luxury of having education seen as a preparation for life, but must make it an integral part of life – 'an instrument of man's evolution' as Julian Huxley once put it. This has led to an all-round democratization of education, the stripping away of those academic hurdles once so confidently used to sort out the gifted and talented, and the modernization of curricula in order to produce as many different types of the élite as a particular country needs, and at different levels. In consequence, the gifted child is increasingly condemned to growing up in a society which is now reluctant to admit either the reality or even the importance of his particular gifts. The watchword would seem to be that the clever child will always manage to teach himself. Initial dissent from this attitude has come not unexpectedly from the USA and perhaps more surprisingly from the USSR and its various satellite countries. It is, therefore, with these countries and their contrasting views as to what democracy for the modern age is all about that we should begin our general survey.

USA and USSR compared

If the launching of Sputnik in October 1957 was seen by Russians as a triumphant vindication of their educational policies, it could only be seen by the Americans as final proof that all was far from well with their own system. It had been under attack long before this for its lack of intellectual rigour and for its false ideas on egalitarianism which centred on giving *all* citizens the same treatment, thus misinterpreting equality of opportunity as identical provision rather than as differential provision according to individual needs. It also came under attack for its otherwise laudable attempt to ensure that all children should complete courses in secondary education – no matter what the content of those courses might be. The result had been an almost total neglect of the special needs of the gifted, and this indeed was combined with considerable controversy as to how they could best be sought out and what kind of special programmes should be devised to meet their needs.

Fortunately there already existed in New York and a few other large cities special schools devoted to their needs. Hunter College, for example, had opened its own elementary school to which entry was competitive on the basis of an IQ ranging between 130 and 150 for children from any social class residing in any part of New York; and in 1938 came the Bronx High School of Science which again admitted widely on the basis of an average IQ of 140 those children betraying special aptitudes in mathematics and science – and which began admitting girls for the first time in 1946. By 1971 no fewer than 21 individual states had passed legislation to deal more specifically with the academically gifted. And in 1973, Johns Hopkins University

(Baltimore) began searching out children around the age of fourteen as promising scientists or mathematicians for whom special programmes, to be worked either in high school or at the university, were prepared. (See Keating, 1976.)

It soon began to be argued, however, that such special schools work best in large communities (such as New York) because the pupils retain a certain anonymity; that they prove less successful in smaller communities where parents can be jealous of anyone seeming to get special privileges; and that they were unnecessary in middle- and upper-class areas where students were shown to be almost all of good ability and where school provision was usually markedly superior. Instead, the general trend has been to seek one of several solutions which do not isolate the gifted entirely from their schoolmates and so mark them out (to their own disadvantage) as in any sense 'special'.

Since 1973, the idea of streaming or homogeneous grouping has become popular particularly in urban areas. There can be special elective programmes or periods set aside for optional in-depth treatment of a subject. There can be part-time special classes for highly gifted pupils displaying all-round ability, these classes usually combining up to ten pupils per class drawn from neighbouring schools and giving enriched instruction from between one to five half-days per week. There are numerous voluntary Saturday or summer vacation schools with which the parents of bright children are invited to collaborate – and senior high school pupils (usually in the sciences) can be sent to study at university summer sessions along with a more sophisticated undergraduate (or graduate) group. There is quite simply acceleration by having a bright pupil jump grades – though this is frequently frowned upon as not leading to good social adjustment. And 'setting', which has for long been commonplace in traditional British schools, particularly for the teaching of mathematics and languages, is also gaining in popularity as in many new British comprehensive schools.

Like the Americans, the Russians are firmly wedded to the idea of a unitary school to be attended by all children, but they do at the same time practise more intensive selection for special schools than any other Western European country. Indeed, absence of selection of the most talented would appear to them as a shameful waste of a nation's most valuable resources. And given the peculiar Russian and Marxist viewpoint of the meaning of democracy and the methods to be used to attain that ideal, this is not surprising. The USSR is still seen as in a process of gradual evolution. At the moment, private capitalism has been replaced by state capitalism. But the ultimate goal is held to be the truly classless society, and in this important contemporary interim period it is the duty of each and every Russian to equip himself, according to aptitude and ability, to help his country move towards that goal. Thus, educational theory stresses the importance of the individual (within the framework of the totalitarian State), insists on the possibilities for greatness that reside in the ordinary man, and urges the release of those creative forces which reside in all human beings and which alone can bring them to the highest peak of human achievement. Talent, it is claimed, is specific and concrete and reveals itself through activity; if it does not obtrude itself it must be diligently sought out.

It is usually after the completion of the basic eight-year school course that specialization for the gifted begins, though the sixteen ballet schools in existence accept pupils from the age of nine to follow a gruelling ten-year course. There are in addition at least one hundred music schools, a large and varied number of theatrical technical schools, art schools, and one circus school situated in Moscow. One interesting venture has been the creation of four university boarding schools situated in Moscow, Kiev, Leningrad, and Novosibirsk open to gifted children drawn from rural areas only. Entry is competitive, and based on success at an examination in mathematics and physics as covered in the eight-year school. Successful candidates then follow the two-year 'complete' secondary school course leading to the maturity examination and will be expected to distinguish themselves sufficiently to pass directly into the university rather than first undergo work experience – a two-year stint that roughly 80 per cent of those sitting the maturity examination will normally pursue. Numerous other schools are allowed to develop a particular bias towards the teaching of mathematics and languages from grade two onwards, but are compelled to recruit from their immediate catchment area before awarding places on a wider basis.

Satellite countries usually conform to the same general pattern which can be summed up as seeking by every means possible to sort out the gifted for service at many levels to the State. Acceleration is frowned upon and is replaced by individual attention in the ordinary class situation, by extra-curricular activities (youth organizations, clubs, and summer camps), by special classes inside the ordinary school, and by the withdrawing of talented children from disadvantaged areas to be educated in special boarding schools.

Western European countries

Western European countries have approached the education of gifted children in a rather different way. The Americans, as we have seen, had for so long geared education to the requirements of the average performer that they were suddenly faced with a real and urgent need to make adequate provision for the gifted. Similarly, the Russians desperately needed all the talent they could muster to restructure their country to their way of thinking and consequently they developed special forms of provision for the gifted. The Western Europeans, on the other hand, have remained confident that their respective systems of education were more adequate to cope with the needs of the bright and talented. Their secondary schools, both private and state-controlled, have been academically and socially selective and have never admitted more than about 20 per cent of an age group ranging between ten and twelve. And this 20 per cent, once embarked on its secondary studies, was faced with a series of academic hurdles which had to be cleared to reach university – or even more prestigious institutions such as the *Grandes Ecoles* in France. The gifted and talented would survive. Democratization of education, however, of which we have already briefly spoken, has led most countries in Western Europe to evolve for themselves their own particular styles of comprehensive education which is increasingly forcing them to begin to take account of the special needs of the gifted. Not surprisingly perhaps, problems are least in the smaller and self-contained countries such as Belgium and Holland which have long enjoyed the privileges of egalitarianism in most facets of day-to-day living, and it is with these countries that we should first continue our survey.

Belgium

Belgium would claim that she still has no particular interest in making provision for the gifted for two main reasons. Firstly, enthusiasm for education has always led the working class to send their children to school and to prolong their education for as long as possible. Today, compulsory schooling extends between the ages of six and fifteen, yet virtually 100 per cent of children are voluntarily in nursery schools by the age of five and about 90 per cent from the age of three, and all but the dullest continue in some form of further education between the ages of fifteen and eighteen. Secondly, it has long been recognized that pupils vary in ability, and as early as 1900 attempts were being made to classify school entrants into three streams: one for those clearly normal and above normal in intelligence, one for the slow or only moderately endowed, and special and remedial classes for the subnormal and retarded. It is on a basis of this early work, pioneered in particular by Dr. Decroly (whose basic educational principles have been largely adopted throughout the whole of the Belgian primary school system), that important psycho-medical centres have been established. These aim to give advice and guidance to schoolchildren and their parents at any time, thus ensuring that each child is individually cared for and encouraged to develop the talents he may already possess or which later manifest themselves. In effect, some form of selection takes place as soon as the child enters his primary school, and even though reforms in education now in process of being implemented are designed to make the school system comprehensive, *l'éducation rénovée* (as it is called) sees to it that there are from the age of twelve subtle and complicated systems of options and electives which can fully stretch the brightest.

Holland

Like the Belgians, the Dutch aim at giving the maximum of freedom possible to all sections of the community. Unity out of diversity is the ideal, it being maintained that a healthy democracy must be based on recognition of and respect for a variety of attitudes and opinions. This reduces the function of the State to that of maintaining uniformity of standards throughout the school systems (of which there are several), and of ensuring that talents of varied kinds are properly fostered. In such circumstances no real need is felt to give special attention to the gifted as such, who, it is maintained, can never constitute more than between 2 and 3 per cent of the population. The aim, as in Belgium and Switzerland, is less to produce an élite of brilliant students than to give all pupils a sound education commensurate with their abilities and in the appropriate school. The watchword – as indeed in most Western European countries – is *suum cuique* (to each his own) and not *idem cuique* (the same for everybody).

In practice, and again as happens almost everywhere else in Western Europe, the brightest progress to distinguish themselves in a variety of maturity examinations which alone can grant the right to attend a university or parallel institution. At maturity level one can distinguish three broadly based categories of curriculum (often in distinct types of schools) designed to prepare able pupils for university entrance. Many of the most able pupils will opt for a traditionally humanistic course which still lays the emphasis on Latin and Greek; other pupils will take a course in which Latin and modern languages predominate; a third group of pupils will take courses concentrating on mathematics and the natural sciences. There are, of course, many variations on this from country to country, but the basic principle remains the same: a pupil at these highest levels must perform adequately not only in his chosen specialities but also in several other subjects, all examined at the same time. Needless to say, a pupil whose talents lie in one direction only is at considerable disadvantage.

France

France is in a special category of her own for a variety of reasons. Firstly, her influence has over the centuries spread far and wide throughout the continent of Europe, including Russia. Secondly, she has remained steadfast in maintaining the superiority of classical studies to the point of considering herself the true heir to all that was best in Greece and Rome. Thirdly, she has never doubted her cultural superiority to most other nations. The ideal type she seeks is a Cartesian rationalist with all the civic and civilized virtues of ancient Rome. Greek and Latin are studied to arrive at a concept of excellence. And the study of mathematics, when added to these, enriches them with a Pascalian quality of logical thinking. Supplement the whole with a fluent command and appreciation of the French language, and you have the basic requirements for that *culture générale* every Frenchman is at heart loath to see go or even modified.

Such an education is not for everybody and the French have always readily admitted that since the Renaissance they have had to be selective and to confer it either on those gifted by nature or on those of a good social background. For the masses they have evolved a sound and thorough elementary education. Today's problems, however, have forced the French to admit that they have done, not too much for the gifted, but too little for the underprivileged from amongst whom they need to recruit and harness all the talent they can find. Excellence must be extended to all activities and occupations. Hence the bewildering spate of reforms in education since 1945 – all devised to this end, but all equally safeguarding the privileges of the gifted minority.

Thus, the latest school plan which began to be operative in 1968 creates a *Collège d'Enseignement Secondaire* (CES) which in theory is a four-year comprehensive school through which all children must pass after completing their primary school course. In practice, however, and though this is intended as a period of observation, children are immediately differentiated by types of course with little interchange occurring. Some 39 per cent of an intake will be found in a traditional academic stream; 36 per cent will be in a modern stream with in-built possibilities for transfer to the more demanding academic course; the remainder are usually taught by general class teachers (as opposed to university graduates), follow strictly practical courses, and will mostly end school at the age of sixteen. Once the academics reach the *lycée* to start preparation in earnest for the coveted *baccalauréat*, they in turn will divide themselves into classical, modern, and technical groupings with the classical side (as heretofore) attracting the best brains.

Yet misgivings were still felt that not enough was being done both to give all children a better deal and to speed on the brightest. So came the much-discussed and highly controversial Haby Plan, supposed to be implemented from about 1980 but at the moment in 'cold storage'. The plan envisages lengthening the primary school course by one year (ages six to twelve) but allowing entry as early as five or as late as seven according to preparedness and so fixing entry to the lower cycle of secondary education between the ages of ten and thirteen. As the lower cycle will still be of four years' duration, a pupil will leave at any age between fourteen and seventeen. All children will follow the same basic course for two years (though there will be streaming for French, mathematics, and a modern language), and for the last two years there will be the 'A' groups placing the emphasis on academic and technological subjects, and the 'B' groups who will have a clear practical and prevocational training. Higher secondary education will be given in two distinct types of *lycée*: the one will last for at least three years and prepare pupils for the various *baccalauréats*; it will also run specialist classes (as now) for competitive entry to the *grandes ecoles*. The second type of *lycée* will run courses leading to the award of various technical/commercial diplomas, but will also allow its promising pupils to earn transfer to its academic counterpart.

How much of all this will later be implemented remains anybody's guess. Put cynically, one can say that the French, whilst afraid of having the label of élitism still attached to them, are deliberately practising it in other guises. They are trying to have the best of both worlds. But who can say that they are necessarily wrong in their approach?

England and Wales

The confused picture presented in England and Wales over attitudes towards the gifted turns primarily on the fact that, whilst the needs of the *able* child have always dominated much of our thinking, there has never been any general acceptance either by public opinion or by local education authorities that the gifted are a category with requirements differing from the needs of the average child. Independent and grammar schools have in any case always adhered closely to the Erasmian ideal, used effective ways of streaming and setting, produced study in depth and in small groups at the sixth-form levels, and have worked on the assumption that any top set in such schools would consist of pupils of such high ability that the most gifted amongst them must get plenty of challenging instruction at their own level. Trouble really began when political decisions were taken to make the entire school system comprehensive, and a position was soon reached, as in West Germany, in which the advocates of comprehensive schooling have had to contend with entrenched attitudes of those who maintain that a well-proven tripartite system of post-primary education must not be endangered in the interests of experimentation. Independent and grammar schools alike have refused to have any truck with a reorganization which would, in their view, seriously hold back a top 10 to 20 per cent of pupils of secondary school age from achieving those standards of excellence of which the country is sorely in need.

As the debate continued, more and more local education authorities either opted for new purpose-built comprehensive schools or converted existing grammar schools over which they had control, and nearby secondary modern schools, into units of a comprehensive system. The pace of change has slowed down since the advent of a new government in 1979 but during the previous fifteen years the face of education in England and Wales had altered dramatically. By 1965, approaching 9 per cent of the total secondary school population were in comprehensive schools, and ten years later the figure was about 68 per cent. The government then turned its attention to those grammar schools not directly under local control and threatened to withhold their grants. The only result has been that, of 173 direct grant grammar schools still in existence at the end of 1975, 109 have been able to secure sufficient financial backing to elect to go independent. In this situation the poor or socially disadvantaged but able young scholar has increasingly been denied an education commensurate with his academic promise – for, some notable exceptions apart, the comprehensive schools have, in my view, not yet managed to match that academic excellence of which the grammar school has over many decades been justly proud.

In such circumstances, it is not surprising that until now no thought has been given to problems of suitably educating the gifted. We have, of course, had our specialist schools for music, dancing, the theatre, and so on, and all requiring all-round ability as well as a special talent – but nothing more, and we have certainly had nothing like the specialized schools of America with the notable exception of Millfield. This is a highly expensive boarding school which runs classes of no more than 10–12 per teacher and devises a personal programme to suit the needs of each individual pupil to combine general academic excellence with room for individual study and pursuit of specialized interests. There are, however, generous scholarships to promising students from non wealthy backgrounds which are awarded on a basis of intellectual promise or talent.

The first real and positive move to consider the gifted came in the 1960s with the so-called Brentwood Experiment (Bridges, 1969) when gifted primary school children were taken from school every Friday afternoon to follow special tuition at the local college of education. The value of this experiment was recognized by the Department of Education and Science which brought the Schools' Council to set up a working party to inquire into *The Gifted Child in the Primary School* (Ogilvie, 1973). There has since been the Gulbenkian Project on Gifted Children which started in 1974 (see Chapter 6) and meantime the DES has instituted a series of special courses for teachers of gifted children, the first of these being held in 1973.

The Scandinavian countries

Among Scandinavian countries, Sweden is always highlighted as having pioneered the introduction of the comprehensive school system into Western Europe and, with typical thoroughness, having spent vast sums of money over many years of research and experimentation. Mounting criticism of the Swedish experience is readily accepted by the Swedes themselves who point out that nothing is finalized, that they are still experimenting, still seeking to improve and build upon what they have so far achieved. Criticism from within Sweden draws attention to how, with the inescapable growth of neighbourhood schools, the child from the lower income groups is constantly disadvantaged; how lack of streaming has led to more attention being paid to the below-average child than to the above average, resulting in a general lowering of standards; how the brightest children, never fully stretched, can become problem children; and how the over-all lowering of standards has adversely affected the universities – formerly bastions of excellence – so that many first-degree courses offer little more than purely vocational training. All this is freely admitted. Much more attention is being given to the needs of the feeble-minded than to those of the gifted. But that is because the Swedes, as yet, lack adequate knowledge on the gifted. As of now, the gifted should emerge during some progressive differentiation begun in the last three years (thirteen to sixteen) of the nine-year comprehensive school (seven to sixteen) and intensified at the *gymnasium* level. They should also hopefully profit from the fact that attention is now turning away from the structure of the school system to methods of instruction.

Denmark and Norway are less draconian in going comprehensive and would seem to be still trying to heed the message of the old Scandinavian dictum that 'there is no better baggage on a journey than much of knowledge.' Both countries, however, now have fully developed nine-year comprehensive schooling from the age of seven, but they do allow for a certain amount of differentiation towards the end of the basic schooling in order to sort out the promising and gifted pupil. Tentative differentiation begins in Denmark between the ages of twelve and fourteen, when pupils are loosely divided into academic and nonacademic groups, and this is intensified for the following two years in an attempt to sort out the pupils who will clearly benefit from a rigorous academic education in the *gymnasium*. In Norway, pupils find themselves separating into broadly based theoretical and practical sides of instruction during their last two years in the comprehensive schools, electives begin to appear, and in the final year those wishing to go on to the *gymnasium* have their courses further stiffened to help them meet the ordeal ahead.

The *gymnasium* in all three Scandinavian countries has a long and distinguished history and can trace its beginnings to the Latin schools of the Middle Ages. During the nineteenth century it was modernized on German lines and quickly became notorious for rivalling the German *Abitur* in the intellectual demands it made on its students as they prepared for the various leaving examinations. With the exception of Sweden, which is now beginning to institute a comprehensive *gymnasium* which combines traditional academic studies along with continuation and vocational pursuits, the other two countries have retained the three upper classes of the traditional *gymnasium*. In Denmark, a broad common-core curriculum during the first year is followed up by specialization along one of six lines for the remaining two years: classical languages, modern languages, mathematics/physics, science, science with social studies, social science. Norway has begun toying with the Swedish idea of a comprehensive form of *gymnasium* and to this end has already introduced technical studies as an option in the last two years of the *gymnasium* course. For the time being, however, there are five distinct lines of specialization on offer of which the most popular, the *Engelsk-linje*, specializes in modern languages with English as the main subject. Then comes the *Real-linje* (physics and mathematics), and after that classical languages, Norwegian history and language, biology with chemistry. The passing-out examinations in both Denmark and Norway consist of both written and oral tests (as with the *baccalauréat* and the *Abitur*) and students must pass at one and the same time in all subjects studied. Sweden no longer has a school-leaving examination, this being replaced by the issue of a certificate (*Slutbetyg*) which lists the average mark per subject (out of a maximum of five) attained by a student during his course.

Concluding remarks

And so, as we finally review present attitudes towards the gifted in our schools, we need to note that in all Western European countries there is evidence of a long tradition of a common culture and way of thinking unlike that of the modern USA or the USSR, and quite alien to what is to be found in the East. It is accepted that the chief aim of education must be (as Professor Jeffreys once put it) 'the nurture of personal growth', and that we must make of education 'an instrument for conserving, transmitting and renewing culture'. From this it follows that the individual worth of persons must be constantly in view; that balance and harmony are essential to achieve proper moral, intellectual, emotional, and spiritual satisfaction; that enlightened leaders are the mainstay of any form of democracy, and that therefore the education of an élite (or élites) is of paramount importance.

It is the Graeco-Roman-Judaic tradition which still remains dominant. By virtue of the intellectual tools he has fashioned for himself, Western European man has come to attach the greatest importance to knowledge which he sees as a system of intelligible truths which can be rationally demonstrated. Unlike the Moslem, he cannot accept that knowledge may not be altered or changed and, though he can accept with the Moslem that we are moving towards the world-to-be, there is no room in his philosophy for the Moslem's fatalism or lack of concern for the future. He cannot accept the Chinese 'cosmocentric' view which holds that perfect harmony should at all times reign between the social and the universal order, neither separating the individual from society as a whole nor isolating society from nature. He can have no sympathy with various forms of Indian culture which would seem to view man's personality as an outstanding obstacle to be overcome if man is ever to attain perfect union with the Absolute. Nor can he subscribe to the Russian attempt to merge the individual with the State to have their aspirations identical, nor to the American urge to make of the individual a kind of cipher for the great American dream.

Throughout Western Europe generally, it is the attitude of 'Speak, Lord, for thy servant heareth' which predominates. Attention constantly paid to individual worth has led to a real demand for high-powered academic institutions. Amongst these the marked success of Jesuit and Benedictine (private) schools led Napoleon to create the French *lycée* which in turn has influenced the development of state education at this level in most other countries, not excluding tsarist Russia. Pupils have been conditioned to look for instruction of the right kind and to register their frustration if not offered it. As one highly articulate French *lycée* pupil once said to me: 'Naturally we want an inspiring teacher. But we will put up with a dull teacher if he is delivering the goods. If he cannot deliver then he will be ragged and that is all there is to it.' For the bright pupil, examination hurdles are no more than exciting challenges which allow him to prove himself to the full. Only as and where standards have begun to slump in sometimes ill-conceived or too precipitate attempts to increase the size of the Erasmian civilized nucleus of the able has the gifted child been put at risk.

In the USA, the early eclipse of the Jeffersonian ideal of an enlightened democracy based upon an educated citizenry which would be governed by an *intellectual* aristocracy soon led to a fragmentation of educational effort – and to a kind of 'two nations' situation. State schools and state universities would cater for the mass of the people, and in catering for the masses would adjust their standards and offerings to meet popular demand. The rich and percipient would organize and run their own private school systems which would steadily feed their brightest products into the so-called Ivy League universities (Harvard, Yale, Princeton, etc.) which in performance have always matched up to the best to be found in Europe. But their contribution is nowadays far too small to meet the requirements of modern America. Hence the pressing need to seek out the gifted wherever they may be found. Hence the urgent plea of James B. Conant at the Washington Conference of 1958 to seek out 'that 15 to 20 per cent of an age group who have the ability to study – effectively and rewardingly – advanced mathematics, foreign languages, physics and chemistry. Obviously the gifted would be included in this broad definition.'

The Russians are a very old people, and if they have managed to make their unitary school system be of service (rather than of disservice) to the gifted it is because of their traditional belief in the value of education allied to the excellent academic schooling (albeit for a minority) fostered by the Tsars from Peter the Great onwards. Realistically, they have not shrunk from opening special schools as the need arose. And whilst deliberately shaping their lives in terms of the Communist ideal, they have wisely built on the legacy of the past.

Part II

Techniques and Strategies in Helping the Gifted

CHAPTER EIGHT

RECOGNIZING THE GIFTED CHILD
Ralph Callow

In any discussion concerning the education of exceptional children there are three fundamental problems – definition, identification, and prescription. It is necessary to restate this truism at the outset of any examination of techniques for recognizing the gifted child. We must try to be as clear as possible about the sort of children we are discussing, and we should realize that any effort to identify such children is largely wasted if no serious effort is made to provide a suitable curriculum for those who are identified. The three elements are closely related and decisions made about one will inevitably affect the other two.

For the purpose of this chapter, gifted children will be taken to mean those capable of achieving an IQ of 130 or better on an individual intelligence test standardized for use in this country. This definition would describe about 2–3 per cent of the school population (see Chapter 1). We might expect such children to have those clusters of abilities which, with proper education and training, would make some the abstract thinkers – philosophers, scientists, mathematicians – and others the most able practitioners – surgeons, engineers – of their generation.

It would seem reasonable to expect that society would be concerned to assist such children to make the best of their abilities, not only for the sake of the children themselves but for the general good of the community. That this has not always been the case is in part due to apathy, part to misconceptions about the gifted (due to lack of accurate information), and part possibly to ill-founded and doctrinaire notions of equality.

The fact of the matter is that a large number of our ablest children are operating well below their ability in school (Painter, 1976, see also Chapter 2). Failure to recognize such children and to give them adequate intellectual stimulation has a negative effect on their motivation, self-concept, and achievement (Malone and Moonan, 1975; Combs, 1964; Kellmer-Pringle, 1970). Social justice and national interest demand that we should be much more actively concerned in the education of our brightest children.

Identifying the gifted

The first requirement is a reasonably inexpensive and efficient system of identification of the intellectually able child. Issues relating to the identification of gifted children at the preschool stage are discussed by Dr. Congdon in Chapter 10. In this chapter we shall be concerned with the development of a system of identification which can be employed in the classroom situation by the practising teacher. I believe that such a system is attainable with our present knowledge. However, as I hope to show, it will depend heavily on the good will and the expertise of the individual teacher for its successful operation.

The use of intelligence tests

There are a number of methods of identification available to the teacher but no single one seems very satisfactory. Since the definition of giftedness has been linked to an IQ score, the use of some form of intelligence test would seen obvious. There are a large number of group tests available to teachers (Jackson, 1971) which are simple to administer and straightforward to mark. There are, however, a number of difficulties associated with the widespread use of such tests. In the first place the group test is held in low esteem by a good number of teachers, because of its connection with the much reviled 11+ examination. Secondly, a comprehensive test programme would be quite expensive in time and money. In addition, it is all too easy for test scores to be misused by those unskilled in interpreting their results. A number of local authorities who are concerned to implement curriculum programmes for gifted children have been unwilling to use group tests for these reasons. The expense would be increased if it ever proved necessary to use a series of tests to guard against the effects of coaching. In addition to this there is no guarantee that a group test would provide an instrument of sufficient reliability.

Nevertheless, as argued in Chapters 1, 3, and 10, the use of group intelligence tests for screening purposes can be very valuable.

Pegnato and Birch (1959) reached the conclusion that 'the group test does not discriminate well between children who are a little above and those who are a great deal above average in learning capacity.' They suggested that a group test would, however, provide an efficient screen but that actual identification '. . . should be left to psychologists employing individual examination methods . . . .'

There is further no guarantee that children who are receiving little stimulation from their school work will be motivated sufficiently to attain a high score on an intelligence test. Kellmer-Pringle (1970) found '. . . that under-functioning and maladjusted children usually fail to do themselves justice in group tests, partly because of their resemblance to scholastic tests and partly because of the absence of encouragement and praise which form an integral part of individual test procedures.'

Individual tests administered by psychologists trained in test procedures are the only sure way of identifying the intellectually able, but cost and time factors would make their widespread employment impossible – even if school psychological services were not already fully stretched trying to cope with other groups of 'at-risk' children.

Using pupil attainment as the criterion

Much use has been made in American programmes of identification by attainment, as shown on school record cards. However, recognition of the able on their record of school achievement can be expected simply to indicate those children who are already succeeding within the school system. Such a method would clearly not identify those performing below their ability. In any case, much of the work in our schools is of a mechanical nature – where obeying rules, neatness in presentation and production of set answers is valued above originality, the ability to classify, conceptualize, or suggest hypotheses (see Chapter 11). Even if the school curriculum were more highly structured and organized so that performance could be related to ability and tested in an objective way, there would still be the problem of the effect of teacher expectation: '. . . children live up or down to their teacher's expectations – as long as their ability remains unrecognised, underfunctioning but able children are unlikely to receive the necessary encouragement from their teachers to reach the much higher level of attainment of which they are capable' (Kellmer-Pringle, 1970).

Identification by teachers

It would be very convenient if the teachers themselves could accurately identify the most able, using their special knowledge of their charges. Unfortunately the majority of studies seem unanimous in condemning teacher recommendation as a method of identification (Gear, 1976). In the context of a grading system in which pupils are promoted on merit, Terman (1925) concluded that it would be more effective to choose for promotion the youngest child on each class register than to ask the teachers to nominate their brightest children. The American studies suggest that teachers can identify about half the most able children (Gear, 1976) and experience in British schools supports this (Tempest, 1974). One study (Ciha *et al.*, 1974) found that a group of parents were three times more successful than their children's teachers at identifying children of superior ability.

There seems to be a measure of agreement about the sort of child most likely to be identified as gifted by teachers. Jacobs (1970), working with kindergarten teachers in America, found that those youngsters nominated '. . . were verbally adept children, who were co-operative and appeared to elicit teacher approval by their actions'. Pegnato (1958) reported that in American high schools 'Teachers' selections are often made on the basis of conforming or pleasant personalities, highly motivated school behaviour. . . .' However fallible teacher judgements have been proved to be, teachers find it very hard to believe they are wrong. One of Dr. Ogilvie's study groups reported that, amongst their members, 'Most teachers agreed that it was their own subjective assessment of pupil potential that was valued most. Test scores were only of interest if they supported the teacher's own assessment of the pupil's ability or capacity' (Ogilvie, 1973).

Certain points must be made, however, about the unpromising 'teacher identification' data. It must be realized, for example, that so far as we know the teachers mentioned in the studies were untrained in techniques of identification – they may have been given a check list of characteristics to look for, but they had had no formal preparation and, more unfortunately, no practice in identification. Some recent research into teacher perception may also help to account in part at least for the poor rate of identification reported in all the studies. It certainly tends to confirm the views of Jacobs and Pegnato quoted above.

It seems likely that teachers develop a fairly rigid set of values by which they judge all the pupils they teach, and that these values are a result of their training and experience. When Nash (1973) investigated the way a group of primary teachers perceived their pupils he discovered that they saw them primarily in terms of 'their work habits, their maturity and their classroom behaviour'. He comments: 'It is very interesting to note that none deals specifically with the child's abilities.' On reflection it is not really surprising that teachers should be so much concerned with these aspects of their pupils' personalities. It is in fact very laudable that teachers should want their children to develop into hard-working, well-balanced people in the atmosphere of an orderly and well-organized classroom.

Hargreaves found that some secondary teachers had a rather similar hierarchy of values (Hargreaves *et al.*, 1975). Personal appearance, conformity to discipline and to the academic role, likeability, and relations with peers were the aspects of behaviour most used by the teacher in evaluating their pupils. The similarities between the two lists are striking. It seems likely that when they are asked to make judgements about the ability of their pupils teachers tend to use instinctively, for lack of anything better, the criteria which training and experience have proved most effective. It seems likely that racial and social class stereotypes may also distort a teacher's perceptions at times.

But is it possible that, in spite of all the contrary evidence, teachers can become more effective? If they could, it would certainly be the most economic approach to identification. There is one piece of published research which suggests that teacher identification can be effective. This is the research of Gayle Gear, of the University of Alabama. A short five-session course was devised for teachers. The package (Identification of Potentially Gifted Programme – IPG) contained 'training scripts for the instructor, correlated instructional media and handouts for the participants' (Gear, 1978).

The workshop sessions were on the following topics:

a) terminology of gifted education;
b) definition of gifted and talented;
c) selection criteria;
d) role of intelligence tests in the selection process; and
e) characteristics of gifted children.

The teachers who took part in the training programme are reported to have proved to be twice as effective in identifying intellectually gifted children as the untrained control group, achieving a success rate of 85 per cent.

It is interesting that in devising an in-service course for teachers with an adviser from a nearby LEA the author had suggested, quite independently, a unit on identification very similar to Gear's. The only differences were the addition of material on the subjectivity of teacher judgements, the phenomenon of the self-fulfilling prophecy, and the inclusion of video tapes of gifted children responding to questions and in discussion situations. This course began in the autumn of 1979 and, if it is successful, may provide a useful prototype for similar courses in other parts of the country. The possibility therefore exists that a growing number of local authorities with a commitment to the education of the very able could, in the near future, be training teachers to identify able children and to implement programmes of curriculum enrichment.

However, teachers trained in this way will still have to use standardized tests from time to time. They will need the advice of educational psychologists and must be prepared to listen to other teachers, and parents, and to their pupils. The fact of the matter is that, trained or untrained in this respect, the teacher needs every clue, every scrap of information he can get hold of.

A strategy for teachers

It is possible (using the information from research studies and the experience gained from work with the gifted children and their teachers) to suggest a strategy which teachers could employ in this field.

General points

Firstly, it is important that the teacher *expects* to find bright children in his school – Ogilvie (1973) found that many head teachers were unwilling to believe that any of their children were exceptionally bright (see also DES, 1977). Yet even on purely statistical grounds we might expect any school with 250 pupils to have about five very bright children on its roll.

Secondly, the teacher must be convinced that it is right for provision to be made for these children in school. This is a matter for his conscience – a decision of this nature requires very careful thought.

Then he must accept that all interpersonal judgements are fallible and heavily subjective, and that clues and hints which might be helpful in shaping judgements must be sought from available sources and carefully evaluated. Teachers are very busy people, class numbers are often too large – yet it is necessary that some extra time is taken to build up as comprehensive a picture as possible about each individual child. The teacher must be willing to talk to the child and, more importantly, listen to his replies. It is more important to try to pay attention to the quality of thought which prompts the child's words than the words themselves.

Observing the characteristics of children in school

Many books about gifted children offer check lists of characteristics which such children are thought likely to possess. Such a list, especially if employed in an unthinking or mechanical way, can prove to be more of a hindrance than a help. If used with discretion, however, a simple list can provide a focus for our perceptions as shown by the study using the Laycock check list reported by Denis Lawrence in Chapter 2. The Laycock check list is set out on pp.51-52. The short list quoted in the West Sussex (1974) Booklet on Gifted Children has proved to be useful to many teachers on in-service courses, and provides a useful basis for a discussion of things to look for. (See also the booklet produced by Devon, 1977.)

The bright child may show exceptional progress in one or more areas of the curriculum but very often we have to look for underlying abilities rather than attainment. Often what we dismiss as silly mistakes or foolishness can mask considerable ability. A child, for example, doing his subtraction wrongly was found on inquiry to have constructed his own subtraction system based on reciprocal numbers. Again, a little boy who tried to relate three totally unrelated numbers because of a pattern he had observed was in fact showing early signs of his considerable mathematical ability. Often the bright child will be concerned, even at a very early age, with causes, relationships, and evidence more than the answers many teachers seem to prize so highly.

The teacher must be alert for the explosion of activity that may follow when some subject or aspect of a topic suddenly inspires a child's imagination and curiosity – the child who shows an unexpected ability to write poetry, or a passionate interest in history or science, for example. Often the bright child will have a good memory and be capable of processing complex information very rapidly – the teacher may have no notion of this until an awkward question or a chance remark reveals it. This ability may be manifested by impatience or boredom if the pace of the lesson is too slow. Many children find it possible to finish with school work very rapidly and spend much of their time in day-dreaming or secretly reading with the book hidden under the desk or playing little mental games incomprehensible to the observer.

Clearly boredom or inattention are not solely indications of high ability but they are signals which perhaps indicate disparity between workload and capacity, and warn that further investigation is required. It is important to realize that all any check list can do is suggest the sort of clues which might indicate a problem – as a bent twig or broken blade of grass suggests to the hunter that some creature has passed.

Investigation of the children's hobbies can often provide useful information. Again it is not only the interest itself but the intensity of interest taken in it, the wealth of specialized knowledge, which provide the clues. The little infant who has a specialized collection of butterflies – can classify insects – knows what missiles an F–18 fighter carries – is so often completely unrecognized by teachers, yet a simple question displaying interest will bring a flood of precise data, informed comment, and intelligent speculation.

Gifted children are often assumed to show signs of advanced reading ability and verbal fluency and these characteristics are usually good indications. Frequently the only objective test result a teacher has is a reading age, and a high one should not be ignored. Not all the gifted are good readers, however, and not all of them are easy and eager conversationalists. Often, too, an accent or frequent mispronunciation, can mask the ability of the child and hinder his ability to communicate. It is the quality of thought, the sharpness of perception which lurks behind the words which we must seek.

Gifted children tend to have a longer span of attention than normal and enjoy working on their own. This characteristic is a crucial element in any discussion of curriculum provision, since a structured programme of individual assignments is a very effective way of providing enrichment materials (Tempest, 1974). It also offers a means of identification.

Observation of the way children tackle an individual assignment – perhaps part of a topic in history, maths, or science – can reveal the child who enjoys working alone, is capable of planning a little research programme and evaluating the results. The negative side of this characteristic is also a useful indicator and also often a source of much irritation on the part of the teacher. Much importance is placed on cooperation in many junior and infant schools. The modern open classroom is structured for togetherness. Tables are placed together, children work in groups, and they are often expected to share equipment and help each other. This can be a good thing, but the bright child is often a rugged individualist who resents the chatter of other children when he has a problem to solve, or objects to being pestered by other pupils to lend them his crayons when he needs them to complete the picture or pattern which is burning with such intensity within his mind.

In the Tempest enquiry (Tempest, 1974) the desire to do one's own thing was so marked that in the first year the little groups of tables, seating three or four children, had to be removed and single desks (fairly widely spaced) hurriedly substituted. This alteration was accepted gratefully by the children and it remained the pattern for the remaining three years of enquiry.

Bright children seem to have a much clearer conception of themselves as people and very definite notions as to what they wish and do not wish to do. This more adult self-concept appears to go hand in hand with quite a fine sensitivity to rebuke or sarcasm. It will be easily seen that such characteristics will often annoy the teacher and that seemingly simple occurrences may provoke quite violent outbursts of temper at times. Like the rumbling of a latent volcano they may prove to be warnings of the fires burning below the surface.

Intense curiosity and desire for novelty can be a characteristic of very able children. Informal occasions when pupils can be introduced to new objects – a piece of machinery, or a fossil or unusual plant, or new ideas – could be used to discover what kind of response certain children make. The response might very well be a joke or a punning reference, for the one characteristic all bright children seem to share is a sense of humour. It can sometimes be a very odd or esoteric sort of humour however. It may sometimes involve rather acid comments on other children, such as the comment 'There is Sylvia fascinating her friends' about a very demonstrative little girl. The comments may even be directed against the teacher, 'We must be going to have a visitor – you've got your good suit on', from a nine-year-old.

The gifted child may produce untidy work, at eight still be reversing some of his letters, and may be totally lacking in imagination so that any kind of creative writing is heavy labour. When he is in the infant school he may be very unwilling to commit any story to paper but, possessing a vivid visual imagination, will produce striking pictures about which he will talk fluently if pressed.

There is no stereotype or blueprint of the gifted child, however, and many of them pass largely unnoticed through their school days because so much lies iceberglike beneath the surface. It would be possible to continue setting down other characteristics and giving examples, but enough has perhaps been written to show the main technique – get to know the children, talk to them, devise situations and material to challenge the unusual response or idea or question, and all the time be on the lookout for the thought, the logic, and reasoning that lies behind the word.

To know your children you must not only talk to them but to their parents. They may be fond or overindulgent but they know their own better than anyone else. In so many schools parents are invited on open days to listen to what the teacher has to say – the teacher should be much more willing to listen to the parents' views and notions. To be effective this process of getting to know the child must be continuous, not limited to a few days at the beginning of each year. Other members of staff should be consulted too. Often informal staff room discussions can be very helpful in transmitting information and clarifying views.

If the child shows some indications of high ability the teacher can then investigate further with standardized tests of verbal reasoning or attainment, or enlist the advice of an educational psychologist.

Conclusions

Practice of a strategy of this kind, commitment, and an attempt at careful assessment by observation, backed up by objective measures and the skills of the psychologist, will not be completely efficient but should be considerably more effective than our present lack of a system. Constant practice should help to perfect techniques and perhaps indicate particular teachers or even staffs of particular schools who are gifted at identification.

It is important that the process commences as early as possible in a child's school career. As in so much else, the role of the infant school is crucial. Many of the children identified as gifted in the Tempest enquiry were already showing signs of disenchantment with school at eight years of age. They had found what went on so boring and pointless that they had switched off. At the age of eight some of our very ablest children were becoming lost to the educational process. This is not to say that the junior school teachers and those in secondary schools have no part to play. Any point of transfer from one stage to another offers a chance to catch children who were missed earlier. Side by side with the new appraisal must go a careful examination of the records to ensure that no one who has given early promise of ability is lost. It is clear that this process will be much more efficient if there exists a friendly cooperation between stages, the easy transmission of unambigious information, and mutual respect.

At the secondary stage much more reliance will have to be placed on the child's school record and the recognition of aptitudes, indicative of high ability in specific subject areas (DES, 1977). The necessary widening of curriculum choices at this point makes possible the identification of some children whose particular abilities or enthusiasm have hitherto lain undiscovered.

Some schools, primary and secondary, already exist where the staff implement identification strategies and they are successful. It is to be hoped that where a few have ventured many will follow. However, no techniques for the identification of gifted children will be of any great use if efforts are not made to devise relevant and challenging activities and curriculum programmes for the children so identified. This issue provides the main substance of the remaining chapters in this section.

CHAPTER NINE

THE DEVELOPMENT OF TEACHING MATERIALS: PRINCIPLES AND PRACTICE
Susan Roberts and Belle Wallace

This chapter is divided into four main sections. The first briefly traces the history of the development of work with gifted children in Essex. In the second we examine the principles underlying the interdependent needs of teachers and pupils in the development of materials. The third section outlines the process of the development of teaching materials which we have adopted in the county working party for gifted children. Finally we describe the extension of this work through the appointment of an advisory teacher for gifted children.

The history and development of work with gifted children in Essex

During the last fifteen years or so the county of Essex has shown a growing interest in the education of gifted children. This interest has developed in a multi-faceted way, springing initially from the professional interests of those working within the education service. More recently, however, the provision of educational resources for gifted children has become an integral part of the county's educational policy.

In the early years of the county's involvement with gifted children much of the interest came from what has become known as the 'Brentwood Experiment', under the direction of Dr. Sydney Bridges.

In 1964 concern was expressed by tutors at Brentwood College that the work students on teaching practice had prepared for their classes was often paced too slowly. For the brighter children, the pace was far too slow, bringing boredom. The college felt it needed to make the students aware of the importance of pacing lessons more sensitively according to the capabilities of the children and especially with respect to the brightest children. The college hit on the idea that those children who have already been selected for grammar school education might be made available to the college to help in demonstrating this fact. Essex Education Authority was approached, and approved the plan. Certain junior schools were contacted and invited to cooperate. Children who had scored over 130 on the Verbal Reasoning Test were nominated and an initial 'pilot group' formed.

These children, 20 in all, were brought to the college for one afternoon a week. Students were invited to volunteer to take them in smaller groups, offering the subjects of nature study, physics, chemistry, maths, and art and craft.

It is clear from the way in which this project was set up that the main purpose was to aid the students rather than help or study the children. Reporting the rationale behind the project, Bridges (1969) states that 'The purpose of the group was to help our students.' However, inevitably some interesting facts emerged about the children and their schooling. One notable feature was that their achievements and effort did not match their potential. Dr. Bridges comments: 'The children had long since become accustomed to a certain level of expectation on the part of their teachers, and also probably of their parents. The result was that on the whole their level of aspiration or demands upon themselves was relatively low.'

Not surprisingly, the educationists involved became fascinated by this problem and decided to extend the experiment beyond their initial aims. They felt that one way to tackle this problem was to choose children from a lower age group who might be less set in their ways. The age of eight years was decided upon, which also gave the college the opportunity to study the children for a longer period of time, say two or three years. Since a ready-made and identified group was not available at this age, the then county educational psychologist was approached for help. This was Mr. George Robb, who had long had a deep professional interest and concern for this type of child, and in fact was one of the founder members of the NAGC. He organized testing in certain schools, using the Terman Merrill Stanford-Binet. Thirty-eight children were selected, 17 nine-year-olds and 21 eight-year-olds, all with an IQ on the Binet of 140+. This group consisted of high-achievers, particularly in vocabulary and reading, but it was also notable that they virtually all were of high socio-economic status. Students were again invited to volunteer to teach the children but some teaching was also carried out by college staff. Attempts to look at and provide extra tuition for gifted children at the college have continued in this or modified forms up to the present day.

Some of the findings produced an awareness in the county inspectorate and administration that these children could be regarded as having special needs in education, which were perhaps not being met. In 1970, therefore, in consultation with Mr. Robb, a senior county inspector and the then divisional education officer for the northeast area of Essex, got together to set up four special classes for intellectually gifted children in that part of the county. Children were to be withdrawn from their normal schools to attend these classes, each group of 4–8 children meeting twice weekly for a morning or afternoon.

It was felt that the classes were necessary in order to fulfil the special needs of these children that the ordinary school was, in the nature of things, unable to meet. Amongst such needs might be, for example, the need for competition (possibly a factor in the relatively low level of attainment described in the Brentwood Experiment); the need to foster interests in depth, and pursue lines of enquiry at length; the need to meet their intellectual peers to obviate the feeling of being isolated or 'different' from others.

In order to select the children, schools in the area were asked to submit the names of possible children to the area office. These were individually assessed by psychologists and those with the highest scores selected. A few children with lower scores were included for social or therapeutic reasons. At least two children were selected from each school, so as to avoid a feeling of being 'different' or 'the only one'. The classes met in secondary schools, so that greater facilities and the advice of specialist staff should be available. The head and staff of the host school had, of course, to be interested in and sympathetic to the aims and needs of the class. Each class had its own specially appointed teacher. However, for various reasons this experiment was not deemed to be the success that was hoped for. After a number of attempts to modify the experiment, the classes ceased in 1972.

Mr. Robb's interest in gifted children did not die, however. On the contrary, he was directly instrumental in the initiation of what has since grown into the present Essex project. As a result of his involvement with the NAGC, one of the association's 'Explorer's' weeks had for some years been held at one of the county's residential education centres. Through Mr. Robb's liaison with the NAGC it became clear that there would be much to be gained from the development by the local education authority of similar courses, using their own resources.

Accordingly Mr. Robb organized a one-day in-service conference on the topic of gifted children, at the end of which he asked for volunteers who would form a working party to organize and run this as a residential course for primary-age gifted children. A group of some eight primary and secondary teachers and head teachers was formed. Early in its career it decided to name itself 'The Essex Working Party on Exceptionally Bright Children'. This was the result of discussions about present attitudes to and provision for the numerous types of giftedness, and a feeling that the intellectually gifted or exceptionally bright were probably the group that teachers found most difficult to cater for, and for whom there was no fringe provision.

The county working party has now run courses for such children since June 1972. Nominations are made by head teachers and individual assessments carried out by psychologists. Children are then selected on the basis of the test results and the opinion of the psychologist.

For the first few years that courses were run, the working party used them as an opportunity to study the children and their needs and interests. However, the working party soon became aware that if their activities were to be of benefit to gifted children in our schools as a whole, some attempt must be made to disseminate their knowledge within schools. Therefore, in 1975 the working party decided that in future the courses were to be in part used as vehicles by which to develop teaching materials for use with such children in ordinary schools. Since then the working party has expanded to 20 people, and we now also run a residential course for secondary-age children, again with the aim of producing materials that may be of use with able children in ordinary schools.

This then is the background to the present 'Essex Project', and it is the experiences of the working party in attempting to produce curriculum materials for able children that is the basis of this chapter.

Principles involved in the development of materials

Four main areas should be considered when analysing the interdependent needs of teachers and pupils in the development of teaching materials for gifted children:

1   The necessity for the development of a comprehensive and acceptable

working definition of what is meant by 'giftedness'.
2 The development of efficient methods and techniques for early identification of exceptional ability.
3 The need to cultivate teachers' awareness and sympathy towards gifted children together with an understanding of the social, emotional, mental, and physical development of these children.
4 The understanding of the organizational and educational implications of making provision for gifted children in the normal school situation.

The purpose of this chapter is to comment mainly on sections 3 and 4 since sections 1 and 2, although of equal importance, are dealt with in previous chapters.

Definition of giftedness

In Chapter 1, Dr. Povey very clearly outlines the difficulty of reaching an adequate, all-embracing definition of giftedness. By common agreement, educationists cannot easily list discrete traits nor compose a comprehensive list of abilities and tendencies of gifted children; it is only possible to build a multi-faceted mosaic of characteristics which may cluster in any combination. However, Ogilvie (1973) suggests that to be gifted is to be outstanding in general or specific abilities in a relatively broad or narrow field. The field encompasses the following areas:

1 High intelligence.
2 Creativity.
3 Outstanding leadership potential.
4 Visual and performing arts.
5 Extraordinary physical talent.
6 Mechanical ingenuity.

While recognizing the importance of all aspects of giftedness, the rest of this chapter will refer to the first area of giftedness, high intelligence.

Identification of exceptional ability

Any discussion of 'giftedness' is essentially linked with the need to develop identification procedures which the teacher can use in the classroom (see Chapter 8). It is, perhaps, sufficient to reinforce the requirement for early identification of potential as essential before the child gravitates to the norm, conforming to peer group pressures and teacher expectation. A teacher can more easily identify the obvious high-achievers or indeed the pupils who manifest associated problems, but gifted children who quietly tolerate the frustrations and who present no obvious symptoms are difficult to identify in a large, busy classroom. As Kellmer-Pringle (1970) suggests, the number of underachieving, covertly gifted pupils can never be known. The more experienced, sensitive, and perceptive a teacher is, the greater will be his awareness of individual differences in ability, temperament, and background amongst his pupils; but as Gallagher (1964), Tempest (1974), and Ogilvie (1973) show, the subjective assessment of teachers is often inaccurate. There is an obvious need for teachers to be trained to administer and interpret wisely and cautiously, valid, reliable diagnostic tests of ability and achievement, thus combining both subjective and objective data.

The teacher's awareness and understanding of the needs of the gifted

> From each according to his abilities, to each according to his needs.
> Karl Marx.

Arguments debating the organizational requirements of an ideal education range between extremes of freedom and control; from Rousseau's Émile to Dicken's Mr. Gradgrind; from More's utopian, democratic, classless society to Plato's selection of 'children of gold'; from the 'environmentalists' to the 'geneticists'. However, one might find an oasis of agreement in the statement that the ideal of education should be to provide every individual with the opportunity to develop fully his potential despite mental, physical, social, or emotional limitations or privileges.

In recent years, there has been an emphasis, justifiably, on the special needs of slow-learning and underprivileged children together with a deliberate move towards a wider, more liberal curriculum. Bridges (1973) suggests that: 'This attitude has developed in part as a protest against a certain educational philosophy which led to excessive stress on the intellectual and relative disregard of the social, the emotional and even the physical' (p.93). He argues that while intellectual development can certainly be overstressed it can also be understressed and perhaps there has been a tendency to think, mistakenly, that intellectually gifted pupils will succeed without special curricular provision.

One can also find a paradox within our society in that certain abilities appear to be more socially acceptable than others; an exceptional athlete or footballer often receives more peer-group acclaim than an exceptional mathematician. Yet the intellectually gifted pupil has latent qualities essential to the future of society. Burt (1975) states:

> It is our duty first and foremost to do the best for the vast mass of the population, who, after all, consist of just ordinary mortals of just average ability. Our next obligation is to provide extra help and extra care for the subnormal and handicapped. Nevertheless, in the interest not only of national survival but of the progress of the race as a whole, there is no escaping the obvious conclusion that in the long run it is the highly intelligent few who can confer the greatest benefits on the less intelligent many, including, it may be, in a time of crisis, the gift of life itself (p.190).

The teacher has the unique opportunity to make provision for the potentially gifted child to develop and mature so that he can eventually become a positive and valuable member of the society which needs him. However, every child should also have the right to develop fully as an individual and the gifted child should be no exception. The specific needs of the exceptional child are closely interwoven and interdependent with those of his teachers, but one can examine the special qualities which *ideally* the teacher should possess.

The sympathetic, perceptive, empathizing teacher would have insight into the child's lack of synchronization with his time, his peers, and possibly his own family. He would understand the feelings of frustration and isolation which can be present when intellectual development surges ahead of the emotional and physical. He would be conscious of the possible disparity between intellectual and social needs, the needs of advanced intellectual development compared with the basic human needs of security and social acceptance.

A teacher of gifted children needs a sufficiently mature emotional development capable of accepting a child with a higher ability so that there is the acceptance of the role of being a learner with the child, the acceptance of uncertainty in new fields. Virgil's famous phrase, *'Timeo Danaos et dona ferentes'* (I fear the Greeks and yet they bring gifts) may well be true for a teacher who is inexperienced and feels threatened and who clings to orthodoxy and predetermined paths.

The teacher needs to be able to participate in creative, intellectual curiosity; to be cognisant of qualitative differences in children's responses; to be competent to identify levels of conceptualization. He should be skilled and versatile in the manipulation of resources and secure enough to ask for help when it is needed.

Undoubtedly, one could argue that all children would benefit from contact with teachers possessing these qualities. However, Ward (1961, cited in Newland, 1976) maintains that since gifted children are capable of responding at exceptional levels, they particularly need contact with teachers of exceptional calibre. He describes such teachers as:

> Men who think as they talk, rather than recall; who speak from the wealth they have learned, rather than from what they have been taught; who argue with a clear recognition and sensitive acknowledgment of the position from which they argue; men who differentiate faith from fact, and label each accordingly; men who in one breath state not only the conviction but its reasoned base – such are the teachers for youth who are critically and analytically disposed (p.148).

There is, therefore, an argument that gifted children require gifted teachers but such circumstances will not always coincide. Mixed-ability classes, for example, are likely to have mixed-ability teachers. In this context the work of the Teacher Education Project at the University of Nottingham School of Education is of interest (see Kerry, 1978). The project is concerned with the development of teaching materials for use by postgraduate trainee teachers and its particular concern is with the skills of mixed-ability teaching in secondary schools. In discussing the needs of the 'bright' child, Kerry (1978) identifies three needs as paramount: the need to help bright pupils develop study skills; the need to encourage the bright pupil to develop skills of higher level thinking; and the need to be rewarded for scholastic achievement whilst at the same time retaining an identity with the class group.

Thus the teacher has to recognize and understand the gifted child's special learning requirements but he must also recognize that the child has *emotional* and *social* needs comparable to his chronological peers. He needs to belong to the group, to play, to be useful and accepted; he needs to indulge in activities for pure fun and relaxation; it must be recognized that he cannot always work to his fullest capacity at the highest level. Nevertheless, it must be stressed that the gifted child needs opportunities to feel normal in a learning situation, to exchange ideas with intellectual peers, to be challenged and stretched to the point of failure. Many are unwilling to face failure, they are too used to success; they tend to avoid a situation in which they might fail and often do not develop work habits requiring perseverance. They need to develop as a whole person, not merely as a collection of talents, and they and their parents often need counselling.

Organizational and educational implications of provision for the gifted in school

> . . . for reasons of policy and administration the school can make it possible or practically impossible for an individual to give effective help to the gifted pupil (Bridges, 1973, p.92).

The organization and philosophy within a school can vary between two poles; at one extreme, rigidity, conformity, and insularity; at the other, flexibility, diversity, and cooperation. The teacher functioning within these limits may be either relatively inhibited or liberated. In addition to this, in a class of 30 pupils where the teacher is committed to catering for individual needs, the diversity of physical, social, mental, and emotional characteristics demands infinite patience, extraordinary energy, and diverse talents. Frequently, inadequate resources and lack of time impose limits on creative, dedicated teachers. Gifted children, because of their special needs, increase the pressures; they devour materials with an insatiable intellectual appetite, and are sometimes careless, untidy, and reluctant to acquire basic skills.

However dedicated and concerned the teacher may be, the motivation of the child himself conditions, to some extent, the response and rapport between pupil and teacher. Burt (1975) suggests that:

> To achieve success in the intellectual sphere the learner needs not only high intellectual ability, but certain qualities of character as well – a stable temperament, a driving curiosity about intellectual problems, a capacity for sustained hard work and a determination to do well together with ideals and aims that look forward to the remoter future and to scholastic success instead of hankering after immediate pleasures or mere monetary rewards (p.182).

While the teacher can appreciate the significance and attempt to encourage the development of these characteristics, the child's home background may be a contradictory force. Terman (1925), in his longitudinal study of gifted children, concluded that a child whose home conditions and parental attitudes conflicted with school and teacher attitudes had a lower level of aspiration and drive to achieve.

Obviously, there is no single answer to the problem of provision for gifted children; any tentative solution must emerge from each school's amalgam of educational philosophy, methods, and organization; the personality, skills, and experience of the teacher; the temperament and background of the gifted child. Nevertheless, in order to move towards a facilitating environment for teacher and pupil, two areas need to be explored:

1   the basic underlying principles which should govern the teacher's preparation of work for gifted children;
2   the strategies in organization and methods which may be manipulated to allow greater opportunities for gifted children to work at appropriate levels.

Tempest (1974) claims that the teacher's main aim should be to teach a gifted child how to learn and he specifies that learning programmes should aim at:

a   intellectual challenge through the quality rather than the quantity of work;
b   developing self-direction and independence of thought and action;
c   encouraging originality and imagination.

Gifted children tend to have a greater capacity than normal children to work independently, they often have the power of sustained concentration, can relate information, interpret, and classify at a very high level. They are usually keenly observant and highly competitive; they need rapid acceleration through basic stages so that they can pursue further enquiry at depth; they make unusual and original conceptual leaps. Practical work may be essential but the minimum is usually sufficient to provide understanding; they have superior ability in discovering and perceiving relationships, manipulating abstract symbols with ease; problem solving presents exciting challenges. Like all children, gifted children need a balance between direction and freedom, structured and open-ended tasks. The teacher tends to underestimate the capacities of the gifted pupil even when the pupil has been identified and the teacher is anxious to make adequate provision for his needs.

Learning is essentially an individual process but a child can either be alone, a member of a small group, or a participant in a class activity. There is a vast difference, however, between being alone because one is an isolate and choosing to be alone in order to pursue an individual interest. A gifted child needs the opportunity to work alone, in depth, following his specific interests. He also needs to work as a member of a group, as a leader and as a member of a team, and an experienced teacher will manoeuvre the dynamics of a group activity to achieve social *and* intellectual goals. A gifted child can also participate in classroom activities when each individual is contributing at his own level, e.g., in story telling, discussions, the making of a class newspaper. It is not difficult to imagine the build-up of frustration in a lesson which depends on step-by-step progress aimed at the average level of the class.

It is generally accepted as conventional and convenient to group all children according to their chronological age but that is the *only* common factor in any such group; the mental, emotional, social, and physical variables create enormous individual differences, a gifted child being, intellectually, *several years*, ahead of others in his class. 'Vertical grouping' (i.e., mixed age range or 'family' grouping) may be seen as one strategy for coping with this problem. Admittedly, in such a situation it is accepted that younger children can work with older ones, but vertical grouping may sometimes intensify problems at home if, for example, a gifted younger sibling is working with an older brother or sister. Moreover, a gifted child could still reach the ceiling of his mixed age range class and show signs of underachievement. This latter point could equally be true of any situation in which pupils are grouped according to ability and the teacher assumes that the group is homogeneous. Even in this situation, each individual has different needs and the gifted child would still be outstanding.

Acceleration is another possible strategy, but even considering whether a gifted child is emotionally and socially *capable* of adjusting to chronologically older children (and acceleration by one year might be insufficient), vital stages in learning might be missed if the child is expected to leap a year and work with the next class.

Extracurricular activities can create opportunities especially for gifted children to explore new and challenging experiences, particularly if the group is small and the activities are unusual or the result of a teacher's enthusiasm or hobby. Often in this situation there are opportunities for the exchange of ideas in an informal atmosphere on a one-to-one basis, the chance to work in depth and breadth.

In the same way, occasional or regular withdrawal of small groups of gifted children from their normal class can provide the stimulus they need. Not only can they have the necessary experience of working with their intellectual peers, but the opportunity for the exchange of ideas with specialist teachers or other experts.

Since many gifted children enjoy and are capable of independent work over a long period of time, it is feasible to encourage them to do individual research in the school library; but they will need experience in the use of references, training in study skills, and careful monitoring of their work.

While browsing through books can be pleasurable, aimless searching through inadequate material is depressing and time wasting. Their work needs to be purposeful, planned, and guided if it is to be worthwhile.

However, strategies such as horizontal grouping, vertical grouping, ability grouping, acceleration, withdrawal, should all be regarded as organizational variations or devices within which the individual should be able to develop towards a rounded intellectual and social maturity.

The ideal solution probably lies in striving towards individualized learning programmes, the gifted child having special need of an enriched curriculum. (This is discussed more fully in the next section and in Chapters 1 and 12.) Dehaan and Havighurst (1961) describe enrichment as:

> the provision of educational experiences that will do two things: first, enable the gifted person to develop his strengths, the things he does best, and second, enable him to fulfil the specialised role he will play in society.
>
> Since children with unusual mental abilities are able to think abstractly, generalise more widely and accumulate facts and principles more rapidly, it is necessary to give them not only more material to learn but qualitatively different experiences. Enrichment means supplying more opportunities for the gifted to delve more deeply and to range more widely than the average child in his intellectual, social and artistic experiences (p.81).

They differentiate between 'intensive, vertical, linear or depth enrichment' and 'extensive, horizontal, lateral or breadth enrichment'. Enrichment in depth encourages specialization in an area of activity at a more mature level; some aspects of subjects such as reading, mathematics, or science having linear as well as lateral dimensions. Depth enrichment also allows the pupils to pursue an activity or develop a skill to a high level of proficiency, to reach saturation point, to feel a sense of completion. It may be argued, however, that this approach leads to a narrowing of vision and encourages 'closed' or 'convergent' thinking rather than widening horizons and developing 'open-ended' or 'divergent' thinking (see also Chapter 1). Enrichment in breadth demands the preparation of work in areas not ordinarily explored rather than the provision of a 'move of the same' approach which produces what Ogilvie (1973) has described as a 'tropopause' curriculum. (See also Chapter 12, pp.174-5.)

It would appear logical to combine both, using breadth where possible and depth when necessary. Both forms of enrichment demand close cooperation between teachers and schools if repetition is to be avoided. Each teacher must be aware of the pupil's learning background in order to prevent discontinuity and the development of an unrelated patchwork of experience and knowledge. The teacher needs to utilize three avenues for enrichment:

1   building enrichment into the core curriculum;
2   developing the child's own interests;
3   widening horizons to include new interests.

This approach enables the gifted pupil to share learning experiences with others, specialize in an area of personal choice, and develop broader interests.

However, there is no set formula for provision and several problems immediately arise when considering the preparation of enrichment material:

1   classroom pressures preclude the teacher from easily providing individualized learning programmes;
2   the gifted child does not automatically respond with enthusiasm to every suggestion;
3   enrichment increases the diversity of demands on the classroom teacher in both material and intellectual terms.

It is, therefore, helpful if the classroom teacher can look for ideas and advice from other teachers and advisory groups concerned with the development of enrichment programmes. The next section describes the efforts of one working party to fulfil something of this function.

The process of developing teaching materials

Bearing in mind the principles outlined so far, Essex had adopted an essentially pragmatic approach to the production of teaching materials. Materials are initially produced for use on one of the courses organized and run by the working party. The courses serve a dual role: firstly, the pupils share the experience of working together and, secondly, the materials can be given a trial run. In the light of this experience the projects can be revised, adapted, and evaluated before teachers try them in schools. Some projects, apparently ideal in principle, are inadequate in practice; the content may be insufficiently demanding, the presentation too complex, or the practical applications too difficult for the teacher to initiate. The opportunity for assessment and consequent revision of materials at a central level alleviates the problem confronting the class teacher who has neither the time nor resources for the preparation and evaluation of similar material.

Teacher expertise and local facilities

In any field of endeavour it is economical and constructive to utilize the skills and expertise of immediate personnel. Therefore, attempts to produce materials have been on what might seem an 'ad hoc' basis, capitalizing on the skills and strengths of current working party members rather than devising a specific framework and expecting the working party to conform to a rigid plan of work. This method of working generates enthusiasm and cooperation since individual strengths and interests are fully exploited.

However, the pupil strengths can also be considered and utilized, e.g., since exceptional verbal skill is often a characteristic of gifted children, a unit on the basics of linguistics has recently been drafted. Scientific topics requiring experimental, problem-solving approaches have been devised, demanding that pupils analyse relationships and draw conclusions. In history projects, great emphasis is given to the use of primary sources with stress on the need to evaluate evidence and differentiate between fact and opinion. Attempts have also been made to make the projects relevant to the local environment and, since Essex has several new towns, a unit based on town planning was constructed. Even children who had not visited a new town understood the problems and essential considerations of planning such a community.

The long history of witchcraft in Essex provided another peg on which to hang a project and, using the principles mentioned earlier, a history topic was produced for secondary pupils which sought to develop powers of analysis and deduction, identifying fact and objective evidence against superstition and subjective accounts. Nevertheless, while using the local environment, care must be taken that the projects are not too specific for general use. Thus, although the grounds of the course residential centre contain a large pond, a project specifically and solely on pond life has not been produced since this would restrict its applicability to schools with immediate access to pond life. Whenever necessary, schools using the kits may contact the teachers (or their replacements) who designed the material so that any difficulties may be discussed.

Practical considerations

The working party has been sensitive to the possibility of 'teacher resistance' to the materials produced. Some teachers might feel inadequate or even threatened by the sophistication of the material itself, or possibly threatened by the presence of a child with exceptional abilities. To try to overcome this, attempts are made to ensure that while the content of the material is sufficiently stimulating and challenging, it is not so esoteric that a teacher would feel inadequate. Topics with titles such as 'Quantum Mechanics' or 'Nuclear Physics' are not so acceptable as 'Bridges' or 'Probability and Game Strategy'. The presentation of these learning kits is essentially simple; many glossy work schemes and sophisticated packages spend their lives in cupboards. The security of being able to say, 'This is what I would have produced if I had the time', generates a readier acceptance.

Materials prepared for use in the classroom must, therefore, satisfy educational needs; they must be practical and economical; they must make use of teacher expertise and local resources; and they must be acceptable to both pupil and teacher. The next section describes some of the projects which have been produced by the working party at the primary school level.

Details of projects based on 'Structure'

The projects based on 'Structure' were devised by a biologist, a physicist, and a geographer. They were prepared for pupils from eight to ten-plus.

Biology   This project is introduced through a study of the basic unit of life, the cell. Slides of plant and animal cells are prepared and studied under the microscope, building up a list of similar and dissimilar cell characteristics. Using cultures of single-celled organisms, the pupil observes and studies a selection of these, referring to advanced reference books as part of the exercise. It is suggested that after studying these specific organisms, the pupil might collect, identify, and study microscopic pond life.

From these simple structures, the project leads into a study of large animal structures with particular emphasis on skeletal construction. Using slides and tapes, the pupil is guided to make an analysis of the purpose of skeletal structure, differentiating between and comparing man and rabbit, fish and bird, carnivores and herbivores, prehistoric and modern creatures.

Another strand of the project develops into an analysis of plant structure with opportunities to classify and build collections of plant material. Yet another aspect explores the evolvement of protective structures of plants and animals. The pupil uses slides, tapes, work sheets, and reference books for individual study, the aim being to develop and encourage detailed observations and deductive reasoning.

An element of fun was introduced with a tape of poems about skeletons, interspersed with selected music.

Physics The purpose of this kit was to explore the variety of bridge structures, analysing the strengths of the designs. Using straws, pipe cleaners, and glue, the pupils are first guided to build basic bridge structures which they test to the point of destruction. Using the knowledge gained, they are encouraged to create a bridge structure stronger than any of the previous ones. The kit also contains a series of slides showing various bridges with notes and questions designed to build up the knowledge needed to classify types of bridges and to discuss the relative characteristics of each type.

The project includes stories and poems about famous bridges, together with suggestions for further research if the pupil is interested and wishes to go into the subject more deeply.

Geography This project revolves around the considerations and planning involved in the structure of a new town. Pupils are introduced to the concepts of distance, area, simple relief, scale, compass direction, and contours. The child is guided to plan a new town using a system of coding, analysing the basic requirements, and explaining decisions taken. To stimulate interest, a series of slides is included, showing various aspects of new towns; notes encourage analysis and suggest possible reasons for various decisions in the design and plan of the new town. The pupil is encouraged to design welcome posters, sculptures, and three-dimensional models of this town. A collection of poems and music is also included.

All the projects aim, basically, at providing individual work, although in practice teachers have occasionally used the kits for group work, encouraging the gifted pupil to tackle the most difficult and demanding tasks. The secondary teachers who provide the subject detail for the projects work in collaboration with primary teachers who advise on methods of presentation. It is impossible to design materials suitable for all children since personality, interests, and needs are unique to each individual. Nevertheless, teachers have found that they can adapt the material, omit some of it, extend certain parts. Reference books are included together with all notes, work cards, tapes, and slides; apparatus is also supplied with the exception of large expensive items such as the microscope. Where a primary school has needed to borrow unusual large items of apparatus, the local secondary school has always willingly cooperated.

Resource materials from other projects

For primary schools wishing to try to initiate project work for the most able pupils, the report of the Tempest (1974) experiment is a helpful source of ideas. Tempest and his colleagues found that pupils enjoyed using work cards which encouraged a systematic gathering of information from books, the examination and classification of such data, and the formulation of general conclusions or hypotheses. These 'Finding Out' work cards were graded in increasing complexity. At first, the questions demanded simple sentence answers, gradually building up to paragraph answers, and finally requiring wide reading from several sources. The pupil would be guided to prepare a detailed piece of work on a central theme.

Tempest also suggests that work cards demanding the use of logic can be very successful. Pupils were encouraged to engage in a variety of problem-solving activities including finding solutions to codes, mazes, and puzzles. They were also presented with a series of open-ended thinking tasks which demanded creative, unusual, inventive solutions.

A number of valuable ideas for teaching materials have emerged from other experimental projects. The work of research teams at Johns Hopkins University in the USA are mentioned by Dr. Bridges in Chapter 11. Several of these research studies are reported in Keating (1976). Another American researcher who has contributed a great deal to the development of teaching approaches for the gifted is E. Paul Torrance. (See, for example, chapter 12 in Gibson and Chennells, 1976). Some of the special characteristics of gifted children are revealed in their unusual ability to explore alternatives, to be adaptable and flexible in their thinking, to foresee future problems with unusual insight and understanding. Torrance *et al.* (1976) suggest that these special abilities could be developed in a very positive way by encouraging gifted children to study the future. Since the present world is changing rapidly, there is great need for future leaders to be able to foresee developments and problems and to work to avoid or alleviate as many of these as possible.

Torrance suggests that gifted pupils should be encouraged in activities such as socio-drama, creative problem solving, redesigning exercises. Certainly highly creative gifted children possess unusual powers of imagination; their constant questions, guessing, and desire to experiment should be developed fully. At a more advanced level, these qualities can lead to studies in depth of such problems as pollution, overpopulation, the effects of advanced technology on the quality of living, etc. Science fiction and philosophy also offer opportunities for deep and creative thinking.

Developments at the secondary school stage

The Essex working party has concentrated on developing enrichment materials for primary pupils but secondary courses were also organized. The first was held in the summer of 1978. Almost without exception, the secondary pupils who participated in the residential course expressed their joy in exchanging ideas with their intellectual peers. They found satisfaction in a learning situation which presented a challenge and were relieved to find themselves 'normal' in their peer group. Topics included philosophy, history, mathematics, creative writing, electronics. The theme of the philosophy topic revolved around the idea of 'knowing what is truth' The insight, understanding, and sensitivity revealed through the subsequent discussion provided evidence of the intellectual stature of these young adolescents. The history topic aimed to develop awareness of the validity and reliability of historical evidence. The topic was centred on Essex witchcraft and pupils were encouraged to discuss the weakness of eye-witness accounts, assess the possibility of inaccuracies and biased judgement due to superstition, ignorance, rivalry, fear, convention, etc.

The mathematics and electronics projects sought to present problems demanding creative, open-ended, original solutions. Creative writing was encouraged by presenting pupils with a science-fiction story which had to be converted into a television play. There was lengthy discussion about the necessary techniques, the limitations of such a television production, the danger of subjective interpretation by the producer, the possibility of restricting the imagination of the viewer.

In developing enrichment materials for secondary pupils, the complexity of a large school organization and the special requirements dictated by subjects can create problems which are not easily overcome. Indeed the primary school in many ways offers a more flexible environment in which to plan enrichment programmes despite its comparative lack of subject specialists and advanced resource material.

However, at secondary level, various strategies may be developed. It would seem desirable for each department or faculty to prepare its own enrichment programme, liaising with other departments wherever possible and organizing group withdrawal when necessary. Unusual subject areas could be explored, e.g., philosophy, archeology, classics. Closer links could be developed between secondary and tertiary institutions to allow for partial transfer of pupils. Various schools could develop as specialist centres so that teacher expertise and apparatus could be shared. Groups of schools could plan extracurricular activities, e.g., Saturday morning clubs, residential courses. Outside experts such as writers, artists, scientists, industrialists have a valuable contribution to make. The report, 'Gifted Children in Middle and Comprehensive Schools' (DES, 1977), examines some of these ideas.

Many of these schemes are being developed in Essex. All teachers involved in this work have full-time school commitments and have contributed their time and expertise voluntarily; they are deeply aware of the problems of gifted children and the difficulty of solving those problems. They are also conscious of the needs of the teacher with innumerable demands and pressures and so have committed themselves to working towards the alleviation of the difficulties of both gifted pupil and busy teacher.

The advisory teacher for gifted children

The county advisory teacher was appointed from September 1978, the encompassing aim of the role being to generate awareness of the needs of gifted children, to disseminate information, and to develop resource material for teachers to use in the classroom. Accordingly, in the twelve teachers' centres throughout the county, in-service education courses have been organized to explore the following questions associated with the education of gifted children:

1   Why is there a need to be concerned about gifted children?
2   What is meant by 'giftedness'?
3   What are the techniques and difficulties of identification?
4   How can provision be made for gifted children in the normal school?

Whenever possible, local working parties of teachers are being established to extend the in-service education and to develop materials and resources for enrichment. Areas of development include the following:

Reading material

Primary teachers, particularly, face the problem of needing to supply appropriate reference books for able children whose intellectual understanding is several years ahead of their chronological age and sometimes also some way ahead of their reading age. Such books need to provide depth and breadth of information without using specialist technical language. Similarly, it is important to provide literature which will challenge the pupils' advanced skills in reading and use of language whilst taking account of their less advanced emotional development and their limitations in worldly experience. There is an obvious need for a review of current literature with this problem in mind so that collections of suitable books can be delivered to teachers requesting such a service. Collections of poems and short stories can also be gathered and possibly recorded on tape with comments to stimulate ideas and follow-up work.

Mathematics

Gifted mathematicians need to move rapidly through basic concepts; they are able to leap through sequential stages and concepts with the minimum of practical experience. A teacher must, therefore, have a very flexible approach, adapting any existing mathematics' scheme according to the requirements of the pupil. There is a need to devise and collect materials which are open-ended, which demand creative problem solving at a high level. Constructional materials of various kinds are essential; a special mathematics box of puzzles, problems, design and constructional tasks, code and logic exercises could provide a gifted young mathematician with a vast selection of challenging activities.

In July, 1979, a three-day mathematics course was arranged for seventy primary children aged from seven to eleven years. The course, incorporating the principles mentioned above, was designed by the head of mathematics at a sixth form college. He was enthusiastically supported by his department who made valuable contributions.

The pupils, representatives from 16 schools in close proximity to the college, attended with their teachers. It was an exciting, cooperative venture, with pupils and teachers being introduced to problems and challenges developed from concepts such as Fibonacci Sequence Patterns, Pascal's Triangle, the Sieve of Eratosthenes, the Golden Ratio. One of the memorable highlights was a lunch-time game of chess, when a European Grand Master played seventeen eager participants simultaneously.

General Courses

At secondary level, groups of schools are cooperating to provide local courses. Time, expertise, and facilities are shared. Problems are discussed, solutions tentatively explored, and ideas are enriched due to the cross-fertilization.

Nevertheless, while it is desirable to provide opportunities for gifted children to meet and exchange ideas, the main emphasis is on trying to provide for these children within their normal school.

Project kits for enrichment

The work already begun by the central working party is being extended through local groups. Experts in various fields are being asked to devise enrichment programmes in areas such as law, geology, pathology, archeology, astronomy, etc. The projects will be tried out locally to carry out the process of adaptation and evaluation before being more widely distributed. It is necessary and desirable to organize regular meetings of groups of pupils using specific projects so that they can exchange ideas and discuss problems with the project designer. These meetings take place during the school day, on Saturday mornings, or during residential weekend courses.

Obviously, there is no real substitute for a one-to-one relationship in learning; any learning 'kit' or structured programme of this kind inevitably has limitations; there is no possibility of anticipating all possible questions and queries; there is no material that has a comprehensive elasticity with respect to opportunity and challenge. Nevertheless, care can be taken to ensure that work cards are well devised, giving essential detail and definitions of technical concepts; that important generalizations are skilfully worded. The tasks specified should allow for the constructive and acquisitive mind, for the inventive as well as the assimilative mind. The gifted pupil should not merely record information but carry out learning activities which demand enterprise, innovation, discovery, invention, originality, and initiative.

In the preparation of enrichment material, the logic and structure of the subject and the sequence of the learning process must be important considerations. Learning kits also need to incorporate appropriate reinforcement material, necessary practice, and evaluation of understanding. (See 'Some Theorems on Instruction' by J.S. Bruner in Stones, 1970, and chapters 4 and 5 in the Schools Council Working Paper 42, 1972.)

In discussion groups, teachers are guided through an analysis of Bloom's *Taxonomy of Cognitive Objectives* (Bloom, 1956). In presenting work to pupils, there is a tendency for teachers to concentrate on the acquisition of *knowledge* and *comprehension* of that knowledge. This is borne out by the recent primary survey, 'Primary Education in England' (DES, 1978b). In preparing work schemes, care is taken to build in activities requiring *application*, *analysis*, *synthesis*, and *evaluation*.

In addition to the development of awareness of need and the development and dissemination of resources, the advisory teacher has the important task of building a network of cooperation and coordination. Members of the county inspectorate are able to contribute a wealth of experience and expertise and are obviously involved in the preparation of curricular materials. The team of educational psychologists have an important function in the development of identification techniques. Area education officers together with head teachers must be closely involved with administrative decisions while supportive services such as the central county library and the central visual aids department can contribute greatly in the task of preparing materials.

Another function of the advisory teacher is that of visiting schools to discuss problems with head teachers and their staffs; possibly discussing appropriate organizational strategies, methods of enrichment, or individual pupil problems. This latter function obviously needs a larger taskforce and points to the desirability of appointing a teacher, within a school, with special responsibility for the identification and education of gifted children. Possibly a group of small schools could share a peripatetic teacher, or a responsibility post already in existence could be extended to incorporate this new dimension and area of concern.

Other aspects of the advisory teacher's role include monitoring the progress of pupils once their potential has been recognized; building up a central resource of materials and specialist reference books; compiling a register of human, environmental, and institutional expertise; and organizing exhibitions of curricular materials.

There is still an enormous amount of work to be done but it is a challenging task necessary to fulfil real, urgent needs of children who could be described as severely handicapped with a burden of brilliance.

In conclusion

In considering the education of gifted children, the teacher must first acquire an understanding of what is meant by 'giftedness'. This necessitates the development of initial identification techniques for use in the classroom. The teacher must be committed to the ideal of providing for the needs of each individual and aware of particular problems and handicaps including that of giftedness. The special qualities desirable in a teacher of a gifted child should result in a learning atmosphere in which creativity, flexibility, tolerance, and mutual respect hold sway.

However, the teacher is limited by the organization and philosophy within the school. Even in a liberal and supportive climate, large classes, insufficient time, and limited resources demand exceptional qualities of patience, industry, resourcefulness, and drive. Gifted children have qualitatively different learning patterns from normal children and the teacher needs to understand and appreciate their exceptional capacities and abilities. The teacher, however well intentioned, has also to cope with the temperamental and motivational strengths and weaknesses of his pupils, together with the influence of home background which can be a powerful force, sometimes negative, sometimes positive.

The teacher also needs to understand the strengths and weaknesses of various organizational patterns and to examine educational methods and techniques, especially the principles underlying curriculum enrichment. Whenever possible he should develop individualized learning programmes for the pupils and in this task he can be aided by the work of advisory groups such as the Essex working party and by reference to 'enrichment programmes' produced elsewhere (see, for example, Chapter 12). Such enrichment programmes devised for the teacher to use with gifted children should thus help to provide for the educational needs of the child and also to alleviate some of the work of the classroom teacher.

CHAPTER TEN

HELPING GIFTED CHILDREN: SOME SUGGESTIONS FOR PARENTS

Peter Congdon

The first World Conference on Gifted Children, which was held in London in 1975, contained some excellent papers (see Gibson and Chennells, 1976). It did not, however, treat in any detail ideas and evidence concerning the influence of family background and parental handling in the upbringing of the gifted and talented. For me this was a significant and regrettable omission and it helped to determine my choice of subject for the paper I delivered to the second World Conference at San Francisco in 1977. This chapter is based on that paper and draws upon my professional experience as a local authority educational psychologist together with the increasing knowledge which large-scale research has put at our disposal.

I would first like to draw attention to some of the research which has taken place in the United Kingdom and in particular to that carried out by the National Childrens' Bureau in London. This bureau is the largest powerhouse of research and information about children in our country. Among its wide-ranging projects is a longitudinal study of 17,000 children born in a particular week in 1958. This has resulted in a number of reports published by Longman (e.g., Kellmer-Pringle *et al.*, 1966; Davie *et al.*, 1972). There have been longitudinal surveys carried out in the United Kingdom before, but none so ambitious and comprehensive as this. It is fair to say that the study contains something uncomfortable for most of us. Those who support women's lib can find little joy in the poor performance of children raised in groups or institutions. Those who emphasize the importance of the child's bond with its natural mother may be equally shaken to learn how much better adopted children, on average, do than those who stay with their unmarried mothers. But the cardinal message is a grim one: namely that inadequate housing, poverty, and above all bad parents affect a child's educational progress and attainments more than any other factor.

Large-scale surveys can highlight trends and present useful generalizations; but it is often the more limited investigation which contains the real-life detail. Such an example is a study by Kellmer-Pringle (1970) of the educational and behaviour difficulties of 103 very intelligent children who had been referred to child guidance clinics in England. These children were labelled 'able misfits'. The IQs ranged from 120–200. Although the investigation left many questions unanswered, a number of common characteristics concerning the parental attitudes and home backgrounds of the children were found. It was discovered that in general the parents were well educated and the majority were professional or nonmanual workers. First-born children predominated. This latter is an interesting point since other studies of children with learning and adjustment difficulties have not reported a predominance of children occupying this position in the family. It was discovered that, despite the children's high ability, less than one in five were rated as having above-average interests and hobbies and almost half of them fell below average. It was also discovered that the majority of these children had experienced limited social contacts with their contemporaries. Despite the relatively high socio-economic status of these able misfits it was found that above-average cultural and social opportunites were only provided by a minority of parents. In only a quarter of the cases did parental discipline appear sensible and inconsistent handling was most prominent in professional class homes. It was interesting to note that most parents showed concern for their child's educational progress but only a minority attached importance to his emotional development. Over-all the investigation indicated that high intellectual ability by itself is not enough to ensure satisfactory scholastic or emotional adjustment. (For an example of one of these 'able misfits' see Part III, Case Study 2.)

When we discuss gifted or talented children we tend to concentrate on the subject of how to identify them, which is important, and how to provide for their formal education, which is also important. But in the past too little stress has been given to the subject of advising, influencing, and supporting the parents of these children. Ultimately, this may well be the crucial factor in their future happiness and success. It is true that despite adverse and tragic backgrounds there are children who soldier on, survive, and in some cases even excel. These are the invulnerable children, but they are in a minority. For most children such conditions would have a depressing and in some cases devastating effect on their whole development.

Since the first World Conference the effects of inflation in the United Kingdom continue to make inroads into the education budget and it is not surprising, therefore, that little extra money has been earmarked for gifted children. The attitude that no extra money and no extra staff is sufficient reason for doing nothing is widespread and it is an attitude in part encouraged by the welfare State. However, in some areas (see Chapter 3) there have been welcome signs of a current development of interest in the problems of the gifted. In the impoverished coal-mining area of North Warwickshire, for example, where I am the only educational psychologist for a population of 16,000 children of school age, we have taken active steps to meet the needs of the gifted. By enlisting the help of teachers, health visitors, social workers, and parents we are in the process of formulating a comprehensive, sensitive, and continuing approach to the identification of gifted children. We have organized conferences and discussion groups and have started a resource centre and toy library for these children. But most of our attention and most of our scarce resources have been concentrated on counselling and supporting parents. We have accepted that in the long term this approach will be the most fruitful.

Discovering the gifted child

Early identification

If we are to help children of high intelligence it is essential to identify them as soon as possible. The early formative years will lay the foundation for their future development. Doctors and official health visitors can play a crucial role in identification. They should be sensitive to the alert baby – the one who raises its head early and follows objects with its eyes. When this is succeeded by excellent coordination, early speech, a minimal sleep need, early bowel and bladder control, a compulsion to explore, the capacity for self-direction and sustained concentration, then the possibility of high intelligence may be suggested to the parents. A wary eye should also be kept for indications of relationship problems between parent and child which could have their origin in unusual mental ability. Early diagnosis must, of course, be cautious. It could breed disillusionment if health visitors or others went around encouraging parents to expect the most from children who will inevitably disappoint them. But if they are trained to open the door gently to the possibility of special intelligence then parents will at least be prepared for later developments.

Parents themselves have a part to play in this identification process. For the young child, observation and especially play observation is a particularly fruitful area. Parents should be alerted to the variety of sounds, both consonant and vowel sounds, which the baby makes. Early language development can be indicative of high intellectual potential. As young babies gifted children will sometimes probe and pinch at food rather like a weights and measures inspector. Some will peer thoughtfully at strangers as if weighing them up. Later they are good at such activities as brick building, bead threading, or pencil manipulation. Some begin to walk at ten or eleven months of age. Most children are at least a year old before they can walk, even when taken by the hand, and independent walking does not normally arrive until fourteen months and onwards. It is helpful if parents of young children are made aware of these facets of development.

Gifted children sometimes run in families and in such cases parents may have little reason to believe that they are different from the average. We have on record a case of a lady in London who has three children each with an IQ of 170. For a long time she had no idea of their exceptional ability. In my own area a family of four with IQs of 130–170 had parents who had little idea that they were gifted. Unless parents and others have an eye for comparing potential it is likely that very young gifted children will go unnoticed. Screening and identification techniques which involve the parent at an early stage help to pave the way for better planning and for a more orderly continuation of the child's education in both home and school. From my own experience, parents, when given the appropriate guidance and encouragement, are often more successful at identifying the signs of giftedness than are sophisticated testing techniques (see also chapter 8). Group tests administered in schools, for example, can be extremely valuable for screening purposes but, unless selected very carefully and skilfully interpreted, they may fail to locate many gifted children. In my own area we use group tests as screening measures. They are helpful, but they are only screening measures and many gifted children only come to light on more individual examination (e.g., by the local educational psychologist).

Breaking the news to the parent

The question is sometimes asked: 'Should parents be told that their child is gifted?' The answer is straightforward. Should parents be told that their child has been selected for the school football team, has been made a prefect, or has been chosen to represent the school at a music festival? Of course they should, and likewise the information that their child has high intelligence should be conveyed to them. There is, however, some point in the question. For some children it may have been better if their parents had never been told that they were gifted; since having been informed they tend to brag about them, pressurize them, cram them, or generally treat them differently from their siblings. There are parents who are genuinely alarmed at the news and feel quite inadequate in the situation. Others are basically anti-intellectual and lack interest. Still others regard gifted children as odd or peculiar and do not believe that their unusual qualities should be encouraged. It is because of the existence of this variety of attitudes that we need to be cautious when breaking the news to parents that their child has extraordinary ability. In order to help combat such problems I have produced a series of little booklets for parents.[1] These are purposely made simple, short, and direct.

In the first place we should discourage overreaction. Above all parents should refrain from changing their whole attitude to the child. There are cases where the parents treat the gifted child in an entirely different way from other children and from his brothers and sisters. This is unfortunate since the child in question may adopt an inflated opinion of himself and this can increase difficulties both at home and in school. It can also expose him to a considerable shock when he does meet his intellectual equals.

Some parents are not happy with the term 'gifted'. They feel that it is too ostentatious a term for their children. They prefer to use the term 'bright' or, if the child is very young, the term 'forward' is quite popular. I must confess that there are occasions when I find such terms more convenient.

Many educational psychologists refuse to impart IQ scores to parents. They feel that the numerical score has little meaning to the layman and is likely to be misused. Perhaps the mental age concept is more comprehensible. My own approach is to explain to parents that intelligence consists of numerous abilities. Some of these abilities are largely dependent on the use of words. We call them verbal abilities. Some are less dependent on words.

[1] Available from the Gifted Children's Information Centre, 941 Warwick Road, Solihull, West Midlands B91 3EX.

We sometimes refer to them as nonverbal skills. An intelligence test samples a number of these abilities and skills and the child's score is merely the record of one performance on one day on one set of criteria. The results are important and can tell us a lot but they do not tell us everything about the child. They can provide us with a tentative indication of the child's academic potential which may or may not be borne out by his later development. The child's ultimate success will depend largely upon his response to school and the encouragement he receives at home. There is also the risk that in emphasizing IQ or mental development we encourage parents and teachers to take a lopsided view of a child. It can be pointed out that high intelligence does not necessarily carry with it a disposition to honesty and generosity and in the long term qualities such as these may be more important.

Reassurance

Francis Bacon wrote, 'The joys of parents are secret, and so are their griefs and fears.' It is a mistaken belief that every parent wants to have a gifted child. This is certainly not so in Britain where many parents are happy to have clever children but not necessarily brilliant or exceptionally gifted ones. Some parents feel shame rather than pride if their children have outstanding intelligence. I well remember the reaction of one mother when her suspicions of her child's giftedness were confirmed. 'All I want is a normal boy,' she said, 'one who will play with his toys like other children.' Unfortunately seven-year-old Simon with an IQ of 160+ was more interested in science programmes on the television or designing a new extension for his parents house or playing chess with his father, whom he regularly beat.

In the first place parents of gifted children often need reassurance. In some cases they are convinced that they themselves are inferior to their child and will be unable to cope. Some are consumed with a guilt complex, believing that they have given birth to something they cannot nurture. They are bewildered by a child who asks difficult questions, needs little sleep, is intensely active, and does not behave as children should. Here it can be pointed out that, however clever their child may be, the parents have the advantage of experience and knowledge of life and unless they make serious mistakes they will continue to enjoy their child's affection and respect. Any undue anxiety can be further relieved by indicating that there are many parents in a similar position to themselves and that the vast majority of gifted children grow up to be happy and useful members of society. It should also be pointed out that parents are perfectly justified in seeking help just as they would have done had their child been suffering from a mental or physical handicap. Once the parents have been reassured the next step is to consider ways of advising, helping, and enlisting their support.

Advising the parents

Responsibility to the child

Usually, though not invariably, parents are highly motivated towards helping their gifted child. In view of the high pupil-teacher ratio in most British schools and the consequent problems of individualizing teaching, it would, therefore, seem wise to capitalize on this largely untapped resource. But for the children to benefit most from this help, it is important for their parents to develop a sensitive awareness of the needs of the gifted.

In the first place parents need to realize their responsibility towards their offspring. This, of course, is easier said than done. It is helpful just to remind some parents that the most important thing they are ever likely to do in their lives is the rearing of their children. What they do now with their children will determine what kind of adults and parents the children themselves become. Their influence, therefore, extends far into the future, long after the parents themselves have died. The importance of parental responsibilities is underlined by the Terman studies (see Terman and Oden, 1959) where it was discovered that many parents of gifted children were involved in a vigorous struggle for economic and social success and in a number of cases this produced resentment of their responsibilities and caused neglect and misunderstanding of their children. This situation still applies today and is relevant to all social classes.

A happy and settled home environment means more to the development of the gifted child than any other single factor. Because gifted children tend to be more sensitive to their environment than other children, their reactions to a discordant and unhappy home are often of greater magnitude. Parents, therefore, hold the key to the gifted child's emotional development which itself will affect his intellectual growth.

Respect for the child

Respect is essential for every child but it is particularly important when trying to understand the gifted child. Parents should accept that highly intelligent children do not necessarily wish to have the usual toys or play the games so popular with their peers. We know, for instance, that at birthday and Christmas time these children can sometimes be very awkward, taking more interest in other people's presents than their own. It is perhaps safer to treat them according to their mental age rather than their chronological age, though it should not be forgotten that physical and emotional development do not always keep pace with intellectual growth (see Part III, Case Study 7). Many gifted children are precocious. They develop and try to express individual opinions at an early age. There are times when they will appear disrespectful and rude. They should not necessarily be allowed to get away with this but it would be equally wrong to suppress their precocity and enthusiasm. Children are expected to respect adults, and likewise adults should respect the individual differences among children.

Avoid overconcentration on the gifted child

We have said that most parents are interested in helping their gifted child. This is good, but at the same time they should avoid overconcentrating on him to the detriment of his siblings. If the bright child is seen to have special consideration his brothers and sisters may become anxious or envious. Such problems should be handled by giving equal recognition to each child's accomplishments.

Parents who talk about their gifted child too much can become very unpopular and run the risk of becoming a 'gifted child bore'. They are also ensuring the child's unpopularity and this may apply however pleasant, modest, and unassuming he really is. The situation should be avoided whereby the child himself is encouraged to believe that he is Einstein reincarnate. Too many parents tend to talk about their gifted child's achievements within his earshot. This is dangerous, as is the situation where brothers and sisters are constantly reminded of his triumphs, virtues, and achievements. Of course it would be unnatural for parents not to talk about their child's successes, but they should always aim to preserve a balance. For every comment made about the gifted child they should make at least one about another child in the family and also make a point of enquiring about their friend's children. Parents should show that they have a general interest in children and not just in their own.

Many parents place great emphasis on their children's education as the key to success in later life, and parents who have had limited educational opportunities themselves are often the most ambitious. (See Part III, Case Study 1.) Sometimes, however, parental pressures can take such a firm hold of the situation that the child's progress can be endangered. There are parents, for example, who see their gifted child as a means of compensating for their own social and educational failures. They may even regard him as the gateway to their own fame and fortune and generally exploit the situation. Such attitudes are unhealthy and are to be discouraged. Associated with this is the danger of giving the child the impression that it is because he has outstanding ability that he means so much to his parents. This can place a tremendous strain on his security. The child should feel that he is important to his parents in his own right as an individual and for no other reason.

Avoid pressurizing the gifted child

There is much truth in the view that the best preparation for adulthood is to have lived fully as a child. Parents of gifted children should never forget this. Accelerating mental development is sometimes bought at the expense of slowing down the pace of social and emotional growth. The result can be a lopsided and maladjusted individual. The British have a warning here in the life of the political philosopher John Stuart Mill who was estimated to have had an IQ above 190. Mill was given a rigorous and rapid education under his father's direction. He was denied a childhood in the usual sense and treated like an adult from an early age. He studied Greek at three, Plato at seven, and Latin at eight. At nine, conic sections, spherics, and Newton's arithmetic were added to geometry and algebra. At sixteen he wrote a history of Rome and published letters in defence of his father's political views. He was precocious, erudite, a successful academic, and intellectually mature. But at the age of twenty John Stuart Mill suffered a mental breakdown. He had become in his own words a 'reasoning machine'.

There are parents who assume almost total responsibility for the education of their gifted child. They organize and regiment his life, march him round museums and art galleries crowding impression upon impression. The child becomes absorbed in educational materials and the private acquisition of skills. No expense is spared for the purpose of stimulating and supposedly educating his mind. Such parents need to be reminded that there are times when these children want to play and act like other children and they should be allowed to do so.

Gifted children, like others, need the contact of other children. Deprived of this they can experience serious social and emotional problems. Children should be allowed a wide education. No event organized by adults can offer the same kind of experience as that of playing with other children. For children, play is work. They grow up socially, emotionally, and intellectually via play. There are times, of course, when parents themselves can share in the play. Otto von Bismarck, the nineteenth-century German chancellor, once made the important observation: 'If you want to get to know a child, then play with him.' I can think of no better advice to give parents.

Time and space for the gifted child

It is far more valuable to give *time* to children than to give *things*, and gifted children have a special need for time. But we must be realistic. Parents have other responsibilities and duties. How far can they be expected to stretch or adapt the family's routine for the child's benefit? Time is a precious commodity especially where both parents go out to work. It may present less of a problem where the child is an only one. Nevertheless, if he is intensely curious, constantly asking questions, and requiring little sleep, his demands may still be formidable. It would seem fair therefore to be prepared to compromise. There is no better investment than to put time aside for the gifted child but it should be made clear to him that there are periods during the day when patience is required and when his parents are busy doing other things. Talking with the child, explaining things, allowing him to participate in your own work, visiting places of interest, even studying together are all ways of giving the child time. We often hear about what parents do to children, but probably what is more important is what they do not do to them. Often they don't talk to them enough or play with them enough; this applies to all social classes. The role of the father is particularly important, especially with boys. Boys are strongly influenced by the attitudes and behaviour of fathers. Besides trying to teach his son practical skills in the home, he should let him know as much as possible about the nature of his own job and his place of work. There is one warning however. Parents should avoid making the gifted child their life's work. After all, it is the child's life and not theirs.

Gifted children, like all children, need space. They need space to create things, space to store equipment, and space for books. Heaven help the child of the compulsive housekeeper who follows the maxim 'a place for everything and everything in its place'.

Very often gifted children are voracious readers. They derive great joy in collecting books such as encyclopaedias and dictionaries and setting them up as it were in a library. Reference books are always a good investment and parents should note the motive of self-defence here. Such books can provide the answers to those awkward questions which intelligent children have a habit of asking. It is also helpful if facilities are provided for the child to perform scientific experiments though, of course, certain precautions need to be taken. Some gifted children will attempt unusual and dangerous experiments. There is the story of Edison's friend Michael who became ill from drinking Seidlitz gas in an attempt to make himself float! The NAGC often organizes its 'Explorers Unlimited' sessions at weekends or in holidays (see Chapter 4) and local clubs may exist (or can be formed by interested teachers and parents) for such activities as 'Junior Chess', stamp collecting, music making, and so on.

Hobbies often provide a clue to a child's emotional and intellectual maturity. Boyton (1941) studied the hobbies of nearly 5,000 children between the ages of nine and eleven. His study showed that children whose hobbies involved collecting tended to have the highest IQs whilst those with no real hobby at all were often below average in intelligence. He found that stamp collectors, for instance, were generally bright and well-adjusted children. It has been said that stamps are like painting: they touch on colour and design. Through foreign stamps you discover different languages, money values, geography, and world history. Similarly, those who become really involved in bird watching or ornithology gain a wide education. The migratory habits of birds involve a study of geography whilst understanding their habitats introduces the subject of ecology. Birds live, so it is essential to understand their metabolism, behaviour, and cryptic colouration. They die, so it is necessary to have a knowledge of predators, pesticides, and climate variations. A particular advantage of ornithological work is the opportunity it offers for children to mix easily with adults and share a common interest.

A hobby can tell you a lot about an individual because generally a person picks a hobby of his own free will. Yet, in order to pursue a hobby successfully, a child again requires space and sometimes extra time from his parents. The home which provides these is encouraging the child's initiative and stimulating his intelligence.

Language development

We know that gifted children ask a lot of questions. Parents of these children often complain that the 'how' and 'why' stage started early and persisted over a long period, the child always wanting to find out more about his world. Within reason parents should listen to their children and try to answer their questions. By asking questions and obtaining answers the child is not only acquiring a vocabulary but he is also building up an understanding of the world around him. He is acquiring language and learning how to think. Have you ever tried to think without using language? It can be done. We know that babies can think before they attach labels to ideas and of course animals can think. But the higher thought processes, those which involve abstractions and concepts, are dependent on words.

Nor should adults be afraid of using more sophisticated language with gifted children. There is a story of the infant prodigy Macaulay who became a famous British historian. As a young child Macaulay was once faced with a patronizing enquiry from an adult: 'Is, iddums didums toofipegs better den.' The young Macaulay replied, 'Indeed Madam, the agony is somewhat abated.' Whenever we are surprised at the high level of a child's language we should raise our own level of vocabulary when talking to that child.

It is important that parents should talk 'with' the child rather than 'to' him about what he is doing. By encouraging the child's curiosity and responding to his questions, parents are not only helping to develop his intelligence but are also reinforcing his urge to learn. It is important to extend the child's comments and thoughts. When he observes, 'Daddy is sleeping', his mother can usefully reply, 'Yes he is tired because he has been working hard today.' In this way she offers an explanation for a situation and gives the child experience of cause and effect.

The development of language is fundamental to the child's intellectual growth and parents have a vital part to play in it. Some years ago a child was referred to me for not speaking. On investigation I discovered that not only did his parents rarely speak to him but they seldom spoke to one another. Parents provide a standard for language development and the one factor which probably contributes most to the development of a gifted child is conversation with his parents. Parents should aim at open friendly conversation in which the child's opinions are respected and in which he is encouraged to probe the unknown.

Variability within the group

Although gifted children as a group have many common characteristics, both parents and teachers should be aware of the high degree of variability they can exhibit. To illustrate this we might turn to the subjects of sleeping and reading.

On the whole, bright children need less sleep than others and often less than their parents. This presents problems not so much for the children but the parents. Some believe that all children require a certain number of hours sleep. Doctors have been known to encourage this by creating tables to indicate sleep requirements at different age levels. The truth is that children, like adults, differ in the amount of sleep they need. No child can be made to sleep more than he requires, though in Victorian England laudanum, which is alcoholic tincture of opium, was sometimes used to put babies to sleep and some parents even turned on the gas taps for this purpose. Today we are much more sophisticated in our approach and use a variety of drugs which in the long term may be even more harmful.

Yet short hours of sleep can be misleading. Some highly intelligent children are lethargic, dreamy, and even sluggish in disposition. The famous British poet G.K. Chesterton was described as a stodgy and sleepy school boy. His teachers complained that he was usually asleep in their lessons and Chesterton agreed that they were probably right.

No other area of early stimulation has been more controversial than early reading instruction. It is well known that many gifted children learn to read long before they go to school. We are told that Madam Curie read proficiently at the age of three and Francis Galton learnt to read at the age of $2\frac{1}{2}$ and wrote a letter before he was four. It would seem that some children are not taught to read young enough. However, just because a child is gifted is not sufficient reason to push him into reading. By all means stimulate his interest in books and offer him the opportunity to read, but if he is basically uninterested in the subject then it may be better to leave it until he goes to school. I have come across many children of high intelligence who were bored by the mechanical processes involved in learning to read. In such cases it would not have been wise to have forced the issue at an early age. Gifted children, like others, can differ widely in their habits, in their characteristics, and in their aptitude and enthusiasm to learn certain processes at particular age levels.

Parental interest in the school

It is essential that parents take an interest in the child's school and there are a number of books which can help to answer parent's questions about their children's schools. (See, for example, O'Connor 1977a, b; Taylor, 1978.) If parents do take a keen interest in their children's schooling then the child stands to gain whether he is gifted or otherwise. Tact, of course, should be observed in relationships with teachers. Comments and questions need to be couched in diplomatic terms. For instance: 'Does Simon ever appear lazy or bored?' rather than 'Simon says he's bored stiff with school.' In this way you may achieve the same result without incurring animosity either against yourself or your child. Nor should parents criticize the school in front of the child. Gifted children especially are quick to understand the implications of criticisms and they become increasingly confused when they are forced to return daily to a school which their parents openly describe as being of poor standard.

Parents are well advised to discover the aims of a school and how far they are achieved. Ideally these should include helping each child to make the most of his own ability and talents whilst cooperating and competing with others. Opportunities should be provided for challenging and stretching the gifted child. Such a child can become resentful when his intellect is not being stimulated and parents should keep a watchful eye for this kind of frustration. A school which merely concentrates on raising the standard of the performance of the average pupil may be the wrong place for him.

Competition is important and gifted children often seem to be naturally competitive. Competition can encourage them to raise their own level of performance and aspiration. But not all gifted children are competitive. This is particularly true of the creative child. The parent should therefore explore how far the competitive spirit obtaining in a particular school is appropriate for her child.

An important question concerns the degree to which a school is able and willing to cater for individual needs and differences. We cannot expect it to meet the child's every requirement, but at least it should offer some degree of flexibility (see Part III, Case Studies 5 and 10). For instance, are there opportunities for a child to be accelerated? Acceleration, grade skipping, or class jumping as it is sometimes referred to, can help to stretch some children (Part III, Case Studies 3 to 7) but it is not always the answer. Acceleration implies emotional, social, and physical development as well as intellectual maturity, and Part III, Case Study 7 offers some interesting observations on this issue from the pupil's viewpoint. For some children an enriched curriculum is more beneficial and the opportunities for this should be explored within the school.

Finally, once a good school has been found, it still needs to be watched with a critical eye. Morale and the quality of teaching within a school can change rapidly. Teachers can also vary tremendously in ability from class to class. A school may meet the needs of a child at a particular age but fail at a later stage and this can be especially true for the gifted child.

The importance of parental interest in the child's schooling is fundamental. In a monumental longitudinal study of 5,000 British children, Douglas (1964) found the most important factor in achievement (over and above social class) to be parental interest and aspirations as evidenced by school visits and the desire for the child to continue his education beyond the statutory school-leaving age. Douglas found that when this factor was held constant, other factors often ceased to show any significant effects.

Sexual stereotyping

The most tragic brain drain in an educational system may be the loss of gifted girls. In Britain, and I understand in many other countries, girls are still conditioned to think that their future lives will not require intellectual development. This is sometimes referred to as the gender trap. From the moment they are born children are under pressure from their parents to conform to the accepted image of either a boy or a girl. This process is later perpetuated in the classroom. Sexual stereotyping runs through our whole social and educational system.

Part of Terman's celebrated longitudinal study of gifted children was a comparison between male and female achievements a long time after the subjects had been identified. The comparison, which took place in the 1930s, reflected attitudes towards women at that time. Whilst many of the men had achieved responsible positions in professional, administrative, and business life, few of the women who were not housewives had risen to similar levels. It appeared that society had not been prepared to use their talents in any way that seemed too masculine. Today, forty years on, the attitude is still prevalent. In Britain too few girls are encouraged to pursue careers in the sciences, engineering, mathematics, or management. If this situation was reversed it could result in the introduction of different methods of thought and expression to these areas and their value might be better appreciated by the taxpayer. On the other side of the coin, society is still suspicious of clever boys with a talent for ballet or other subjects normally associated with girls. It would seem essential therefore to warn parents of the dangers of sexual stereotyping.

A final comment

I am sure that many of the statements I have made on the subject of helping parents of gifted children appear axiomatic. However, experience has warned me that what seems patently obvious to the professional or to the outsider is not always self-evident to the parent. The importance of the home should never be underestimated in the development of the gifted child. A warm, active home in which adults share in the intellectual and social activities of the child is a source of enduring motivation the like of which cannot be provided in the school.

CHAPTER ELEVEN

EXPERIMENTS AT CAMPION SCHOOL
Sydney Bridges

Background to the experiments

When the team at Brentwood College began the experimental work with gifted children in 1964 the problems that emerged were mainly concerned with the lack of challenge which resulted from the gifted being in large classes of relatively mixed abilities (Bridges, 1969). The schools from which these children came for their weekly session in the college were all well-run junior schools, but classes tended to be of about 45 children. Some of the buildings were old and they lacked the facilities for many of the activities which were commonplace in some of the more up-to-date buildings. The success rate in obtaining places in very good secondary schools, of which some were 'direct-grant' foundations, was very high and many parents moved into the area to take advantage of the success of the local authority junior schools.

It became obvious very early in the experiment that, although all the children had performed well on the Terman Merrill (1960) Intelligence Test (the original cut-off point was 145) or on what we believed then to be 'creativity' tests, almost all the children had some notional target in their school work, which they often hit, but the target was manifestly below their capabilities. Relative success in the work set for the class had helped in this conditioning so that it had become almost second nature to the majority of the children. On the whole they would perform adequately according to the expectations of their teachers but they would not voluntarily exceed those expectations. (Little blame for this situation could be attached to the teachers who were striving to deal with a fairly wide range of ability, often in rather crowded classrooms. One very bright boy indeed once suggested that if more children entered the class all would have to wear corsets!) This tendency to do just what was expected and no more we then called the 'stint' and this stint has characterized many and probably most of the experiments carried out subsequently at Millfield (Bridges, 1975) and in Greece. The existence of this condition and its constant reinforcement by the circumstances prevailing in the classrooms meant that the first task in the college sessions must be to break down attitudes, a task which proved more difficult than we had expected. Normally these children were capable of technical correctness but they rarely allowed their imagination any scope. The principal difficulty lay in persuading them that their correctness was not enough and that much of the work they produced was boring to intelligent people. It came, and indeed had to come, as a shock to many of the boys and girls that what would earn an 8 or 9 out of 10 in their schools was rated at about 3 or 4 in the college.

The children who attended were all from primary schools and were accustomed to having the same teacher throughout the school day. Obviously there were subjects which could not be adequately covered by a teacher in such circumstances and so it was possible to make the college sessions largely enrichment courses in various subjects of the curriculum. This was not so in the case of the Millfield children. Firstly they were on the average three years or so older than the Essex children and most had been accustomed for some time to specialist teaching. Again a fair proportion also had been accelerated in a way not normally possible in primary schools. Moreover, all had a wide variety of subjects and there was no question of the experimental work being an enrichment of those subjects. The programmes inevitably became of a different nature and more attention was paid to the developmental aspects of the children's education. As in the case of the Brentwood children, these Millfield youngsters were likely to be available for at least two or three years and so a relatively leisurely procedure could be followed. In consequence studies were made in intellectual and creative activities and also in self-understanding and in relationships with other people. Personality tests were also used. (After the conclusion of the Millfield experiment it was discovered that the Johns Hopkins University in Baltimore, Maryland, was employing the same battery of tests on their highly gifted young mathematicians. See Keating, 1976, and Stanley *et al.*, 1977.)

Despite the very different circumstances of the Brentwood and Millfield experiments, however, there were certain similarities in the results. For example, both sets of children showed behaviour characteristic of the 'stint'. At first the Millfield groups tended to treat the work as something not too serious since it did not lead directly to an 'O' level. They soon settled down, however, especially those in the preparatory school. When they did so they revealed much the same characteristics as the other children in trying to sum up the expectations of the experimenters and in subsequently settling themselves to work up to those expectations, but not beyond. Those who were obtaining high marks in several of their subjects were doing so without a major effort and some showed a little resentment when the assessment of some of the experimental work was more severe than they were used to. One technique which was used in the case of some of the creative work was to have a second group of pupils assess the scripts on various criteria without knowing the names of the authors of the scripts. When the scores were communicated to the first group they sometimes had a salutary effect as the writers realized, perhaps for the first time, that other people agreed with the assessments of the teacher. When the technique was repeated with the position of the groups reversed there was a temptation to take some sort of revenge so that the assessments tended to be even more severe. Some pupils felt rather chagrined when they received their results, but there was no doubt that the message was driven home and at last some of the children seemed to become aware that they were being challenged in a way to which they were not yet accustomed.

The experimental setting

The school itself

When Pitman's published *Gifted Children and the Millfield Experiment* (Bridges, 1975), they stated that the author was deputy head of Campion School, Athens, and that he was trying to set up similar experimental work in Greece. It was not realized at the time, however, that this statement was really contradictory. The school population at Campion increased in size from 100 pupils to over 1,200 in five years and in these circumstances no deputy head could possibly find sufficient time to look after the gifted. Only when the author reverted to full-time director of studies was it possible to look at the children of superior ability.

Campion School is an American foundation run on English lines rather like Millfield. Originally it was only a secondary school catering for American and British children but now the school has a full age range and includes pupils of fifty nationalities. The school is organized on a grade structure (kindergarten and then grades 1 to 13). Grade 6, with pupils aged nine to ten-plus, is the first class in the 'secondary school'. The range of abilities of the children is wide but many of the children are bright and have been brought up in circumstances favouring school success.

Despite the presence of children of high ability, however, the nature of the school posed a number of problems for anyone wishing to initiate experimental work. The first of these was the enormous turnover in the foreign schools in a capital city. For example, in one year over 300 children left and some 500 entered. Again, the school caters for children from a variety of cultures and the majority do not have English as their mother-tongue or speak it outside school. In school however, lessons are taught in English and pupils have to accommodate to this situation even though, for some, English may be their third or fourth language. There is, therefore, always a limited time to help any of the gifted and much of the available time is required for a mastery of English since the majority will eventually sit 'O' and 'A' level examinations for one of the British examining boards.

Finally, many of the children have a Greek background or come from countries where children are expected to be learning at least three languages by the time they go to school at five or six years of age. The parents of the majority of the children believe that children attend school to learn and not to play and that the main function of the school, or indeed of any school, is to make sure that their children acquire the necessary pieces of paper to ensure entry into a college or profession. Any activity that does not manifestly help to achieve that 'consummation devoutly to be wished' should be discouraged. Many of the children are so indoctrinated with this belief that they query any nonexaminational activity, except perhaps physical education if that term means soccer. The result is that even where it does prove possible to bring together some of the brighter ones there may be a certain amount of resistance at first. 'Why do we have to do this stuff?' was the expression used by a very bright boy from Poland.

Setting up the experimental class

In face of these difficulties it was decided that the best approach was to form a full-time class of children, all of whom would have been regarded as very bright if the medium of instruction and learning had been their vernacular instead of their second or third language. More stress was laid on their mathematical ability which did not suffer so much from linguistic problems but all had to have a satisfactory pass in an English comprehension test requiring reasoning ability. A test was devised in the school for this purpose. Little attention was paid to chronological age which is of less significance because of the varied backgrounds and frequent transfers of the children than in Western schools with more stable populations. Of the first 14 children who satisfied the criteria, 13 were girls ranging in age from 9.2 to 11.6 years. The solitary boy was 9.4 years and was included because he scored well on an intelligence test. His promotion to the secondary school had been the result of a report from the primary department that there were some problems at home. He was asked to present himself for testing: his appearance, that of a small fair-haired boy in neat blue shorts, seemed to belie his alleged misbehaviour. On testing it was found that his IQ on the Wechsler Intelligence Scale for Children was in the 140 range (WISC-English version revised 1974) and that he was underachieving in the 'grand manner'. He was promoted two grades – drastic action, as it seemed – but it has ultimately been justified.

Obviously the class had to be balanced, but there were few boys available of the right age and so some older boys, three of them being somewhat limited in English as it was in each case their third language, were drafted into the class. All were bright and all were doing well in mathematics and in their first and second languages. What we did not realize at the time was that one of these boys of Greek origin (seven nationalities were represented in the class) was highly gifted socially and soon had a wonderful effect on the class. Partly because he was older than most of the children, but largely because of his social capacity, the class passed in quite a short time from a number of bright individuals to a group of 20 children with an ethos of its own: each was a member of the team and no longer just an English, Australian, Greek, Lebanese, Rhodesian, or Yugoslav boy or girl placed by chance or some authority in class together. This did not prevent some rivalry when the class was divided for various activities into groups based on the results of a sociometric test, but it was a very friendly rivalry which added to the challenge required by these bright children. (On the use of sociometric tests see, for example, Evans, 1962.)

In Campion the sixth grade, as already mentioned, is the first class in the secondary school and children are aged from about nine to over ten. The classes have, except for languages, art, and physical education, a class teacher responsible for most of the teaching. In the seventh grade the classes normally have a class teacher but they also have a greater amount of specialist teaching leading up to full-time specialist teaching in grade 8. In the case of the experimental class in the seventh grade (identified as class '7.3') it was decided to introduce specialist teaching from the beginning and each department was asked to allocate one of their best teachers. The departments were told that the children must be constantly challenged and that there was no reason the syllabus for the year should limit the progress of the class. Departments interpreted these ideas in their own way, the mathematics department in the most literal way so that the class managed to cover the eighth-grade syllabus as well as the seventh. The participating teachers found considerable satisfaction in working with such bright children as a social as well as an intellectual unit and the form or homeroom teacher, although not teaching the children as her field was remedial work, played a great part in welding the group into a unit. The departmental teachers also came to realize that there were probably more of their pupils who could move faster than they had been previously expected to do. Since then more children have been promoted and faster groups have been formed at various levels.

Before going on to consider some of the special activities it may be worth while here to make some reference to the reaction of the parents and also to the subsequent history of the children. At first there was some puzzlement amongst the parents, but most of this was cleared up at the next parents' evening when a substantial proportion turned up to find out exactly what was happening. Most were delighted that their children had been placed in the class: one or two felt that class 7.3 must be less prestigious than 7.1 or 7.2. And some felt that an undue strain might be placed on the children, especially on those whose English was not very strong. Where there was obviously a real anxiety, an attempt was made to allay this by promising some extra coaching in English. These reassurances had their effect and later, even where children were finding some difficulty in keeping up with the rapid pace of the class, most parents assured us that the experience of being in such a group far outweighed any of the academic problems that had arisen. This was indeed one of the sources of encouragement to the staff concerned (and some of these had been doubtful of the venture although they were participating in it) that in the end all the parents believed that it had been a privilege for their children to be members of the class.

The subsequent history of the group was an illustration of what occurs in schools like Campion. Four children, including the highly gifted Greek boy who had proved himself a natural leader, left with their parents for other countries. The girl who had been the outstanding leader amongst the girls was moved up two grades because she was older than the others but had remained voluntarily in the group because she enjoyed it so much and because she had enhanced her powers of leadership. The others moved into the fully specialized eighth grade where in most subjects it was no longer possible to keep them as a unit.

The departure of one of the girls highlighted a problem which can occur in any community which believes in giving gifted or very bright children the chance to move up the educational ladder at their own pace. What happens if the child moves to another area or country where there is little enlightenment? This girl was the youngest of all in the class and was just ten when she completed grade 7 and left for her own country. She was in all ways a remarkable girl, high IQ, socially well developed, calm, conscientious, but still a small girl, full of fun. She had shown herself capable of fitting in intellectually and socially with children two years older and while she was rarely at the top of the subject lists in examinations, as she would have been if she had been kept with her coevals, she made excellent progress at the rapid pace of the class. Despite her chronological age and her relatively diminutive size, she was intellectually and temperamentally ready to transfer to at least the first year of a grammar school of the old type. But the area to which she was going had a middle school system up to thirteen and seemed to lay more stress on the chronological age than on the other more important factors. Such a placement in a middle school could be like a two-year retardment, involving the temporary dropping of certain subjects which the girl was capable of studying. It seems that in some countries, including Britain and the USA, it is largely a matter of the luck of the draw whether such children will be intelligently placed on returning to their own country.

The methodological approach

Insofar as the various academic subjects were concerned, each department was responsible for the teaching of the subject and, as the teachers were specially selected by the departments, the methods were those chosen by each subject teacher. Apart from being encouraged to be as adventurous as possible, the teachers were given the responsibility of using what they considered appropriate methods. But it has been clear for years in those countries which have developed an interest in their more gifted children that many bright children can be well taught and still show some of the effects of the conditioning referred to in the opening paragraphs of this chapter. For this reason three periods on the timetable were allocated to 'general studies', a term which has the great advantage of being acceptable to parents but which can in fact be used to mean whatever one likes. These periods were taken by the present author, and he conducted them in the same way as he had done formerly in Brentwood and Millfield.

On first encounter with groups of this kind the author usually has asked the class a number of personal questions such as the name favoured, position in the family, languages spoken, and, in Campion especially, the language normally spoken in the home. After twenty questions or so the children have been provided with a piece of paper and told that they may in their turn ask the teacher a question or two which must be written down. This has always proved to be something unusual for the children and so the questions are often of this type – 'How far is the sun from the earth?' In latter years the children have been told that the questions must not be of the type that can be answered from a dictionary or an encyclopaedia. In many cases the children seem to be nonplussed and sometimes blank papers are handed in. Some of the children respond to a reminder that they have been asked a lot of questions and now it is their turn. Thus encouraged, some will ask personal questions, such as 'How old is the teacher?', 'Where was he born?', and so on. Or again others will ask why the class has been formed and what work they are going to do. Even then, some of the questions can be categorized as defensive. However, when the process is repeated a few weeks later, few of the difficulties remain and the result gives some indication of the mutual trust that has been built up between adult and youngsters. In Campion, as in Brentwood and Millfield, this mutual trust is considered to be fundamental. This would apply in the case of most children but it seems to be even more important with very bright children who can often see through the actions of adults in a most disconcerting way. Occasionally, when the author has been certain that he has wrapped up some personal query in a skilful manner so that no child could possibly penetrate the secret, he has been shattered by some such remark as 'We know what you are trying to do', or, as in one instance, 'Why don't you ask us outright what our attitudes are to certain studies or teachers?' Even when the child's perception is wrong or distorted one feels that one's defences are threatened.

Another technique which has proved useful from time to time with the very bright and sometimes also with the less than bright has been to start off the group with a few simple mathematical questions, including such a question as, 'Write down the square roots of 9 and 16'. Almost invariably

that he considered that he had learnt something of value from his father who frequently remarked that he firmly believed that 'Honesty is the best policy'. For example, on the previous day 'A' had found a 500 drachmas note. At first he was tempted to keep it as it is often difficult to find who has lost a banknote. Then he reflected that if he did keep it he might be discovered and later accused of stealing the note. Therefore he handed the note into the school office on the grounds that 'Honesty is the best policy'.

The instruction read: 'As far as you can, evaluate the action, motives, and attitudes of "A".' Incidentally, the instruction had first to be explained to both the older and younger children, but care was taken to ensure that the explanation did not affect the direction of the discussion. As in the older group, the discussion amongst the experimental group tended to concentrate on the incident of the actual finding of the note. The distinction was made between a note and coins since the latter were much more difficult to trace to their owner. In other words, the action was the easiest part to deal with. However, some of the children did place themselves in the position of the person who had lost the note and suggested that this was their main motive in urging that the note should be surrendered to the authorities. When the group was asked to look again at the proverb, 'Honesty is the best policy', one or two of the group stressed the fact that the boy had acted more out of fear than out of any feeling for honesty. This they said was his real motive and they considered it inadequate. However, it still proved difficult to direct their attention to the assessment of the proverb although they had now reached a point very near to where the discussion was intended to lead.

At this point the author had to make use of the same technique he had used with the older children, who were five or six grades ahead in the school and for whom therefore the technique was much more appropriate. This technique was to invite the children to imagine that they had suddenly became fifteen years older and were in the position of finding themselves parents. It was pointed out to them that at certain stages in life one has to take certain decisions which require careful assessment of one's attitudes and beliefs. Such occasions occur on entering a profession or undertaking a duty, and especially on accepting a new role in life as in marriage and parenthood. Since this was so, and several showed understanding, one quoting the case of a boy or girl becoming a school prefect, they were invited to imagine that as parents they had to decide whether they would teach their children that 'Honesty is the best policy'. In this fresh situation the majority of the group studied the proverb much more closely and much more critically. One girl from a home in which the parents were devout, practising members of one of the English-speaking churches began to challenge the word 'policy' and brought up the analogy of an insurance policy. One took out such a policy against a risk. Another girl followed up by pointing out that the boy had really handed in the money since he was afraid of the risk of holding on to it. These expressions of view led ultimately with a little guidance from the teacher to the idea that as parents we should teach our children to be honest, not just because it might protect one, but as a positive way of life. Surely this is a suitable conclusion for youngsters learning in a school in the city where Socrates taught.

It has sometimes been suggested to the present writer that discussions of the kind just described are really beyond the capacity of young children, however bright. One critic maintained that the discussion must inevitably be led by the teacher and that the theme was beyond the stage of development of the children. This criticism was maintained despite the point made by the author that by nine years of age or over children should have some idea of a quality such as honesty. However, seeing is believing, and the sceptic was invited to attend a session with the experimental class. The topic on this occasion was from a passage which was taken with slight adaptations from the Saturday morning edition of the *Daily Telegraph* and was written by Bishop Appleton under the title 'Unexpected Blueprint'. The bishop had referred to St. Paul's great hymn of love in the thirteenth chapter of Corinthians and to the translation by James Moffat. He stated that he would not have recognized the work as Paul's if he had come across it anonymously. Of Moffat he wrote that he was a dour Scotsman and an austere scholar, perhaps as tough as Paul. He quoted:

> Love is very patient, very kind, love knows no jealousy, love makes no parade, gives itself no airs, is never rude, never selfish, never irritated, never resentful; love is never glad when others go wrong, love is gladdened by goodness, always slow to expose, always eager to believe the best, always hopeful, always patient, love never just disappears.

Bishop Appleton concluded his article with the paragraph: 'Somewhere among all the sermons I have listened to and the books I have read, I came across the suggestion that I should put my own name in place of the word 'love' in this passage. The result was devastatingly humbling, and still is when I repeat the exercise. Try it yourself.'

The exercise had already been tried out on a mixed-ability group of twelfth and thirteenth graders who responded very disappointingly, some being apathetic and others not being accustomed to the evaluation of ideas.

It was, therefore, with a certain amount of trepidation that this was tried out on a much younger group, especially in front of a rather sceptical observer. In this instance, as with the older children, there were some who did not immediately grasp the purpose of this exercise, which incidentally in a group of seven nationalities containing several Muslim children was not presented as a form of religious thought but rather as a study of oneself. Those with limited mastery of English had to have the quotation explained to them. Meanwhile, those who had understood at once the meaning of the verses proceeded to carry out the instruction to fill in their own names.

When the others were ready, the discussion began with some of the children remarking that they fell a long way short of the teaching. One girl who combined a high IQ with a great deal of common sense gave an example of her own impatience with other people, while a boy confessed to the glee he had felt a few days before when one of the class had made a rare error and had been humiliated. The boy admitted that he had rubbed it in. After the period of examples of their own shortcomings the discussion gradually moved on to ideas and how far behaviour might be regulated according to ideas. As the children were showing signs of having spent a little too long 'on yonder mountain height' the discussion was ended with the promise that a similar type of discussion would be arranged soon.

The observer was invited to express his reaction with a view to improving the programme for the children. He admitted that he had been pleasantly surprised that some of the children had been able to start the discussion. He had noted that the response to the challenge had varied considerably and that the boys on the whole had contributed less than the girls, perhaps because boys are less interested in such matters. He also remarked that the word love had been accepted by the group without the reaction that might have characterized a group beyond puberty. Actually the examples put forward by the keener children had been taken mainly from themselves in relation to their parents, siblings, or schoolmates. In consequence, the discussion had been for the most part practical and therefore relevant to their own lives and some of their problems. But he felt that there were two conditions necessary for undertaking this type of work with children so young: one was that the group had to be kept together and allowed to develop as a team and the other that the teacher had to have a close relationship with the group and an understanding of the timing of the work so that the challenge was not carried beyond the physical as well as the intellectual capacity of the children. Otherwise the activity might lead to a feeling of strain or to boredom and so do more harm than good. This seemed to the author to be a caveat that any bold worker with the gifted should keep in mind but not to the extent that he becomes too timid in his approach.

Conclusions

Despite the inevitable brevity of this account and the limitations outlined above on the Campion experiment, it is possible to draw some conclusions or to strengthen some of those drawn in former experiments.

One such conclusion concerns the tremendous importance of the quality of the teacher and the teaching. As Dr. Meldon pointed out in *Gifted Children and the Brentwood Experiment* (Bridges, 1969), the gifted and the very bright really require better teaching than do more average children. The teacher of the gifted requires a very fertile mind and a liveliness of manner which demands and ensures an equally lively response.

Another conclusion is that programmes must be adaptable and must not crystallize into something which revives the conditioning of the 'stint'. On the other hand, just because these children are so demanding, a basic programme can offer useful guidelines and also lessen the burden on the imagination of the children. Programmes of this kind devised by Dr. Ogilvie and his team (Chapter 12) are likely to be of greatest value where the school population is reasonably stable and where the number of gifted children is too small to justify special groupings.

Again, in those cases where it is possible to have special groups, even if it is possible for only a limited time each week, the teacher of the group must be able to inspire those colleagues who take the children for their various school subjects to use their most stimulating methods. In some instances it may be advisable for him to demonstrate his own techniques.

Finally, it is evident even amongst the brightest children entering Campion School that in the majority of cases insufficient effort has been made in their previous schooling to distinguish between principles and details. Time spent on this aspect of learning is well spent. Indeed it is one of the greatest pleasures and most rewarding experiences in a teaching career to watch the brightest children gradually come to appreciate the economy of learning derived from the mastery of principles in place of the wasteful attempts to memorize largely inchoate masses of detail.

CHAPTER TWELVE

THE SCHOOLS COUNCIL CURRICULUM ENRICHMENT PROJECT
Eric Ogilvie

Origins

The Schools Council Curriculum Enrichment Project for Gifted Children in Primary Schools originated in the findings of an earlier investigation into provisions for gifted children (Ogilvie, 1973). Although space does not permit a thorough review of the 1973 report, it is worth attempting a brief summary of the main points in order to provide the essential context within which the later work occurred.

The concept of giftedness

The position in schools in 1970 with regard to the concept of 'giftedness' almost defied description. Some teachers felt very strongly that the whole idea smacked of élitism, and hence were reluctant even to discuss it; others were equally certain that the only real difficulty lay in problems of reliability of intelligence tests. The very suggestion that there might be useful but alternative ways of looking at 'giftedness' outside the area of 'general intelligence', or the 'g' factor, was almost always rejected out of hand. In sum, the investigation revealed that the idea of 'general intelligence' had become deified in the minds of the vast majority of teachers and indeed in society generally. What might be termed the 'IQ approach' had attained the status of a natural law, and whilst it was, and still is, easy to stimulate discussion of the sterile 'nature-nurture' controversy, it was, and still is, almost impossible to persuade many teachers to envisage an education system freed from the conceptual strait-jacket that our powerful attachment to this approach has produced.

All this is not to deny the need for categorizations of one sort or another. On the contrary it helps to emphasize that the systems of categorization we adopt must be justified by their utility. The total arbitrariness of most categorizations, however, needs constant emphasis and reemphasis.

Any human categorization will be imprecise and assume an often spurious agreement about what is 'normal' in regard to, say, attainment or ability.

Thus the original Schools Council investigation, whilst retaining the proposition that some children might be, or seem to be, generally gifted, also included in its definition the statement 'any child who is outstanding in . . . specific ability, in a relatively broad or narrow field of endeavour'. It further noted that 'we were concerned with those conditions, results, and evaluations of learning which were of particular relevance to teachers and which relate specifically to problems arising directly or indirectly from the presence of outstanding or potentially outstanding pupils within a school' (Ogilvie, 1973). Clearly then, the development of any kind of talent and the teaching conditions appropriate thereto became the focus of attention rather than the traditional topics which recur ad nauseam in work conditioned by the 'general intelligence' or 'g' approach.

Provision for gifted children in primary schools

Given the general attitudes outlined above, it is perhaps not surprising that the position within schools regarding provision for the gifted was found to be such that few generalizations could be made. The basic question posed was simply: 'To what extent can any child pursue his/her own bent without let or hindrance?' Or alternatively: 'Are there any brakes on an individual's pursuit of maximum achievement in any or all curriculum areas?'

That many brakes on optimum progress do exist is perhaps self-evident. That many are in fact institutionalized and avoidable without the expenditure of large sums of money was not so clearly recognized prior to the publication of the 1973 report which drew particular attention to the following characteristics of the school situation:

1 Teacher attitudes, whilst ranging from plain antagonism, through indifference, to equally plain ignorance, resulted in a general failure to appreciate that some, perhaps many, children were actually being held back in school. The influence of teacher expectations was grossly underrated.

2 The nature and complexity of individual differences was misunderstood, unappreciated, and underplayed in many schools. For example, the widespread move towards mixed-ability grouping was not necessarily and invariably accompanied by mixed-ability teaching systems. If anything, the change sometimes reduced the degree of individualized learning that the children were able to undertake since straightforward class teaching continued unabated.

3 The nature and complexity of the many brakes on progress within the system were largely unrecognized. They were specified in the 1973 report as follows:

  a Lockstep curricula and teaching programmes.

  b Rigid adherence to achievement levels based on traditional teacher methodologies, standard texts, etc., which formed the bases for teacher expectations.

  c Failure to attempt actively to match learning situations to individual needs either by curriculum overstructuring (as in a above) in accordance with group norms, or by understructuring, as entailed in an overreliance on so-called 'discovery' and 'project' methods.

  d Inarticulations between home and school, school and school, and even class and class.

  e Overemphasis on teacher qualities other than specialist expertise in particular curriculum areas. This was associated with a concomitant failure to recognize the need for teachers to be seen and appointed to schools as members of teams rather than as individuals who essentially replicate rather than complement one another.

  f Persistent overestimation of the actual time available to teachers with classes of thirty-odd children for guided discussion with individuals or even small groups of pupils. Teachers were happy to state that they 'individualized' as much as possible, but very reluctant sometimes to admit that in practice the 'possible' meant very little.

  g The concept of 'enrichment', whilst receiving general approval as a mechanism for providing special help to gifted children, nevertheless remained unanalysed and imprecise. In particular, teachers often failed to appreciate that in no way can procedures which merely involve 'more of the same' be termed 'enrichment' in its full sense (see also DES, 1977). 'Enrichment', to be truly such, must involve qualitative as well as quantitative change; or, as the 1973 report put it, 'depth' as well as 'breadth'. The danger of the 'more of the same' approach is that it produces a 'tropopause' curriculum whilst appearing to remove the 'ceiling'. It often looks as if the pupil is engaging in further 'depth' study but what really happens, as I have described elsewhere, is that he 'proceeds rapidly through Book IV and then effectively bumps up against a "tropopause" and has to engage in "width" studies' (Ogilvie, 1973).

Proposals for change

The 1973 report proposed a number of possibilities which might be considered as at least partial responses to its criticisms of the status quo. It is not intended to review these here but one of the possibilities discussed by the report is of particular relevance. This was the suggestion that perhaps the one way in which teachers could be given positive help to extend the degree to which individualized learning actually occurred, as distinct from being said to occur, was for somebody to provide them with learning packages. These packages would themselves need to be designed in accordance with certain clearly articulated principles of individualized learning if they were in fact to achieve their fundamental purpose in reducing the hindrances to pupil progress. Thus the council funded a second follow-up project dedicated to the creation of a set of exemplar or prototype packages which would help teachers to use their time more effectively. It is the task of the following section to describe this follow-up work involving the development of the Schools Council Curriculum Enrichment Projects (Sceps).

The Schools Council Curriculum Enrichment Project for Gifted Children in Primary Schools

Sccep construction

The work of package construction does not proceed in simple linear fashion. It is not a process of decision making whereby a first judgement leads directly to a second, and so on. The Bruner (1966) concept of a cyclical system is more appropriate in that it implies continuous reflection back from one set of decisions onto others taken earlier. Its weakness is perhaps that it implies progressive development throughout the whole design, whereas in reality some initial proposals have to be adhered to even when wisdom after the event would make us change, and others prove to be impractical. The main point is that the following review is, for convenience of exposition, more sequential and discretely divided than was the work of the project itself. The length of any individual section does not necessarily reflect the time or importance devoted in practical terms by the project to its subject matter.

A bank of Scceps

Clearly the vision of an education system free of brakes on individual pupils presupposes a school organization which has as one of its basic resources a 'library' of individualized learning kits at least as great in numerical terms as the book libraries are today. Just as in the best schools every class has its own library which complements the school library, so must each class come to possess its own bank of Sccep-like materials as part of the 'school bank'.

It is equally obvious that the Schools Council could not fund a large-scale production line to provide for the schools' requirements with respect to individualized learning materials. It was thus decided that the number of Scceps to be produced should be sufficient to illustrate and highlight the need, and not in any real way to provide for it. Considering all the circumstances, seventeen Scceps were deemed necessary, though not sufficient, and the 'grid' in figure 12.1 indicates the pattern evolved.

As our earlier discussion has emphasized, it was essential for the Sccep pattern to reject quite explicitly the idea of 'general' enrichment. The goal of the Scceps could not be deliberately to encourage the development of 'g' men: they had to be seen to be aimed at relatively specialist curriculum areas. Hence four divisions were recognized in as nonarbitrary a manner as possible. Our investigations revealed a perhaps surprising consensus, in fact, that mathematics, environmental sciences, humanities, and expressive arts taken together form a reasonable basis for any core curriculum. (Arguments are also sometimes advanced for the inclusion of moral education as a separate unit. See, for example, Lawton, 1975.) Unfortunately, however, each term is highly generic and much of the debate about the core curriculum revolves around the selection of particular content. 'Expressive arts', for example, clearly encompass a wide range of skills including music, pottery, and painting; and each component of this subsection of the 'seamless web' is important in terms of talent development. The project's solution to this 'particularity' problem will become apparent in what follows; all that we need to notice at present is the fact that our seventeenth Sccep

Figure 12.1 Sccep Production Grid

	A Mathematics	B Environmental Science	C Humanities	D Expressive Arts
4	13 The Adventures of Alison and Sandy	14 Space	15 Understanding History	16 The Man Who Made Pictures
3	9 Now you see it Now you don't	10 Settlements	11 English – Poetry and Story	12 Masks
2	5 [17 Mathematics and Nature] Variations on a Theme	6 Living Things	7 Discovering History	8 Carvers of the Long Night
1	1 How Far Can You Go?	2 The Earth	3 English – Building with Words	4 Follow This Thread

Age-related difficulty level (1 easiest; 4 most advanced)

('mathematics and nature') was inserted in the grid as a matter of deliberate policy. The objective was to show that whilst a Sccep designed in accordance with our principles of enrichment must be seen to cover some definite and recognizable part of an accepted discipline, it does not follow that Scceps cannot be interdisciplinary in content or goal. They must, however, relate to the developmental features of some well-defined content area in one or several disciplines.

The vertical axis provides the age-related basis for the Scceps, the higher the box the more advanced the level of work. The numbers 1 to 4 originally referred to fairly broad age groups which were to have included infant as well as junior groups – but the former were omitted owing to inadequate funding. The numbers then came to refer loosely to the four junior school age groups. It is important to note that whilst some such basis had to be adopted as a guide for the production programme, nobody knew just what some children somewhere might accomplish at any particular age. The whole tenor of the project denied the idea that any particular level of work should become attached to any particular age group, and again we return to the precept that the relation of one Sccep to another is in terms of its developmental patterns of thought and content, not in terms of age suitability.

Perhaps a final point is that of all the possibilities which are missing from the grid we felt that technology was the most important. One advantage of the 'Sccep system', if such a term is justifiable, would be that curriculum innovation would be far easier to bring about than is currently the case. Technological studies are to all intents and purposes entirely absent from our primary schools and will remain so if we have to wait upon the training of a new and special generation of teachers. Given a good supply of 'technology' Scceps, however, one could envisage a very rapid increase in technological knowledge and understanding not only on the part of pupils but also their teachers. Indeed the provision of 'technology' Scceps might well stimulate the appointment of teachers with technological expertise, a practice which is currently remarkable only for its total absence.

The design team

One of the valuable outcomes of choosing four definitive curriculum areas is the guidance offered in terms of choosing a Sccep design team which, by the very nature of the different expertises encompassed, would inevitably concentrate on Scceps which called upon and developed manifestly different skills. It may be recalled that attention was drawn in the 1973 report to the inability of a 'generalist' primary teacher, however good in that particular role, to provide work at levels beyond his own personal competence. And yet there was a clear need for Scceps to involve activities which qualitatively went well beyond current expectations if they were to perform their essential function of extending outstanding pupils. Nor was it a matter of simply stretching pupils at their current stage of development. Clearly the requirement of 'depth' can only be said to be a characteristic of any particular Sccep if it not only embodies progression within itself, but also can be shown to be an integral part of a much larger continuum even to, say, degree-level work. Thus the project team appointed recognized experts in a number of particular fields: mathematics, biology, earth science, English, history, art, and pottery. All the people appointed were practising tutors in their subjects at college level and beyond.

That could not however be the end of the matter. Unhappily 'experts', say, PhDs in whatever, are not often found teaching in primary schools. Even more unfortunately they do not always reveal a practical or even

Figure 12.2 Sccep Design Team Organization

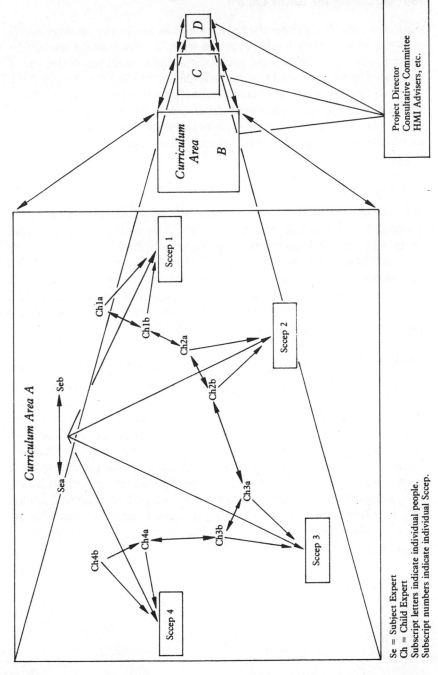

Se = Subject Expert
Ch = Child Expert
Subscript letters indicate individual people.
Subscript numbers indicate individual Sccep.

theoretical interest in either the learning of their subject by younger pupils or in the ways primary teachers have to work. In short, whilst the subject 'expert', *ipso facto*, knows his subject, he knows nothing of the young children who were our main concern. It should be clear therefore that the Sccep design team had to include teachers of substantial experience in working with the age range eight–eleven years. In the event, two 'child' experts were appointed to work with each subject expert in the design of each Sccep so that the team organization can be diagrammed as shown in figure 12.2.

A Sccep examined

We have noted that enrichment involves the provision for related experiences at both intra- and inter-Sccep levels. The total syllabus or overall schema in any curriculum area is envisaged as a network of relations, of separate but complementary skills and the like, within which are embedded the micromesh of individual Scceps. Enrichment is thus provided in both depth and breadth. The general intra-Sccep pattern is shown in figure 12.3 and the project team's general ideas for the environmental science Scceps (curriculum area B) are illustrated in figure 12.4.

Methodology and materials : Environmental Science Scceps

The main objective of Sccep 2 p.182 is to heighten children's awareness of the earth materials around them and convey specific impressions as to the contribution these materials make to the development of both landscape and man. Extracts from the students' tape scripts are perhaps the most economical way of showing how the goal of providing a variety of learning situations has been achieved (see pp.182-5). It is important to note that our tapes are used not merely to provide for the high-achieving poor reader but also to relate stories and aid the imagining child with suitable background effects. Work sheets are incorporated in most Scceps and examples are shown below. The extracts from the students' tape scripts indicate something of what the work sheet tasks involve.

Figure 12.3

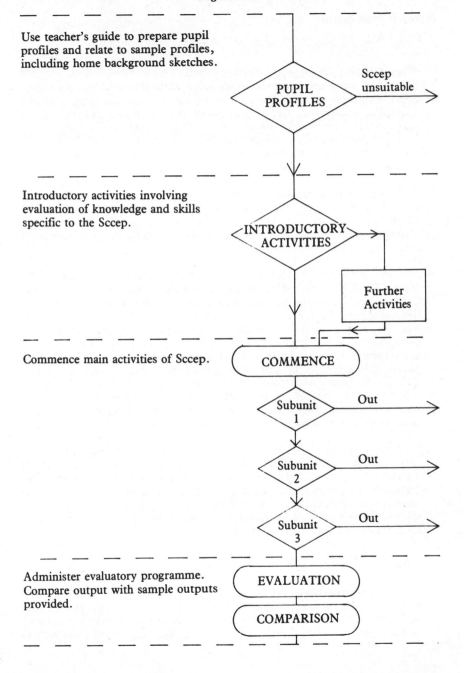

Use teacher's guide to prepare pupil profiles and relate to sample profiles, including home background sketches.

PUPIL PROFILES

Sccep unsuitable

Introductory activities involving evaluation of knowledge and skills specific to the Sccep.

INTRODUCTORY ACTIVITIES

Further Activities

Commence main activities of Sccep.

COMMENCE

Subunit 1 — Out

Subunit 2 — Out

Subunit 3 — Out

Administer evaluatory programme. Compare output with sample outputs provided.

EVALUATION

COMPARISON

Extracts from scripts

Sccep Two: Subunit 2. Crystals.

We made it ten sides altogether. Crystals of minerals are made up of things called 'molecules' – they are sometimes round, and so small that we can only see them with a special microscope. Here's a way we can find out something about the shape of mineral crystals. Get seven round beads of marbles and plasticine. Roll the plasticine out then make patterns by pressing the beads into it. Page 4 of the Picture Book shows some of the patterns that we made. Try to make the smallest pattern that you can with the seven beads, and draw the plan of that pattern in the top half of work sheet 3.
STOP.
Ours seemed to have six sides. Write the number of sides yours had, in the box on work sheet 3.
STOP.
Can you tell us by writing your answer in the bottom half of the work sheet, why crystals tend to have flat sides?
STOP.
Now look at the postcard picture of a group of mineral crystals on page 5 of the Picture Book, How many different shaped crystals can you see? I can see three. One that looks like cube sugar, some long white ones, with points on the end, and then those at the bottom which look like gold. It isn't gold really, in fact, it has iron in it and is called 'iron pyrite' or sometimes 'fool's gold'. If you look carefully, you can see that the crystals in it are very thin, like needles. Now look at the cube crystal. It looks as though it's made of glass, doesn't it? But it's a mineral called fluorite. Do you know that all these crystals tend to split in a different special way when you try to break them open with a hammer? With the fluorite, the corners fly off. On page 7 of the Picture Book, you can see a cube and below it a drawing of what the fluorite looks like when the corners fly off. How many sides do you think it has now?
STOP.
We make it fourteen. If you wanted to make a model of the cube, we could make a shape like that on page 7 which shows all the sides of the cube flattened out. Do you think you could make drawings like this for the white crystals on page 5 of the Picture Book? This mineral is called quartz. If you think about it you will need to know how many sides the crystal has before you can start your drawing on work sheet 4. To help you find out the number of sides there is a drawing of some of these crystals on page 7 of the Picture Book.

Sccep Two: Subunit 3. Rocks. Work sheet 4

Rocks formed from hot (or sometimes called 'molten') liquid are called 'igneous' rocks. (The ancient Latin people had a word for fire called 'ignis' and we have used part of it for these fire-formed rocks.) The ancient Greek god who lived deep in the earth was called 'Pluto', so rocks that cool deep in the earth we call

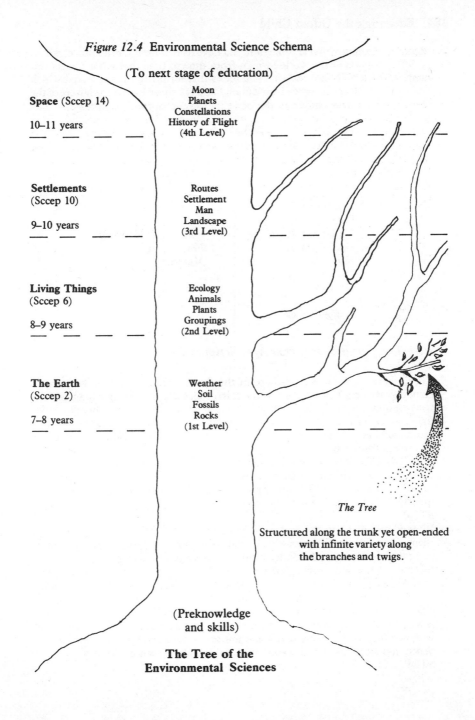

Figure 12.4 Environmental Science Schema

(To next stage of education)

Space (Sccep 14)

10–11 years

— — — —

Moon
Planets
Constellations
History of Flight
(4th Level)

Settlements
(Sccep 10)

9–10 years

— — — —

Routes
Settlement
Man
Landscape
(3rd Level)

Living Things
(Sccep 6)

8–9 years

— — — —

Ecology
Animals
Plants
Groupings
(2nd Level)

The Earth
(Sccep 2)

7–8 years

— — — —

Weather
Soil
Fossils
Rocks
(1st Level)

The Tree

Structured along the trunk yet open-ended
with infinite variety along
the branches and twigs.

(Preknowledge
and skills)

**The Tree of the
Environmental Sciences**

'Plutonic'. I am sure that at some time you have read or been told about volcanoes in different parts of the world, which from time to time throw hot sparks and lumps of rock high into the air. The rocks that form from hot material which oozed out of volcanoes, we call 'volcanic'. On work sheet 4 write the letters of the specimens you have chosen in the boxes at the top of the descriptions.

Work sheet 4

(Specimens of 6 different rock types are provided in the kit)

□	□
Igneous rock	Igneous rock
Plutonic	Volcanic
Cooled inside earth	Cooled outside earth
Coarse grained	Fine grained
Minerals	Minerals
Used for:	Used for:
Name of rock	Name of rock

Sccep Ten: Subunit One. Iron Age. Script and Work sheet 4

Look, there's a woman over there in the far corner, can you see her, she is combing her long hair in front of the mirror and she is wearing a long greyish woollen dress, she must have woven the material on a loom – yes, there's a loom in the corner. The dress is fastened by a brooch on the shoulder and she has rush sandals on her feet. Isn't that a beautiful necklace she is wearing, do you see it glinting in the fire-light? It's made of gold I think, and its called a torque, that's T-O-R-Q-U-E. Write it down at the bottom of your work sheet 3.

Now stop again, this time we have quite a number of slides to look at. I want you to look at Slides 5, 6 and 7, in turn, and then take the work sheet 4 and answer the questions on the sheet which all refer to those slides.

STOP.

It's cold and damp in this hut, let's move over to the fire in the middle of the room. There is something cooking in that large clay pot, doesn't it smell good, it makes me feel hungry, I wonder what it is, have you guessed? Yes, it could be that bullock that was being killed outside the hut couldn't it. There are many pots stacked near the fire, some are large and some are small, they must use them for all sorts of things, I imagine they make the pots themselves. Oh good, the chieftain's woman is going to give us some meat on those large flat clay dishes, she is cutting off some pieces of meat with her knife, I suppose we will have to eat it with our fingers. This is good. I was hungry – were you?

When you stop this time I want you to take Slide (8) out of the box.

STOP.

Work sheet 4

IRON AGE STAGE   *SETTLEMENT SIMULATION GAME*
Write your answers to these questions in the spaces provided.

1a   (Slide 5) This is an Iron Age mirror; how could it work without any
       glass? . . . .
1b   What tells us that we are looking at the wrong side of this
       mirror? . . . .
2   (Slide 6) Look at the slide carefully then write what you think this article is
       and what it could be used for.
       Article: . . . .
       Why? . . . .
       Use: . . . .
3   (Slide 7) This article, made of solid gold, was ploughed up in a farmer's
       field in Norfolk. Write how you think it was made and its use as a piece of
       jewellery.
       How it was made: . . . .
       Use: . . . .
       Why? . . . .

In Sccep construction, as already mentioned, particular emphasis has been placed on developmental features. This is so even in curriculum areas such as expressive arts where programmes of work are based upon the exploitation of a quality, a technique, or an experience from a number of different perspectives. The skills involved, for example, in the production of a *papier mâché* model or a painting might be analysed from the viewpoint of developing techniques at 'observational', 'intellectual', or 'manipulative' levels. Consideration can be given to the various qualities involved (the use of colour, tone, texture, etc.) and to the development of aesthetic awareness. The contextual setting of the topic can also be examined (e.g., in Sccep 12 reference is made to the historical/cultural climate in which masks are prevalent).

It is perhaps also worth drawing attention to one particular facet of Sccep construction not mentioned earlier which relates especially to the known psychology of 'gifted' children. It was to be expected that many of the children the project had in mind would not wish to be overly constrained to a 'linear' progression. On the contrary, they would frequently wish, and should be encouraged, to extend their scheduled activities into related fields not covered within the Sccep itself, at any rate as initially designed. At the same time aimless wanderings into 'dead ends' and 'inert avenues' must be discouraged in positive ways. The clear implication is that every Sccep should be designed with a good number of useful 'diversion' activities or 'branching' programmes actually built in; with others perhaps not actually provided for but certainly borne in mind as immediate possibilities which children could be expected to 'discover' for themselves. Thus the 'tree branches' in the environmental science schema diagram are intended to show that certain divergent possibilities are not merely envisaged but actually inherent in the way the 'trunk' work is organized.

Scceps and self-assessment

The more we engage children in individualized learning activities the more important it becomes for teachers to be sure that learning, as anticipated and expected, does in fact occur. It is equally vital for pupils to experience their own sense of worthwhile achievement if our packages are to meet the essential requirement that they be largely self-motivating. The most elegant and economical way to satisfy both these needs is to build in, at convenient points in each Sccep, programme 'check points'. The forms of evaluatory feedback available to Sccep design teams are numerous, ranging from straightforward tests of one sort or another to witnessing the simple fact of a pupil's finishing an activity. We concentrated on the inclusion of 'game' activities as often as possible in order that the pupil on the one hand would find maximum enjoyment in his work and the teacher on the other would feel a minimum need to test and evaluate in a formal atmosphere. There would be little advantage to be gained from the frequent conversion of a teacher from an informal group teacher to a formal group tester.

An incidental advantage of built-in evaluatory 'games' is that they can frequently be designed to engage the 'Sccep' pupil in activities with certain of his classmates. The introduction of Sccep procedures on a significant scale would undoubtedly reduce the group 'discussion' sessions which currently occupy so much school time. Indeed it is specifically designed to increase individual work. The Sccep procedure need not, however, be an instrument of pupil isolation. On the contrary, a well-designed Sccep will focus pupil interaction on matters which have developmental significance and stimulate the sort of cooperative action which produces worthwhile results.

Other aspects of Sccep design and use

It should now be clear that our project, albeit founded in what we conceived to be sound psychological and pedagogical theory, was intensely practical. Space does not permit detailed explication of all that was done and such an account would, in any event, prove boring to those who wish to use Scceps rather than construct them. It is convenient at this point, therefore, to change our style of discourse somewhat and slant attention to the kinds of questions potential users of Scceps might be constrained to ask. Only brief answers will be given here, since full discussions are or will become available in relevant Schools Council publications. In no sense are the questions posed below to be seen as complete: they indicate the type of issues which need to be borne in mind by all Sccep constructors and users.

1 *Will the incorporation of Sccep work in my teaching programme necessitate major alterations to my customary and generally preferred ways of working with my class?* The straight answer here is that the introduction of Scceps entails no change whatsoever in many common school situations, and certainly very minimal recognition in others. Traditional class teaching can proceed without hindrance at the same time as a portion of the group is working freely through Scceps.

This is particularly true where earphones are available, but such additional equipment is not vital. Certainly where the best progressive open-classroom situations are a feature of any teacher's work then conditions approach the ideal. Scceps are then complementary components in a teaching organization which is based fundamentally on the assumption that Scceps and other similar materials are in fact available. Thus no teacher ought to reject Scceps on the grounds that their introduction is impractical in his particular circumstances. On the contrary, whatever systems are in vogue, all can be improved to a greater or lesser extent by the introduction of Scceps.

2 *How do I recognize the children in my class who might most readily be expected to benefit from any particular Sccep?* It is obvious that the more closely any Sccep can be tailored to the needs of a particular individual the more effective will consequent learning become. Unhappily the conditions for producing perfectly matched Scceps must wait upon an ideal future, and what we have to achieve is simply the closest approximation to the perfect match that our particular circumstances permit. Thus, if we assume for the moment that the contents of the Sccep are familiar to the teacher, then a series of preliminary questions require to be put.

a Has any child demonstrated a high level of interest in the particular field covered by the Sccep?
If affirmative, then:

b What relevant preexperience has he/she had, and how do current achievement levels in basic skills match up to the requirements of the Sccep itself?

These subquestions are difficult to answer. It is not too much to say that they summarize, in fact, the whole art of effective teaching. Leaving aside for the moment the possibility that some children have a capability to profit from a Sccep without having demonstrated an obvious interest in its subject or activity matter at either home or school, it seems clear that the most valuable information required by a teacher is contained in the achievement profiles of children who have already demonstrated good matching by working through the Sccep successfully. But which dimensions of achievement are relevant? Since Scceps differ in their subject matter and the nature of the activities involved, it is difficult to generalize. In any event, different teachers place different degrees of emphasis on different kinds of capability. Despite what we have argued about the dangers of 'intelligence' testing, some teachers will consider an indication of IQ absolutely essential, others will be far more interested perhaps in 'creativity' or 'mathematics' scores. In these circumstances all that can be done is to provide as much available information as possible, and thus enable each teacher to make the best of it from his special point of view. Typically, each Sccep handbook contains a detailed case study.

3 *How can I be sure that Sccep work would suit at least some of my children?* The plain truth here is that no prior assurance can be given. The Scceps have been tried out and progressively refined so that we know they 'work' with some children extremely well. We know further that an examination of their content by one group of teachers led to their rejection without trial as being too difficult for any of their children. Concurrently another group in a different area found them ideally suited to their best pupils. One psychiatrist made the criticism that the content of one Sccep included imaginary situations which would give children nightmares, whereas others actually making use of our materials have found them helpful and even manifestly therapeutic when offered to disturbed and difficult pupils. The message should be obvious: any teacher not wholly satisfied that all his problems of teaching individuals are yet solved might well feel able to risk exposing some of his children, already recognized as able, to some of our Scceps which examination shows to be possibly well matched to their interests and/or achievements.

Conclusion

As director of the project, it is perhaps appropriate for me, having extolled, however inadequately, the virtues of our products, to conclude by addressing two different groups of readers. To those open-minded, ready experimenters who fortunately abound in teaching, I would simply say: Beware! There is no such thing as a perfect Sccep and we must expect each one to take us only so far on the road to better things.

To those who reject our Scceps through mere inspection, however well experienced they conceive themselves to be, I can only record our own surprise at what some of our young 'guinea pigs' – including some who didn't read too well – did in fact achieve. We sometimes set our sights too low. We believe that any child who demonstrates a capability for working by himself, or with a friend perhaps, more or less regardless of his current levels of achievement in general terms, ought no longer to be denied the opportunity of attempting Sccep work at home and in school.

Part III

Individual Case Studies of Gifted Children

CASE STUDIES

Editor's note

I have compiled these case studies from original material (3, 4, and 8) and from existing texts. Since the studies from the National Children's Bureau are so very carefully and fully documented, I have included three detailed cases from one of its research reports, *In Search of Promise* (Hitchfield, 1973). Case Study 2 offers another detailed study drawn up by the current director of the National Children's Bureau, and included in her report of an earlier university-based project, *Able Misfits* (Kellmer-Pringle, 1970). These four are the most substantial studies. Case Studies 5, 11, and 12 are from Dr. Ogilvie's (1973) Schools Council project; 6 is from *Gifted Children and the Millfield Experiment* (Bridges, 1975); and 10 is from *Gifted Children and their Problems* (Rowlands, 1974). I am most grateful to those people who have contributed original material and to the authors and publishers for permission to include existing case study material.

The cases are arranged in the following manner: the first two illustrate the contrast between high intellectual ability which is translated into recognizable achievement, and high ability which is almost unrecognizable. In Case Study 2 Albert is functioning at an ESN level in most subjects and high intelligence in his case seems unable to surmount the obstacles (amongst others) of emotional disturbance and difficult home circumstances. Cases 3 to 7 show a variety of examples of children requiring some adjustment in their patterns of schooling (e.g., an early start to their education, an 'enrichment programme', or acceleration into a higher class). The next two studies (8 and 9) are examples of intellectually gifted children who are disadvantaged in some way. In particular, Brian (Case Study 8) lacks a stimulating home background, and in Case Study 9 John's ability has remained unrecognized at school, resulting in a generally low level of teacher expectation. In comparison with Case Study 2, however, these cases illustrate the resilience of many intellectually gifted children in the face of adverse conditions at home or in school. Both Brian and John could end up amongst the legion of gifted children whose intellectual promise has not been realized. In each case, however, 'native wit' is still alive and kicking and it is quite possible that the timely intervention of a perceptive and interested teacher could ensure its translation into high achievement. Finally, Case Studies 10 to 12 illustrate some of the issues relevant to the emergence of talent in music (Case Study 12 offering an autobiographical account by an outstanding young musician).

Where 'social class' categories are referred to, this relates to the following classification: *Social Class I* comprises children from families in which the male head of the household is 'higher professional'; *II*, 'other professional and technical'; *III*, 'other nonmanual and skilled manual'; *IV*, 'semiskilled manual'; *V*, 'unskilled manual'.

Unless stated otherwise details of the tests named in the case studies can be obtained from the publishing company of the *National Foundation for Educational Research*, Darville House, 2 Oxford Road East, Windsor, Berkshire, SL4 1DF.

Case study 1

Paula

Identified as 'gifted' on both attainment and intelligence tests at seven years of age. On the Wechsler Intelligence Test Paula gained a full-scale IQ of 154+ (Verbal, 155; Performance, 146). At age eleven, a reading test showed her to be in the top 2 per cent of her age group, while a mathematics test placed her in the top 5 per cent. She enjoyed all of her school subjects, finding none boring, and her interests were reading, sport, and playing outside. She claimed to have no interest in painting or chess. Her family background was of social class III, manual (see editor's note).

At birth Paula was a healthy first baby. Her father was a factory worker and her mother a shop assistant. Both parents had happy childhoods, but knew the difficulties of financial insecurity. They determined to give their children openly expressed affection and a secure home. They left school at fifteen years of age but continued to educate themselves at night classes.

At seven years of age   Paula made a quick start at school and by seven was considered in the top 5 per cent of her age group on all subjects. She had one sister.

At eleven years of age

INTERVIEWER'S REPORT

Paula was one of the most mature-looking children seen. She looked especially grown-up in facial features and expression. Her ability to laugh at herself and her own ideas was rather unusual, for most of the very intelligent children seemed to be serious about their own purposes.

She was a child who was completely absorbed in school and school work; it obviously had provided the outlet for her abilities. Reading was her dominant interest.

SCHOOL REPORT

Paula was rated in the top 5 per cent of her age group for mathematics and the top 6–30 per cent for general knowledge, use of books, and oral ability. Her teacher said: 'If not quite outstanding, her work in both mathematical and creative writing spheres is very good. She is very friendly and a good-natured child who can be both serious and humourous when the occasion merits it. The most serious weakness, which she is overcoming, is an inability to take second place. She does not like to be beaten, but is overcoming this.'

There were no indications of any social adjustment problems on the Stott scale.

PARENT'S INTERVIEW

INTERVIEWER: Does she enjoy school?
MOTHER: She loves school. On the whole we're quite happy with it – it's a comprehensive school. There's a tendency to merge good and bad; they don't push enough children in front. There's no way of knowing whether she's progressing as well as she did. We know she's still doing very well, but

now she has an A pass (80–100) in her report card. Before she had 98 per cent. I spoke to the teacher recently about it; I think it's better from a personal point of view if she's still in a competitive atmosphere. They were streamed in her previous school. At first when she came to this school, she wasn't too happy. In the other school she collected all the prizes; that was good from her point of view. When she moved to this school she felt she had missed her prizes. This head doesn't believe in prizes. To him this is a personal attitude; he just doesn't believe in it. Both of us would prefer a more competitive atmosphere. She thrives on competition – she wants to be top. She blossoms under pressure; she really comes to the fore under strain. It's a different type of education from what we're used to. You don't seem to be able to accept it. The results speak for themselves; she seems to me far in advance of a child of her age. She converses about subjects far and away above her. She seems to be in advance of everybody. When I go to the PTA I'm told this. She's good at maths and creative writing; she has the ability to put down on paper what she's thinking about. She loves maths. She comes home and sits doing these for days. It is a challenge to conquer. She reads a lot, she's a great reader, she can tackle anything. Several teachers have said she's a joy to teach – a teacher's dream. She's really interested, no matter what the subject is. One teacher at the PTA said she just had to see me again to say what a joy it was to teach her. Teachers seem to like her; she's a likeable nature. It's not just academic subjects she's good at. She knits her own jumpers. She could write her name and address long before she went to school. She always wanted to, so we did teach her. She's quite artistic – she draws and makes things. She's not terribly interested in music – we had to take her off the violin in the school orchestra – she cried and cried, she wasn't interested. The teacher said it was a pity, she was doing so well.

INTERVIEWER: What type of secondary school would you like her to go to?
MOTHER: Grammar school. But the choice is very limited as far as we are concerned. Our area has the comprehensive system. We would have chosen grammar school. I would tend to push her academic interest – a greater percentage go to university. It's essential at school to mix with children who want to go to university. The parent has to keep reminding the child that they want to do something better when they're mixing with children who all they want to do is to get out and earn money. For different children – different things. It's important for her to find out the subject she really excels in and decide what she's going to be and keep at that. I think one reason the grammar school is better is that they're more aware of social problems and modern insights into modern history and modern problems,

whereas these older schools tend to plug away at 1066. The grammar school has a good scientific background.

INTERVIEWER: Could you tell me something about her – what sort of person is she?

MOTHER: She's very obliging, quite a good nature, better than she used to be. Two years ago she was very withdrawn and very reserved. We said she worked too hard at school; there was nothing we could do. Now she's mastered things she can relax. She's got a sense of humour; she can talk and hold her own. She's quite witty. We've always encouraged them to talk. She's a very grateful child – she appreciates it if you buy her anything. I think she's an awfully good, intelligent child. Never a day passes but she tells you that she loves you. It's a great thing to see her and her sister playing together – they very, very rarely disagree.

INTERVIEWER: Is she easygoing, or inclined to find life difficult?

MOTHER: Quite easygoing, but some time ago I used to think there were problems inside her life. She was moody and used to cry a bit. She couldn't explain it to us. Now in this past couple of years this has gone. She doesn't need people, she does not like being fussed over. She used to be apt to cry when people fussed over her.

INTERVIEWER: Have you thought what kind of work you would like her to do?

MOTHER: I think she'll be a teacher. She has great patience and she enjoys showing children how to do things. Her father thinks she'll do something mathematical or possibly something in science. He doesn't think that teaching is good enough for her.

PAULA'S INTERVIEW

INTERVIEWER: How much do you like school?

PAULA: I enjoy everything.

INTERVIEWER: What is your favourite subject?

PAULA: Oh, nothing really, I don't think I have any preference for subjects in school. I enjoy doing projects – I did one on our country and I not only enjoyed that but I did another one about the president. I like to go and work on my own; I like looking up facts about all these people; it's quite difficult to find some information.

INTERVIEWER: How much do you enjoy reading?

PAULA: I enjoy reading books quite a lot.

INTERVIEWER: Do you read more than most children?

PAULA: Well, according to my friends I seem to. I do really enjoy reading – that's one of the things I enjoy most. I've read all the paperbacks and all the Enid Blyton books in the school library and I can't get any more and there was none in the public library the last few times I've been up.

INTERVIEWER: Do you choose to read information books?

PAULA: Yes, quite often I do. We've got a big encyclopaedia in the house and I hear something on the news – something someone's talking about – and I read it. Mother says I don't know what I'd do without my encyclopaedia.

INTERVIEWER: Tell me about your other interests.

PAULA: I write to my pen-pal quite often, she's in France. And I go to see football matches and I sometimes go to the baths, and I play netball in the school team, often going away to play. Finally I took an awful interest in sketching or drawing all over the place but it went off again. I knitted myself a cardigan and jumper.

INTERVIEWER: Do you collect anything?

PAULA: Yes, I collect stamps. I was really getting quite a good collection but in the last couple of weeks I haven't really been bothering.

INTERVIEWER: Tell me about your friends, and the things you like to do together.

PAULA: Well, I've got all the girls in the class. We've all started clubs. I hate it if I'm in anything if I'm just one of a crowd. I like to be up in a committee or something like that.

INTERVIEWER: Have you a best friend?

PAULA: Yes – I've always liked her.

INTERVIEWER: What does a 'friend' mean to you?

PAULA: A person you go about with, a person you like, a person who sticks up for you in arguments.

INTERVIEWER: What are the other members of your family interested in?

PAULA: Well, my sister's been trying to get through to the netball team this year and I've been trying to help her. There's a type of ring in the garden up on the wall – we use that as a shooting stand and I give her tips on how to play. My dad, oh, he's football mad – we all go on Saturday. My mum, she goes to the Women's Institute. They voted her president, she's mad about it. My dad goes to the Union, he used to be chairman or something.

INTERVIEWER: What do you want to be when you grow up?

PAULA: Earlier I wanted to be a vet but it's just a fit you take.

INTERVIEWER: What else have you considered?

PAULA: I've taken an awful fancy to be a cowboy a wee while ago – my

teacher she'll say – what do you want to be this week! *(laughs)*.
INTERVIEWER: What kind of a person are you?
PAULA: Well, quite fiery tempered at times, but I try to calm it down. I used to get up in the morning, couldn't look at anyone – but I just lie in bed now and say – you don't get up until you're going to behave yourself!
INTERVIEWER: What do your friends like about you?
PAULA: I don't know – they like I can laugh at a joke and we usually agree instead of just arguing – I just try to avoid an argument.
INTERVIEWER: What might they dislike about you?
PAULA: I don't like being bossed around, I hate being bossed around – I like to be the one doing the bossing around!
INTERVIEWER: Do you ever think about serious things, grown-up things?
PAULA: No I don't usually. If I'm on my own I just sit and think about friends and things that have been happening.
INTERVIEWER: Politics, religion?
PAULA: Yes, specially when I did the project on President Kennedy. I seemed to think about politics a lot then.
INTERVIEWER: Did anything puzzle you?
PAULA: Yes, why some of the parties had certain ideas on race relations, that always used to puzzle me, because we're all people really – why couldn't they get on together, all the people of the world. I always seem to think we're silly that people of different religions can't get on together as well, especially Catholics and Protestants because they're both Christians; it's stupid to fight over that, they're not really thinking about it as religion – just as a thing. I think they should think about religion as religion and not something to fight over.
INTERVIEWER: Are you looking forward to being grown up?
PAULA: No. I don't want to think about being grown up – too much responsibility. As a wee bairn you can enjoy things without having to worry about what'll happen.

Summary   Paula showed clearly how school had satisfied her intellectual interests. She was almost wholly orientated towards traditional school subjects in her interests and without stimulation from teachers in this respect might well have been a less happy child. Her parents were ambitious and encouraged an attitude of competitiveness in an academic setting; they looked to the school to foster their daughter's abilities, though in the final resort teaching as a career was not thought good enough for her. Her fine sense of humour ensured her a welcome in most groups and her personal qualities and social maturity suggested that she would be one of their leaders.

Case study 2

Albert

At the age of seven years seven months Albert had a Mental Age of ten years six months and an IQ of 139. His attainments, on the other hand, were very limited. He had a Reading Age of only five years eight months, a Spelling Age of five years three months, and he failed to register a score on a standardized arithmetic test. He was referred by the school for psychological assessment because of personality difficulties and serious backwardness.

The child   Albert was most unprepossessing in appearance: small, weedy, with ill-fitting spectacles and large, protruding ears; added to which he had a squint, an ungainly posture and walk, made worse by a limp and a quite noticeable stammer.

Establishing the necessary relationship with him, prior to undertaking the psychological assessment, proved a most difficult task. He was extremely ill at ease, blushed crimson whenever he had to make a reply of more than a monosyllable, never looked me in the eye, and remained tensely anxious despite explanations as to what would take place during the interview. When all reassurance proved ineffective and he was taken to the playroom in the hope that there he might become more relaxed, this was no more successful in easing his tension and lessening his painful self-consciousness. So, reluctantly, I decided to make a start with the intellectual assessment.

It then transpired that it was only in response to a relatively impersonal, intellectual challenge that Albert could overcome his almost crippling inability to establish contact. To say that he enjoyed thinking might be going too far if only because some deep anxiety continued to lurk just beneath the surface; but at least he would speak much more freely and the stammer grew less incapacitating. It also became quickly apparent, that he was an exceptionally able boy and that any obtained IQ was bound to be an underestimate because of the restricting effect of his emotional condition.

Because it was only towards the end of the morning that Albert had become relatively relaxed and able to talk fairly spontaneously, a second diagnostic session was arranged. Before that a physical and neurological check-up was carried out which indicated that the squint, limp, and stammer had no detectable organic cause. Though his EEG tracing was markedly abnormal, Albert had never had any convulsive fits nor did any appear during the following twelve years; however, the EEG remained abnormal.

Despite his very good intelligence, Albert was practically a nonreader and his understanding of arithmetical processes was nonexistent. Moreover, he disliked school with an intensity bordering on hatred. The main reason for this appeared to be that his extreme timidity, blushing, and stammering had led to his being ridiculed and bullied by his classmates.

At home, too, he was the odd man out among three younger sisters. According to him they were boisterous, talkative, and rather stupid; at any rate they had nothing in common and he tried to keep out of their way as they too enjoyed tormenting him.

Once Albert became able to talk his wide vocabulary and power of self-expression were most impressive; all the more so considering that he came from a practically illiterate home. His critical appraisal of others – whether parents, teachers, or contemporaries – was of a high order too. Though he was painfully aware of his deficiences, especially in the educational sphere, he also realized that compared with contemporaries his general knowledge and particularly his scientific understanding were far superior.

The puzzling question was how or where he had acquired these. The answer turned out to be simple: by listening to the radio.

School Albert was due to go up to the junior school at the end of the term and the head mistress feared he would completely fail to cope there. Hence her decision to refer him for psychological examination. She described him as the strangest child she had ever dealt with: 'You cannot get through however hard you try; attainment is low enough for an ESN school and he hardly makes any contact with the other children; yet here and there he comes out with an extraordinary remark when he happens to be alone with his teacher or no one else is listening. But in class he refuses to take part in oral work and his ability to cope with written work is practically nonexistent. His teachers find him wholly unresponsive; they are aware of his being completely rejected by other children.'

The head mistress added that she had become concerned about him in his very first term but did not believe such a dull child could benefit from psychological help. Since the only other alternative to her mind was a residential ESN school (a day one not being available in the area) she was reluctant to take action as she was against sending so young a child away from home even if it was an unsatisfactory one.

Teaching methods used in the school were rather rigid and in reading the approach was exclusively a phonic one. This was believed to be the most suitable for the less academically able child for whom the school largely catered. Discipline and general classroom management were similarly old-fashioned so that there was little opportunity for individual guidance and maximum use was made of competition. For a child like Albert this was misery since he found himself invariably at the bottom of any mark list.

Nor could he find relief in P.E., games, or art, since his clumsiness, poor coordination, and awkward gait presented serious handicaps. Thus he had no escape in school from constant failure and isolation. 'A really pathetic boy who doesn't know how to smile' was the class teacher's summary.

Family circumstances The father, an unskilled labourer, had difficulty in holding down a steady job, partly because he had a rather quick temper; so the mother worked as a cleaner to supplement the family income, but she too was temperamentally rather erratic and in and out of jobs. The father's mentally defective brother lived with the family and his dirty habits, incontinence, and childishly demanding ways caused much quarrelling and recrimination between the parents; however, the father refused to let him go into a hospital. Albert had to share a bedroom with his uncle who distressed and disgusted him. The youngest sister slept in the parents' bedroom and the other girls in the living room. Thus the house was not only overcrowded but there was perpetual chaos; the mother was chronically 'trying to catch up', partly because she was a poor manager and partly because she simply had too much to cope with.

Parental attitudes The handling of all the children was very unpredictable and inconsistent. There was a fair amount of shouting and ineffectual slapping which appeared to have little effect on the girls but worried and upset Albert. He was clearly the mother's favourite because 'he was a boy and so different from his three sisters'. The father's attitude was a mixture of bemusement and irritation. The former was caused by Albert asking questions to which he could not find answers; for example, at the age of three years Albert went through a period of not going to sleep for long hours and showing evident distress about it. Eventually he said to his exasperated father: 'If only you would tell me where I go to when I have to go to sleep, then I could try harder.' The irritation was caused by his son's 'stubborn, sullen, and superior ways'.

The three girls seemed quite ordinary and were making reasonable progress at school, compared with Albert's severe backwardness. 'Yet I know he isn't stupid,' was the father's comment, 'he sits for hours listening to the wireless. There are rows about it because he wants everyone to shut up. His favourite programme is science survey which I don't understand myself.' Both parents were worried lest he be sent to the 'daft school'.

Summary and recommendations   There could be no doubt that Albert was an exceptionally able as well as a seriously maladjusted boy. The long-term solution would probably have to be boarding school because his home was so incapable of meeting his needs; currently it was particularly harmful because of the effect which the mentally handicapped uncle was having on the boy. However, we shared the school's view that it was undesirable to remove such a young child from his family. Therefore, Albert was accepted for remedial treatment and play therapy though there was little likelihood of basically modifying his home conditions.

Subsequent development   After several months' work with the parents, especially the father, it was agreed that for the sake of Albert and his mother, admission to a hospital should be sought for the uncle. It then took another year to bring this about. Meanwhile the boy had 'discovered' reading. Switching over to a combination of a look-and-say and kinaesthetic approach had quite dramatic results: within a matter of a few months Albert became a fluent reader and revelled in his new-found skill. Just as radio before, so books now opened new worlds to him. However, his spelling improved at a much slower rate and his handwriting remained a problem to him for many years; it was ill-formed, slow, and cumbersome. Thus it constituted a barrier between his excellent vocabulary and power of speech (the stammer gradually disappeared) on the one hand, and his incapacity to cope with the mechanics of writing on the other. This discrepancy was likely to constitute an increasingly serious handicap as he grew older.

Once he became confident enough to converse freely, the real extent of his facility with words and ideas became apparent. For example, children were given free milk during their two-hour session with us. Albert's comment on this was 'I regard it as extraordinarily generous of the authorities, considering this is not an ordinary, educational establishment.' No wonder that when eventually he became able to talk with other children, he got himself nicknamed Professor. Arithmetic remained a closed book to him mainly because he was bored by the subject. Though there was also some slow improvement in his capacity to cope with life's stresses and strains, these remained too difficult for him to surmount entirely. His parents' personal and intellectual inadequacy; the squalor and chronic muddle of his home; the lack of privacy on the one hand and of opportunity for widening his horizons on the other; all these limitations were too severe, particularly for a child who had become so vulnerable because of the deprivation and emotional stress he had experienced from very early on in his life.

Though scholastically he was catching up, he had too much leeway to make up to succeed in the selection examination; moreover, he was a poor examinee, getting extremely worked up and hence slower than ever in his written efforts. However, it proved possible to obtain a place for him in a residential school for maladjusted but highly intelligent children. There he went for the following seven years. He made good progress but always slipped back, especially in adjustment, during school holidays. Throughout them his mother would spoil him 'for not being with us normally', to the extent of letting him stay in bed every day as long as he wished, not expecting him to give any help, and not even suggesting he should do at least some homework – she knew he was expected to complete a number of assignments and essays. Thus he slipped back all too readily into the passivity, aimlessness, and chaos of the parental home.

Eventually he obtained several 'O' levels but kept failing 'A' level examinations until the local authority decided that payment of fees could no longer continue.

First of all, Albert obtained a post in a solicitor's office, but he walked out after a few weeks because he became bored and lonely. Then he tried his hand at photography but did not like it. Next came training for market research and then the export trade. When we last heard of him he was still very unsettled and unfortunately the periods without a job were becoming longer.

Prognosis   Not hopeful. Attempts were made to find a hostel for him so that he could live away from home. . . . While he had never completely slipped back during the past eleven years there had always been adults available to counteract the demoralizing influence of his home conditions. It now looked as if without such support he would not be able to make out despite his very high intelligence.

Case study 3

Steven

Steven is the eldest of three young and active boys. His father is an engineer and his mother had worked as a secretary before having children. At the age of four years one month, Steven was referred to the Child Guidance Service on account of hyperactivity and behaviour problems. A psychometric assessment indicated a child of very superior intelligence (Stanford-Binet IQ 184). He was a fluent reader having apparently mastered the process for the most part on his own. When assessed at the time of referral his reading age fell at the eight years six months level on the Burt Word Recognition Test.

Steven was always an active child, full of curiosity and forever asking 'how' and 'why' questions. He also showed an unusual interest in puzzles and construction toys at a very young age. He needed little sleep, had tremendous energy, and seemed to grow up very rapidly. His parents hardly remembered him as an infant or toddler, and they couldn't recall him using baby language such as 'puff-puff' or 'bow-wow'. Despite his mental maturity, however, Steven could relapse into normal childish behaviour, throwing temper tantrums, for example, when frustrated. But these never lasted for long. He could also present a difficult management problem, running wild at times with his brothers.

The head teacher of the local First school was interested in gifted children and sympathetic towards the harassed mother. She agreed to admit Steven to her school as an early admission (a practice which is often regarded as one of the best forms of acceleration since this does not involve the child in leaving his friends to move into a higher class). Throughout his three years in the first school Steven presented no particular problems. He responded well to discipline and the 'controlled environment' of school. (This is also true of his younger brother who is also very bright – IQ 130 on the Stanford-Binet.) Even though Steven was nearly eighteen months younger than his classmates he coped easily with the work. He soon rose to the top of the class and was regarded as being emotionally and socially mature.

When the time came for Steven to move on to the middle school stage of education with the rest of his class, some of his teachers expressed the wish that he should stay in the first school with them. They were, however, unable to offer any strong scholastic or social reason for this and it may be that 'teacher politics' had entered the scene, the school wishing to keep its numbers up and not, therefore, particularly keen to lose one of its prize pupils prematurely. Despite the reluctance of some of the first school staff, however, Steven was accelerated to the middle school stage where his teachers are trying to offer him an individualized and enriched curriculum. He appears to have settled in well.

Case study 4

Jane (Campion School)

An interesting but not too uncommon type of case is that of Jane who was tested at the age of eight when she was already in grade 4. Her teacher had noticed that she was not being stretched and so she was included in a batch of children who were being tested with a view to early promotion from grade 5 to 6, i.e., from the top junior class to the first secondary school class in which the age range is from about nine to ten. Jane's marks for English and arithmetic were both over 90 per cent in internal tests and so she was promoted to grade 6 and put into the brightest section. She was still a very small girl from a family of above-average ability. This family ability was fortunate since for social reasons it was now felt wise to promote an older sister from grade 6 to grade 7 and this older sister showed herself to be capable of coping with the problems arising from the unexpected promotion. Jane herself was and is a placid girl with an unusual social development which has always helped her to fit in with her coevals and with her older intellectual peers.

At the end of the school year Jane, now 9.2, was duly promoted to grade 7 to a very bright section with specialist teachers who were encouraged to work fast but also to do some work in depth. This group was tested several times during the year and Jane's scores were as follows:

Age 9.2 : Graded Arithmetic and Mathematics test. Vernon Miller. Maths age 11.10 (English norms). Standardized score 130. Percentile 97.

Age 9.2 : Bristol Achievement Tests (published by Nelson). Level 2 Mathematics. Standardized score 120. Percentile 91.

Age 9.2 : Bristol Achievement Tests. English level 2. Standardized score 132. Percentile 98.

Age 9.9 : A H 4 (Intelligence) test. Score 65. No norms under 11 but equal to about 65th percentile for 13-year-old comprehensive school children.

Age 9.9 : Wide-Span Reading Test (published by Nelson). Version 'A' First occasion. Total score 53. Percentile 99+.

Although she was the youngest girl in her class, which eventually covered a substantial part of the eighth-grade syllabus as well as their own seventh, her place was always well above the average of the class with end-of-term results mainly in the A and B categories. Four reports follow, all contributed by specialist teachers.

English   Jane is quick to learn new techniques. Good vocabulary and spelling. Reasonably imaginative, Very good at poetry, analysis, and summary work. Very good reader. Despite only average creativity is developing rapidly. By no means passive amongst older children: very quick, articulate, and logical. An example of Jane's response to a stimulus passage in her general studies is included at the end of this case study and the reader can see for himself the relevance of the report in English.

Mathematics   Jane is an extremely clever child with an academic ability far superior to that of most of her peers. She is naturally inquisitive and her regular questions during lessons display the depth of her thinking and her appreciation of the nature of mathematics. She takes very little for granted and requires a quite rigorous justification. This approach usually develops if at all at a later age and so it is doubly pleasing to find it in one so young. Fortunately Jane has lost none of her childish charm and the combination of this with her mature reasoning makes her both a pleasure to teach and an asset to the class atmosphere.

It should be noted that in her class the mathematics included all the work normally covered in the seventh and eighth grades and also some ninth-grade topics. Moreover, considerable time was spent on discussing first principles and fundamental axioms which would usually be dealt with in much less detail. Her final mark was 80 per cent and she finished third in the class behind two bright girls who were a full year older.

Science   Characteristics. Jane was studious, friendly, humorous, helpful, good worker. Actually she worked rather slowly but what she did was perfect. This meant that she rarely did all the questions in an examination.

Normally if she did not understand, one explanation was sufficient for her to master the difficulty. When set to classify objects she was one of 3 who quickly saw the point of the exercise. She was able to put biological ideas (things needed for an organism) into inventive situations, e.g., in designing a Martian man. Moreover, she saw seeds as living things while others found it hard to regard them in this way. Outside school in bush walks she tended to 'boss' her sister who was $1\frac{1}{2}$ years her senior.

General studies   Jane was in the experimental group which is referred to in Chapter 11 on the Campion Experiment. She played a full part in the group and in a subgroup. The subgroups were formed after the class had expressed their preferences on a sociometric test. One stipulation was made that each boy and girl should nominate at least one member of the opposite sex. Jane was chosen by three girls, all mutual choices, and by the most popular boy in the class, who was easily the most frequently chosen pupil in the whole class. In discussion she spoke as the spirit moved her and always sensibly. An example of her work in general studies is shown below.

The stimulus passage was as follows :

The boy stood in front of the furniture shop looking at himself in a mirror in a show-case. He racked his brains trying to remember who he was and where he had come from. There was nothing in the pocket of his short-sleeved shirt or in the pockets of his shorts to help him. The sun tan on his face, arms, and legs suggested that he had spent a lot of time in the sun. Through his mind echoed the words 'Seventeen today' but he was not sure that he was a boy of seventeen.

'What shall I do?' he asked himself. 'Shall I go and ask my mother who I am? But where is my mother and who is she?' He hesitated for a moment and then thought, 'I suppose I will just have to try and work it out myself. It's just like doing an equation.'

Looking at himself in a mirror which was in a furniture shop he saw that he had a tan all over him. 'Aha!' he thought, 'I must have been living in this country for quite a long time. Perhaps I was born here. But what is this country? That is another thing I have to find out.'

This country must have always been a hot country otherwise I would not have known to buy myself a short-sleeve shirt and shorts. And that is another reason why I might have been here long.

Suddenly he got a brain-wave. Quickly he searched his shirt pocket and found nothing there. He searched his shorts pocket and found nothing there. 'That means that this could not have happened before.' He said out loud. He racked his brains to see if he could remember anything at all. Then something came to his mind; the words were 'I am seventeen. Well that does not help much,' he thought. 'I am completely stuck. What I must do is to go around asking people who I am.' So he started to walk down the street. He had been walking for about 10 minutes when someone smiled at him and said : 'Hello Robert, how is Andy's leg?' 'Excuse me sir but I do not know who Andy is and who I am' he said. Before he got an answer he woke up finding it was nothing but a dream.

Like most bright children Jane counted up the words written from time to time. The last number recorded at the side of the paper was 227 but Jane carried on until all were told to stop. The children were told to complete the sentence they were writing. This explains Jane's rather banal final sentence.

Case study 5

Peter

By his fourth birthday Peter could read easily and do quite a lot of sums and number games; I taught him for a short while each day as he seemed so keen to learn . . . we decided to start Peter at the kindergarten when he was $4\frac{1}{2}$. His class teacher was herself a trained psychologist with four children . . . she surprised us by saying she thought Peter was far more intelligent than her own and guessed his IQ to be around 165. This was the first inkling we had that he might be a 'gifted child'. He loved school and settled down happily into a group about a year older than [himself] and was quickly learning to do addition and subtraction, writing stories and poems, telling the time, and reading anything. Because he was interested he also learnt his tables himself.

At five, after much insistence on his part, Peter started violin lessons which he took to with great enthusiasm and an obvious ability as he progressed rapidly. He was a quiet child, not very sociable or outgoing but very happy and completely absorbed in whatever he did, whether it was writing stories, designing maps, or playing in the sandpit with a plastic truck.

We [had] to move again when he was five years eleven months and on the advice of his former teacher (who felt a state school would not be adequate to cope with him) started him at a preprep school. This proved to be a mistake: he could cope with the work and was indeed moved up so many times that after a year he was with boys of $8\frac{1}{2}$ and he still came top in everything. However, it was a very formal school with no facilities for games or sport or even adequate playing space and no importance attached to arts subjects at all and we felt he was becoming far too much of a book worm; he was now wearing glasses and seldom wanted to do anything other than the three Rs. Moreover, he did not *enjoy* school.

We were recommended our local primary school which we went to see and were immediately impressed by the head mistress and the whole informal yet working atmosphere of the school. As soon as we transferred Peter we noticed the difference in him; he became far more sociable, keen to play and participate in physical activities, learned to play chess, and joined the thriving school orchestra. It seemed as though everything was attempted at the school and Peter was delighted to have so much to interest and occupy him. The head mistress gave him extra English and there were always plenty of interesting projects on hand for him to work at with a wonderful choice of books in the school library. Children were always free to come and use these books and were constantly moving from room to room or popping in to see the head mistress. There was an atmosphere of busy activity everywhere. The head herself talked to us about his intelligence and at this point we decided to join the NAGC (having read about it in the *Guardian*) although we had no problems at all.

Unfortunately we had another move. . . . After our happy experience with the primary school we automatically sent Peter and his younger sister to our nearest primary school. Before we moved, however, we visited the head master and told him that Peter's previous head mistress wanted to send a report and a personal letter about the child and his ability. The head agreed to get in touch with her before term started and we did make the point that Peter was doing more than most of his classmates although still kept with his age group.

However, some weeks after term started at the new school, because of increasing apathy from Peter and general unhappiness at home, we went to the school and asked to see his form teacher She never seemed available so we went to talk to the head teacher. He had not written to the previous school and said we were making a fuss as the child was perfectly all right. At the parents' evening the form teacher told us Peter was a good, quiet boy, no trouble at all. We asked again if he could have rather more stimulating work or if he could bring his own books to read; we enquired if there was a chess club or any music group; football or swimming – but there seemed to be no 'extras' at all. He was doing hundreds of simple sums and expected to get 60 right at a time, otherwise he had another set – work he had been doing at five or six. We were pleased to hear a class newspaper was to be started for which Peter was a writer but when he produced an article on Vietnam, he was told that sort of thing wasn't suitable for children.

At home he did nothing. He became quiet and morose, lying in front of the television, not reading or writing or taking an interest in anything.

We had another useless interview with the head master who thought we were making a lot of fuss over nothing and told us that there were 'several' children in the class as bright at Peter so the work was quite adequate and stimulating enough. We then went to see an education officer who agreed that Peter must be seen by an educational psychologist and have his IQ measured. Peter enjoyed this immensely – one of his 'best days' – and the result was found to be over 170 (Stanford-Binet) and just below 160 on the WISC. We then met the head master and education officer together to discuss how his work could be made more interesting. The psychologist had suggested he be moved up a year but this was turned down as being quite impracticable because of the fuss which would be made by other parents. Nothing new was suggested at all and we felt to continue like this would be disastrous.

Very reluctantly we decided to consider a private school. The head master tested and interviewed Peter and took him the following term, putting him in a higher class at once. Immediately the change was obvious: he came home smiling, rushed to do homework, chatted enthusiastically over tea about all the sports and team games, house competitions, etc., and then started to work on projects in his bedroom. Now he takes part in everything. He learns French, Latin and science, plays several games, goes swimming, plays his violin with the choir, belongs to the chess club, and the work is sufficiently difficult to keep him interested. There are some bright boys in his class and he certainly doesn't come top in everything but this is a very good stimulus for him and he seems to thrive on competition. The educational psychologist has visited the school and agrees that, although formal looking and old-fashioned in some respects, it is certainly far better for Peter than the primary school he so hated.

Case study 6

Carole

Carole gained a full score of 133 on the WISC, the performance score being well under the verbal score. When she was about $2\frac{1}{2}$ years, her best friend, a four-year-old girl, began to attend nursery school and so Carole was deprived of much of her companionship. Carole was keen to go to the nursery school, which admitted children at four years. Her parents explained to her that she could not go to school until she was able to read and write. A few months later, to the discomfort of the parents, Carole had acquired these arts and demanded to be sent to the nursery school to join her friend. By dint of much persuasion the head of the school agreed to admit her.

She had been talking from about a year old, and soon began to show a liking for quite long words. She was brought up in a household where the parents never talked down to her. At the infant school stage her attitudes to her parents and baby brother were favourable, but she sometimes betrayed some irritation with slower children and tended to form friendships with older children. Her favourable attitudes to her parents have been maintained and she appears to put up with her younger brother with a kind of amused tolerance. Her friendships still tend to be with children older than herself. The sociogram suggests that her coevals find her rather mature for them. In the 'Guess Who' type test, three boys identified her as the girl described.

Other signs of precocity were her beginning to learn chess at about four years, her keeping of a travel diary on a trip to Venice at 5½ years, her acquisition of some swimming medals by the age of eight, and her being promoted to the top group in her village school by the time she was eight years old. It is not surprising that she usually made friends with older children. After testing by a local psychologist, she was sent to Edgarley, where the challenge was likely to be greater than in the village school, although she received there much help and consideration.

Another common characteristic of very bright children is their capacity to exist on a minimum of sleep, and Carole, at least at home, sleeps well under the average for children of her age.

Case study 7

Mark

Identified as 'gifted' on both attainment and intelligence tests at seven years of age, on the Wechsler Intelligence Test Mark was found to have a full-scale IQ of 154+ (Verbal, 154+; Performance 154+). At age eleven, reading and mathematics tests both showed him to be in the top 1 per cent of his age group. Finding no school subject boring, Mark preferred mathematics, science, and sports. Uninterested in drawing, painting, and belonging to clubs, Mark's major interests were science, reading, sports, music, inventing games, collecting, making things, and playing outside. His family background was social class II (see editor's note).

At birth   Mark was the firstborn child of young parents in their twenties. He was a normal baby in every way. His father, who came from a working-class home, was working as a factory supervisor. He hated school and left at the earliest opportunity at the age of fourteen; he gained promotion quickly and all the time felt ambitious to achieve more. Mark's mother came from a similar social background, but stayed at school until she was sixteen. She started a professional training but discontinued it when she married, though she continued working in a clerical capacity until near the birth of her baby.

At seven years of age   Mark was continuing to be a healthy child. By this time he had a brother and a sister. His parents had improved their circumstances by going into business for themselves, something Mr. M wanted to do very much. ('I couldn't get out of the factory gates fast enough.') Mark started school at 4½ years of age and was said to settle down quickly within the first month. His progress was rapid and at seven his teacher recorded, 'This particular child is so bright that he is in a class above his age group.' He was considered to be in the top 5 per cent in relation to all children of seven in oral ability, awareness of the world, reading, creative skills, and number work. It was noted that he frequently preferred to do things on his own rather than with others and sometimes seemed to be restless and inclined to worry, but in social adjustment to adults and children he was considered normal.

At eleven years of age

INTERVIEWER'S REPORT

Mark was a very handsome boy of average height and weight. He held himself upright, perhaps a little stiffly, and when talking took a stance somewhat like a lecturer about to address a large meeting, which made him appear rather formal in behaviour. There seemed no need to spend time easing him into the situation, he was ready for anything and asked intelligent questions about the survey and its outcome.

He was a boy who could not be hurried, he seemed to have his own pace for everything and whether he was answering a straightforward question or eating a biscuit he did it in his own time, unmoved by pressure from outside to hurry or slow down. It was not necessary to suggest break periods, he decided for himself when he wanted to stop and when he wanted to begin again.

He tackled everything with interest, and had exceptional powers of concentration; once he started to do something or say something he went on until it was completed; it seemed that he could not do anything casually. He made jokes and appreciated jokes but did not laugh openly: he would give a controlled smile and a look of acknowledgement at the interviewer.

He spoke slowly and deliberately as if reflecting on each phrase.

SCHOOL REPORT

Mark was promoted to a grammar school one year early. He was put into the first year 'A' stream.

He was rated in the top 5 per cent of his age group for general knowledge, use of books, and oral ability, but one grade lower for mathematics. He was considered 'outstanding' in poetry.

His teachers described him as 'Enthusiastic about everything', but inclined to be 'concerned with his own importance and sometimes extremely serious'. His score on Stott's Social Adjustment Guide was 10, showing some 'unsettledness'.

PARENT'S INTERVIEW

INTERVIEWER: Does he enjoy school?
FATHER: He absolutely adores it. He moved to the high school last September, he's a high flier. They couldn't teach him any more at primary school. I can certainly say he received every attention there; he's enjoyed every teacher he's had. One made, what I consider, a most startling statement, 'If I'm not careful I find him running the class and I come second!' I put it down to inexperience. He was one term in that class and then moved up. He's always been eighteen months to two years younger than his friends. Physically this made it a struggle for him; physical status is very important to a youngster.

He enjoys everything hugely, nothing doesn't interest him intensely. We were a little apprehensive when we moved to the secondary school, because he was so young, but he didn't seem to be particularly perturbed at all. After his first term last Christmas his average was 80 per cent on all subjects, so obviously he's not disturbed at all. The advantage of the high school is that there are different teachers for different subjects. He still finds it confusing but it gives him a chance to progress at his own individual rate. I don't like all this streaming business, I think it tends to set a child; on the other hand I'm very pleased for my son that he gets the best advantage to bash on at his own rate. He's in the top class, it seems to be a sort of exclusive club where he gets the best of everything. The rights and wrongs of this I won't go into, but he enjoys it.

There's a wide gap between juniors and high school. I was a bit appalled at the gap between what they're expected to do there and at the high school. His friend who went up with him struggled and was very bewildered by it, but he's settled down. It was more a spur to my son. There's his physical age, I used to be a bit of a sportsman locally myself, he tried tremendously hard to get into the rugger side, he was a terrible failure, he's not that way inclined. We've coached him in cricket as much as possible and he's useful at it, and he seems to have made the first eleven cricket team. One teacher said he's full of his own importance in class, he shouts the loudest, he feels he's *got* to shout to make himself heard, to come up to their level. If he does well in cricket it will prove to him that it doesn't matter being younger. He usually enjoys P.E. It's most important that children should be allowed to progress at their own rate, it leads to happy children not out of their depth. The variety of subjects covered at that school is quite remarkable, the facilities are first-class for any hobby such as drama; the teachers are quite dedicated there to helping the children.

INTERVIEWER: What are his interests at home? Does he get bored easily?

FATHER: He gets bored during the holidays, he thinks they are a waste of time. Like most bright children he thinks he's got to be occupied every minute of every hour of every day.

He likes all sports, cricket, football and, to a lesser degree, swimming. The thing he's least interested in is art, but he will sit for hours in his own bedroom working out maths problems, he loves drawing graphs, charting the progress of various things. His interests cover almost everything, he has an intense interest in just about everything that goes on.

He occasionally helps me at work but he likes all the glamour jobs, the chores, it's virtually impossible to get him to do. I usually end up saying, 'For goodness sake go.'

He's very absent-minded, he's dependent on his mother anticipating what he needs. He's more of a hindrance than a help in the house.

He likes reading, he'd read a toffee paper, anything from Biggles to the most serious subjects. He gets himself lost in geographical books, he tries to understand biographies, he likes to understand why they were trying to achieve certain things in their lives. He still has comics every week, anything that comes to hand.

INTERVIEWER: What sort of person is he?

FATHER: He's favourably optimistic about things, he's inclined to be temperamental, occasionally difficult from his mother's point of view. He will argue right down to the last minutest detail, to the last and finest point. He drives his mother frantic at times. He has a marked lack of urgency whenever it's required, he leaves twenty minutes to go three miles to school, he wouldn't worry, something would save him. He can be extremely rude and he can be extremely thoughtful on occasions. He's most generous. His ego! He knows he's good, he's got bags of confidence. He's quiet and well spoken. There have been several occasions where he's had to stand up before an audience, and he's quite unmoved. He gets very passionate about things he's interested in, his team lost the cup final, he worked himself up all the week to Saturday afternoon, it fermented inside him, and when they lost he folded up. He went to bed, he didn't want to speak. It was amusing from our point of view, but we understood it from his.

He very rarely lies, on the only few occasions he did he was full of remorse afterwards. He's open, that's one of his good points. He detests cruelty of any sort.

INTERVIEWER: Have you thought what kind of work he might do?

FATHER: He appears to be academically biased rather than engineering and technical subjects. As long as he's prepared to go on we will back him to university if possible. I'm sure whatever he does do he will go fairly near the top.

MARK'S INTERVIEW

INTERVIEWER: Tell me about your interests.

MARK: Swimming's really my interest, and drama. I'm quite good at drama, I played quite a part in the school play. Then there's cricket, I'm doing quite well in the first-year squad. And there's violining, playing the fiddle, I don't play in the orchestra, I'm only learning. I make a few kits, plastic model kits, and I've got a kit I had in two stages, it's an electronic kit. I had the basic kit, that's number eight for Christmas, and Dad promised me if I could do well with it I could have the second kit for my birthday.

INTERVIEWER: What is it about?

MARK: Well, it makes electronic gadgets, like a burglar alarm; it's got a little resistor, the resistance of which alters if you catch light on it; if, say, you put a book on it, while it was attached to the circuit and then you lifted the book up, because of the light falling on it you make the circuit whistle and then you'd know that the book had been picked up. And you can use this, say, on a door, make a little hole at the top of a door and put it in and when the door was opened the light would fall on it, you know, it's a sort of electronic bell. It was with the second kit; with the first you could make an elementary morse set with just one earphone; it was just a one-way tapper, and you can make with the second kit a two-way morse tapper with loud speakers; and even an electronic organ – it doesn't work very well though – very difficult – as you press the metal key down it completes a certain part of the circuit, according to which part, that creates a pitched whistle. I've made an intercom, I listen to the radio at night the odd time, and television, perhaps a football match that sort of thing, and its been quite successful.

INTERVIEWER: What about art?

MARK: I do quite well in art lessons. I don't do it very much at home, not really.

INTERVIEWER: Do you collect anything?

MARK: I've got a small collection of coins, a lot brought back by relatives who've been abroad; we find some in the till, we found a Chinese coin in the till once, somebody thought it was a penny, it was a ten cash coin, that's where we get the word cash from apparently. I've got about forty coins, some old British including an 1806, I keep that specially; it's worth about a pound now. Then I collect stamps, I don't find all that much time for putting them in but I've got a lot on the waiting list.

INTERVIEWER: Which school do you go to?

MARK: I'm at the high school at the moment, since last September. I'm under age. When I was in the infants' school, well, I had about half a term's start, with a few other children; well, I was sent up to the junior department a year early, and then in my second class I was put back where I should be 'cos it was thought I couldn't cope with being the year ahead, but I was ahead of the rest of the class really in my own year; and then I was put up to the top class a year before time with another lad and then I went up to the high school.

INTERVIEWER: What is your favourite subject at school?

MARK: Well, I like them all really. The one I'm not keen on is religious knowledge; for one thing we have it last period on a Thursday which is a bit boring and the teacher doesn't care one toss if you're not learning it, he doesn't teach the sort of teaching that drives it into you. I enjoy most of the lessons, I prefer maths and science. I particularly like the maths as the maths teacher we have puts it across so enjoyably, he may be unorthodox but he teaches us quite well, he gets across to us and we *enjoy* the lessons. I am jolly good at maths, I came fifth in the form at the end of the first term.

I'm not particularly good at the crafts, metalwork, and woodwork, although the art teacher thinks quite a lot of me.

INTERVIEWER: How much do you like writing things down on paper?

MARK: I don't like that quite so much, you know, as actually *doing* something or *making* something; not so much as mathematics 'cos when we do put that down I feel I've made something.

INTERVIEWER: How much do you use books?

MARK: Well, I do read quite a lot, I've got seventy-odd books, it's touching on eighty at times when they're all in the bookcase. I've got quite a lot of Enid Blyton books – not the Noddy sort – the ones like the *Secret Mountain*, that sort of thing and *The Boy Next Door*. I've got five or six of those and I've got quite a lot of the Biggles books by Captain W.E. Johns and I have read some of these other books about space. I've got one very nice book which I had as a present; it's quite fascinating, the story of speed, how travel's developed right up to the space ship from running.

INTERVIEWER: Do you think you read more than other children?

MARK: Well, I won't say that, but I would think I do read rather better than other children in my class because – well, to recall one incident at the primary school, well the infant part of it in my last but one class I think it was, I was the only child in a class of forty who could read.

INTERVIEWER: What kind of a person are you?

MARK: That's a difficult question! Well, being underage I do get . . . I don't compare quite so well with children I live with, you know, although in certain games I do catch up with them and in some things overtake them, like in maths, that sort of thing; but no, I don't think I'm put out by the fact that I *am* underage, like my friend is, he's older than me, he's not so much underage and he's completely put out by the fact. I'm not going in for any school sports (athletic events) I won't make it, but I've made the cricket squad and I feel I'm up on level terms with the other children. I'm not rough in my ways, quite quiet really, just like other children around, apart from being underage.

INTERVIEWER: Is there anything you'd like to change about yourself?

MARK: Well, if I could I'd like to be a bit more wholehearted about football. I go in for football a bit delicately, I'd like to change that a bit and feel on equal terms with everybody when I barged in. I'd like to be as strong as the other lads, that sort of thing, it's about the only thing I'm really lacking in, I think . . . physically.

INTERVIEWER: What do you want to be when you grow up?

MARK: I don't really know, I'd like to go into a job, perhaps scientific or one which involved mathematics, but I wouldn't like to be stuck up in an office all day. I would like to go to a college or university after I leave school, of my own accord . . . or, like I say, something I'm interested in, maths–science something like that.

INTERVIEWER: Are you looking forward to being grown up?

MARK: I don't know, I'll be sorry not to be a child, but there again I'll have to wait and see when I'm grown up what it's like.

INTERVIEWER: You're eleven now, you've lived quite a few years, what do you think about life?

MARK: I think it's a bit mixed up, and it can turn around on a pinhead, it changes all of a sudden, like when my sister was taken into hospital, and my grandad died, these sort of things upset me quite a lot and they did change me.

Summary   Mark was doing exceptionally well all round, at home, at school, and in his own estimation. He had every support from home and plenty of encouragement from school.

The one thing that was a source of unease to him was the fact of being 'underage'. He referred to this time and time again. He was not as well developed physically for his age as he was intellectually. He was in an 'A' stream with children who were twelve to eighteen months older so that competition was keen for him especially in sports and P.E. His teachers needed to be very much aware of his individual circumstances if he were not to be underestimated in relation to his age. The following extracts from the sentence completion test revealed further his anxiety:

> Other children . . . sometimes leave me out of things as I am underage. My greatest worry is . . . that being underage will make me left out of school activities, although I compare quite well with the other boys in my form. My greatest fear is . . . that because of me not having very many friends of my own age at home I will feel alone and left out of life in the village.

The fact that he scored 10 on the Stott's Social Adjustment Guide also revealed his teachers' awareness of some 'unsettledness'. He appeared to be overdemanding which could well be so because as one of the youngest and smallest in the class he felt himself to be in a highly competitive situation and had to strive to draw attention to himself. He was well aware of his teachers' views as a sentence completion showed:

> My teachers think I am . . . rather concerned that I am important, very good at the subject they teach me, and some think I'm just another pupil in IA.

The overall picture was one of an exceptionally able boy of strong personality with a wide range of abilities and interests which were likely to lead him on to the university and a professional career.

Case study 8   *Think about W. S. checklist.*

Brian

Brian is the illegitimate son of a mildly subnormal mother who bore him when she was nineteen. Father is known to the family but has never concerned himself with the child. Two years ago when he was ten, mother gave birth to a second illegitimate child, a girl. Brian was badly shocked by the birth of his half-sister and for a while felt rejected. He wanted to leave school at break times and lunch times to check that his mother had not deserted him. During this period he developed a number of psychosomatic complaints. At his comprehensive school he is sometimes teased by the older boys and when the pressures become too hard for him to bear he truants.

It was clear at the beginning of his schooling that Brian was gifted. For example, he gained a score which placed him at the $97\frac{1}{2}$ percentile on the Ravens Matrices test and always scored highly on standardized group tests, though he tended to rush and become careless. It was also appreciated that problems were likely to arise because of his background. As a result the educational psychologist and school medical service were asked to take an ongoing interest in his development. Despite this they were unable to help counter the emotional shocks of the last two years. Brian's development through the primary school is interesting. He was extremely articulate from his earlier days and his grammar, which was free from local colloquialisms, was noteworthy for its correctness and breadth of vocabulary. This is quite remarkable when one considers his background.

As an infant Brian was slow to read 'openly' and was easily distracted by more interesting things. At the age of six he declared that he could not be bothered reading school books (initial reading schemes) because he could make up better stories himself – as indeed he could and did, orally! However, he soon discovered that the school had thousands of books and he immersed himself in reading. By the age of nine he had a mechanical reading of fifteen-plus. His ability to extract and collate facts was extremely good and he excelled in setting down his own ideas in diagrammatic form and then discussing them at length with an adult. Towards the end of his junior school years he had begun to turn his skill into the invention and solution of either actual or imaginary problems.

As an infant and lower junior he developed enthusiasms about specific subjects. For instance, he was a most accurate mine of information about British birds, prehistoric animals, space travel, military aircraft, warships, and equipment generally. Towards the end of his junior career he became almost morbidly interested in everything to do with Hitler and Nazism.

As Brian has grown older he tends to seek the company of adults in the school with the express purpose of engaging them in conversation. Some members of staff regard him as an 'articulate odd-ball' and 'attention seeking'. He regards all organized games as a waste of time and as a result tends to 'pop up' in odd places during play times to see if he can help, e.g., the boiler house. He is at his happiest when in the library either working on his own or in a small group.

Efforts to extend Brian during his infant and junior career would appear to be only partially successful. He was given access to a wide range of books and materials but his teachers seemed unable to cope with the examples of creative thinking he continually placed before them. There was a tendency to steer him into mundane activities instead of encouraging his mind to range widely and freely. The problems he now has in the secondary school are in many ways worse.

Badly handled — soc probs.

Case study 9

John

On the Wechsler Intelligence Test John's full-scale IQ was 143 (Verbal, 131; Performance, 147). At eleven years of age, a reading test showed him to be in the top 25 per cent of his age group, and a mathematics test placed him in the top 18 per cent. In school his favourite subjects were craft, art, science, and games, while he found music boring. Not interested in collecting, writing, music, or clubs, John enjoyed making things, painting, drawing, science, and playing outside. His family background was social class IV (see editor's note).

At birth John was a firstborn child. His birth was prolonged and for the first month of his life he suffered from convulsions. His father worked on an assembly line in a factory and his mother also worked in a factory before marriage.

At seven years of age When the record from his teachers when he was seven was consulted, it was found that he was considered *below* average in oral ability, reading, number work, and awareness of the world, although his results on the test of reading and that of arithmetic suggested he achieved more than appeared (21/30 reading score 8/10 arithmetic). From the Stott social adjustment guide, some clues are obtained about his behaviour; he was reported to be shy, wanting adult interest but could not put himself forward, could not concentrate for long, was too restless ever to work alone; however, he was a good mixer with other children, never fought and was liked. He was also reported to be attractive, well-dressed, and healthy.

At eleven years of age

INTERVIEWER'S REPORT

He brought with him a drawing of a complicated electrical experiment he had invented consisting of batteries and wires, etc. He was very cooperative in the tests, quick, competent and insightful on scientific, spatial, and nonverbal material. His drawings showed originality. He was slow and deliberate on verbal questions, his answers were restricted but generally to the point. His chief interest was inventing things and he was very definite about this, he wanted to be an inventor, 'to invent things that move'. His standard of English was low, spelling and sentence construction weak.

SCHOOL REPORT

His teachers rated him as in the middle 40 per cent of the age group for general knowledge, use of books, oral ability, and mathematics. His test scores indicated higher achievement and so did the fact that he was in an 'A' stream class (there were 45 children in it). No answers were given to the open questions about future school and job performance, nor to the personality questions on virtues and faults. He had a low Stott score so there was no indication of 'unsettledness' or 'maladjustment'.

PARENT'S INTERVIEW

MOTHER: He's a very quiet child. Well-mannered – it just seems to be natural although I keep him to it. He's got feeling for others.
INTERVIEWER: Can you say what it is you most enjoy about him?
MOTHER: He's a good child, he doesn't give much trouble.
INTERVIEWER: How does he react to being punished or corrected?
MOTHER: He gets very upset if he's shouted at for something serious, when his report was not so good. We said, 'How has this happened, you're slipping?' He got very upset. He said he'd tried and he didn't know what had happened. If he knows he's done his best and it's not up to scratch he gets upset.

INTERVIEWER: Is there anything that worries you about him?

MOTHER: Sometimes I think he hasn't as much confidence as I think he should have – just with children of his own age – he can stick up for himself if anyone picks on him, but he'd sooner forget it and not trouble.

INTERVIEWER: Does he enjoy school? What is the school like? What do you think about it?

MOTHER: Oh! yes – quite enjoys it. It seems all right, I don't seem to have too much confidence in it.

INTERVIEWER: How does he get on with school work?

MOTHER: It's very easy for him. The head master said he was about average. English is not as easy to him as arithmetic. He doesn't seem to do so much painting and drawing in primary school as he'll get at secondary. He does the sketching and painting for the school paper – he's very interested. There's no science rooms in the primary school so he can't practice – he's got a microscope I bought him the Christmas before last, a small one. He loves watching things, but not at school. I think he gets a bit bored at school.

INTERVIEWER: What type of school would you like John to go to?

MOTHER: Secondary modern, but if his ability is better he would go to a selective school. At first he was keen to go to a selective school. Now he's changed his mind. I suppose because of his friends. They don't have woodwork at grammar school and they have a lab in the secondary modern; I don't know much about the grammar type, but he's got just as much a chance, if he's got any ability, of it coming out in secondary modern as they are now.

INTERVIEWER: What sort of things does he like to do in his own time?

MOTHER: Since nine years of age his main interest is to potter around at home with a hammer and nails. He made a table – very rough – his dad helps sometimes with difficult bits of Leggo or inventions. He loves his microscope and drawing and printing. He likes to play out like other boys.

INTERVIEWER: It's early yet, but have you thought what kind of work you would like him to do?

MOTHER: No, I haven't because it would only be something he was interested in. He's always drawing – perhaps he should be a draughtsman, follow it up; only once he said he wanted to be an architect. I don't know if he really knew what it was, I said 'You've got a long way to go!'

INTERVIEWER: What sort of things does he read?

MOTHER: Comics, encyclopaedia he's got, he's always looking that up. Not the daily papers at all, not news.

INTERVIEWER: Where does he get books from?

MOTHER: I buy them, not the public library.

JOHN'S INTERVIEW

(The efforts of the interviewer to encourage John have been omitted, only questions immediately preceding his responses are quoted.)

INTERVIEWER: How much do you like school?

JOHN: Don't like it much . . . not very keen on school.

INTERVIEWER: Which subjects do you find interesting at school?

JOHN: Science, art, crafts . . . games . . . that's all.

INTERVIEWER: Which subjects do you find boring?

JOHN: Music.

INTERVIEWER: What about the others? (*He had a list in front of him. No response*.) English?

JOHN: It's all right.

INTERVIEWER: Mathematics?

JOHN: Not very much.

INTERVIEWER: What is your favourite subject?

JOHN: Crafts.

INTERVIEWER: Can you say what has made it your favourite subject?

JOHN: I like making things.

INTERVIEWER: How much do you like getting things down on paper?

JOHN: Not very much.

INTERVIEWER: What are your interests, tell me about them.

JOHN: Inventing things . . . drawing . . painting.

INTERVIEWER: Anything else? Tell me some more about your hobbies. (*No response.*) Do you ever invent games?

JOHN: Yes – invented one.

INTERVIEWER: Tell me about it.

JOHN: I forget.

INTERVIEWER: Do you ever write stories or poems at home?

JOHN: No . . . only at school . . . don't like writing them.

INTERVIEWER: How did your interest in inventing things start? (*No response.*) What do you invent? Tell me a bit about it.

JOHN: I like inventing things that move . . . I like seeing things that move, you see, so I make them meself. . . . I like seeing things that work so I make some meself.

INTERVIEWER: Is there anything you would like to do as a hobby but haven't had the chance?

JOHN: Invent a computer . . . or a robot.

INTERVIEWER: How much do you use books?

JOHN: Use them a lot in school.

INTERVIEWER: Tell me the names of some books you've read recently, say in the last month.

JOHN: Don't think I've read any.

INTERVIEWER: How many books have you of your own?

JOHN: None . . . reading books, just reading books? I've got an encyclopaedia and atlases.

INTERVIEWER: What are the other members of your family interested in?

JOHN: My brother and father are interested in football.

INTERVIEWER: Anything else, and what about your mother?

JOHN: I don't know.

INTERVIEWER: What kind of person are you?

JOHN: Person who likes inventing things.

INTERVIEWER: What do other children like about you?

JOHN: I can draw good.

INTERVIEWER: What do you want to be when you grow up?

JOHN: An inventor.

INTERVIEWER: How does a person become an inventor?

JOHN: Start when he's young.

INTERVIEWER: You've lived eleven years now, what do you think about life?

JOHN: Interesting.

INTERVIEWER: Have you ever puzzled about something because you couldn't decide whether it was real or not real?

JOHN: . . . yes . . . drawings that can be seen from two angles.

(An interesting answer, but no further elaboration evoked. His definitions of different subjects were just as brief and sporadic.)

Summary In comparisons between the test scores of a sample of specially selected gifted children John did well. His IQ and high scores on divergent thinking tests put him in the top fifteen boys. He performed on achievement tests at an above-average, but not superior level. His shyness may have been due to his difficulty with verbal expression or vice versa, but these two things go together and seemed to be preventing him from revealing more of himself in school. Although his teachers rated him as only average, he was in an 'A' stream, he received no special help of any kind though it was obvious that he needed it in English. As one of 45 in a class he was unlikely to get the individual instruction he needed to improve his spelling. He had a keen interest in science and was supported by a mother who did the best she could for him, but he needed more active help in pursuing his ideas about inventing and more contact with books if his interests were not to wane for lack of stimulation.

Perhaps John should have the last word. His essay showed the difficulty he had with spelling and sentence structure, but he had ambition and a positive outlook for his future life.

His approach to the essay was rather original, few children using a story form for their answer. He conveyed his interest in science and awareness of its special approach, he saw himself as a professor and managed to include reference to the satisfaction and pleasure of inventing.

'Imagine that you are now twenty-five years old. Write about the life you are leading, your interests, your home life, and your work at the age of twenty-five.'

> I start out from the house at seven o'clock, my work is fifty miles away and I go by car. My car is a rover and I get to work about twenty to nine. My work is in a Laborty and my name is proffesser J. I work mostly with the microscope looking at backtria and other things like it. Today I am going to try to find or make something to cure a sertian germ. I use lots of diverent things, mixing them together and – writing down each time I add another sustence what it is, and how much I use.
>
> Every time I add something to it I test it whith germs by puting them in it puting them and the subsence under a microscope and then looking at it for a few minutes and when it does not work I sterile it and add another subsence, I then do the same as I did to the one before. Just before I have my lunch I find somthing, after a while, evrything is – still. I then eat my lunch firly quily but when I came back I found it only knocked them out for a bit but the next subsance realy killed the germs and I whent home very pleased with myself.

Case study 10

Gerald

In his second year at primary school Gerald's teacher declared that he was a bad influence on the rest of the class and should probably be removed. To what, exactly, she did not specify. She seemed at the end of her tether.

He has never, apparently, been a very easy child to get on with. At seven, he was particularly puzzling. A typical day might start with his refusing to eat breakfast and claiming to be ill. Dispatched to school despite this, he might start by emerging from the cloakroom with his arms tucked down the sides of his sweater, and inside his trousers belt. 'I can't do anything today, Miss! I've got no arms.'

A chorus of other voices would greet him with a mock groan and comments like 'Don't be a lemon!' and 'Trust Gerald!' (He made his classmates laugh sometimes but more often he contrived to exasperate them.)

The teacher might say 'Who wants to get on with their cowboy and Indian pictures?' This referred to a frieze that was being painted in sections as part of a project on the Wild West. She might offer some alternatives and, while little groups formed in different parts of the room, Gerald wandered vacantly from one thing to another.

'*You* didn't finish your Indian camp bit, did you, Gerald? It was coming on awfully well . . .'

Coaxed, Gerald approached it.

Some time later, the teacher might be collared by a tearful girl, anxious about the future of the project that she and her friends were so proud of: 'Please, Miss Harding, Gerald's spoiling it all.'

'Oh, Gerald!' Pause. '*What* is that?'

Gerald would be half nervous, half delighted about what he'd done. 'Well, you see, Miss, a tornado came up and destroyed everything.'

The black whirlpool he had drawn over all his efforts of the previous afternoon was distinctly tornado-ish, once he had explained it. But Miss Harding and his classmates could only see it as a blot on what would otherwise have proved an impressive wall-full at the parents' open day. 'They do have tornados in America,' he added, as a defence against the scorn surrounding him.

Later, in a little group making careful progress towards reading, he would be conspicuous for yawning heavily, and achieving nothing. He distracted some others who tired quickly of reading, and they laughed at him. He wasn't popular with them, however, or with any of the others for that matter. He was somehow *different* from them.

In the yard, at break, a fight might develop. Sorting the opponents out, Miss Harding would very likely find Gerald at the bottom of the pile.

While others made neat houses with cuisenaire rods, and wrote down the dimensions of the walls, doors, and windows, Gerald obviously had other ideas. 'What kind of house is that, Gerald?'

'It's a *prison*, Miss.'

Although Gerald explained it was easier to measure dimensions if the cells were all the same size and you were looking down on to the top of the prison, it was clear to Miss Harding from his tone of voice that he meant it as an insult too.

The part of school that he liked best was when there was some form of music. He had been known to slip out of his own classroom when he detected that the two senior classes in the school would be listening to some music on the gramophone in the assembly hall. Here he sat in the corner, trying to be as unobtrusive as possible. His habit was discovered in the end when his teacher became suspicious that he was taking about twenty minutes to 'go to the toilet'.

At home, he was equally difficult. He never seemed to listen to prohibitions: if he was curious about the controls of the television set or the car, he twiddled them. His father had the feeling that punishing Gerald did very little good. He cried, he said he was sorry, then he repeated the act. It seemed possible that Gerald was not so much naughty as mentally handicapped.

His teacher and his parents discussed him, and the possibility of an ESN school was mooted. But this very serious step could not be made before consulting an educational psychologist at the local child guidance centre. This was arranged, when he was just eight.

When it came through, the report staggered everyone. Gerald had proved well above average on a basic intelligence test (involving understanding and use of words, shapes, numbers, and general knowledge); he was 'not suitable' for assessment on reading, because he had a specific reading problem; on a mosaic test, in which his use of materials of different kinds was observed, and his explanation of what he was doing was noted, he revealed a higher intelligence than any child the psychologist had ever tested. The report also mentioned a suspicion that he might be musically gifted, that he was an artistic and original thinker with little respect or time for formal teaching, and that he had abnormal emotional problems.

'Well,' said his teacher, 'all this doesn't make him any easier to teach.'

All the same she took advice and gave him some individual help on reading, which took account of the fact that he tended to see words in the reverse, as opposed to their correct order. And she looked for signs of 'artistic and original thinking' in what he did. His parents asked him whether he would like to learn the piano or the violin, and he said he would prefer a French horn (he wanted to be the wolf in *Peter and the Wolf*). He was allowed to join a recorder class higher up the school, and he attended a music centre run at the town hall on Saturday mornings.

Gerald is now thirteen. He is not much more popular than he used to be, but other children recognize that, although he is poor at team games, he is clever at some things, and not just 'odd'. His schoolwork, at a large comprehensive school, is very moderate. His spelling cannot match the kind of expressions he tries to use. His spoken French is reasonably good, but he finds writing it very difficult. Mathematics he enjoys in fits and starts. He has not done much science, but is regarded as promising.

But it is in music that he shines most. He plays the flute really well, in addition to three different types of recorder. He still hankers after the French horn, and will no doubt try it some time. He was found at the music centre to have a very fine singing voice. His ear is very sensitive, and he can recognize notes and reproduce them precisely and beautifully.

His parents get on with him better. But, although they like music, they do not play it, and they feel they do not have much contact with their son. Nor are they confident they are doing the best thing in keeping him at his present school. They feel he needs a balanced education – but more music too. They are surprised and rather frustrated that he is not doing better at his school work, or at making friends. This would make it difficult for him to transfer to a public school, even if they could afford it. They approached a specialist music school, but he was not up to their standard.

Their worry is that Gerald will emerge from school with, say, three or four 'O' levels, and possibly one at 'A', which will not be enough for him to go to university. At the same time, he will continue to be very good at music, but not sufficiently trained to make any kind of career in it. 'He looks like falling between two schools,' his father says.

Case study 11

Ian

At the lower junior school stage Ian gained standardized scores of 126 on a Sentence Reading test and 135 on an English Progress test. He performed less strongly on a Picture Intelligence test, gaining a standardized score of 100. At the age of eight his overall achievement was sufficiently good, however, for the school to place him in the third year junior class which was a year ahead of his own age group. He showed a good adjustment to this move.

He began learning the violin in 1965, at age ten. When his teacher left, he was sent to a neighbouring school one afternoon a week until his parents and head teacher objected to him losing half a day's schooling for half an hour's violin lesson. When a new teacher was appointed Ian was able to resume his study of the violin.

He was a quiet, self-contained boy, regarded as a 'character' by the other children because he disliked games and preferred to play, or even read about, music. With the assistance of his music teacher, Ian learned to compose and harmonize, and soon passed grades 2 and 3 in violin exams.

Even though under age, Ian passed the entrance exam to a special music school and was immediately placed in the junior and then senior orchestra. At the music school Ian was accepted as an LEA place-holder and was sent twice weekly to a college of music.

The musical director of his school describes him as 'very gifted', and says Ian has been 'coerced' into learning the piano as well as the violin. But the director also thinks Ian needs 'building up' in personality. Although he shows great technical achievement, he is too self-effacing and lacks confidence in public performance. One of the youngest boys in the fourth form, Ian ranks third musically and plays in the quartet and orchestra with older boys.

This case is of great interest from several points of view. Apart from showing how relatively 'unbalanced' and yet well 'integrated' Ian is, despite or because of his acceleration to a higher group, there is evidence of the possibly oppressive effect of parents and teachers. Here they combined to prevent the child from spending one half-day per week in another place to pursue a fairly obvious talent. Insufficient information is available for us to question this decision: it was no doubt wise in all the circumstances of the case. There is a clear need, however, to stress the implications for provision at this point; they are twofold at the very minimum:

a School staffing must be on a team basis so that all essential expertises are represented, even if peripatetic help is required to complete the team.

b Extramural provision will minimize the need to place 'general' and 'special' aspects of education in contradistinction and competition.

It needs no imagination to appreciate that without an adaptive and robust temperament, coupled with an enduring interest in the violin, we have here a case where talent could so easily have been destroyed. Had Ian been average at 'ordinary' school work, one cannot help wondering whether his musical talent would not have gone by the board altogether.

Case study 12

Anthony

The earliest contact with musical education that I can recall was a short series of private piano lessons when I was six years old. Although I was not forced into these, by any means, they were short-lived and came to nothing.

It was probably an interest in practising and theory which was lacking, rather than an interest in music, for I continued to play about on the piano, without having any actual lessons.

At this stage, the thing that made the most impression on me was my first hearing a Gilbert and Sullivan operetta at the school an older brother was attending. This became an annual event, and before each one I would take out the musical score from the public library to go over the words and music – the latter of which did not mean very much to me.

Music at the primary school consisted of hymn singing as far as I remember. There was no opportunity for instrumental music whatsoever. The only exception was one particular year (I was about ten years old) when we had a young and enthusiastic teacher, who formed a choir, taught us part songs and motets, and gave us the chance to perform before an audience. This teacher also 'discovered' that I had quite a good voice and often had me singing solo parts.

On the results of the 11+ examination I went to a secondary modern school and was placed in the 'grammar stream'. As far as music was concerned here, the emphasis was again on class singing. As for theory of music, I learned nothing in the first couple of years of secondary education. At this time my rather vague and undirected interest in music took various forms. I tried to compose 'operas'. (I would make up stories, often in verse, and put tunes to them, although I could not actually write the music down.) The tunes were in my head and I could manage to play them by ear on the piano – the melody line only, of course. I also tried taking the piano to bits to see how it worked!

By now, we had a record player at home and I was beginning to hear a few of the more familiar classics.

Eventually the music teacher began to form a small orchestra, and I discovered that a boy in my class was going to a music class and he suggested that I should go with him. This was in the evenings and was run by Mr —. On my first visit they lent me a violin so that I could practise at home. I was then fourteen years of age.

This actual involvement with music making led to a widening of my interest, and my first visits to concerts and operas.

During the following year, I realized that music was my main interest, and asked to do the 'O' level music course. Since music was not taught as an academic subject, I had the benefit of some individual tuition, which gave me the chance to make up for lost time. At this time I joined the schools orchestra, and, on the recommendation of my music teacher in school, was accepted in the youth orchestra. I toured Germany with this orchestra, giving three or four concerts in different cities. This involvement with these two orchestras introduced me to many musicians, professional and amateur, whereas previously I had known hardly any.

During my studies for the 'O' level music, the music teacher left the school, and I was left more or less stranded. However, I continued my studies alone and gained the examination.

Unfortunately, I had not passed sufficient 'O' levels to transfer to a sixth form, so my family decided to let me spend another year in the secondary school. By the end of this second year I had gained seven 'O' levels, and was transferred to the sixth form of a grammar school.

Here I received the main stimulus to my musical interest, as there was an extremely active music department, which involved me with opera, chamber music, and orchestral playing, as well as the normal class studies leading to 'A' level music. With this sudden change of the situation, however, I found myself lagging behind the others, whose musical backgrounds had been less turbulent than my own, and I realized that it meant I would either have to 'pull out all the stops' so to speak, or give up. However, with the encouragement I received I managed to catch up and finally gained three 'A' levels with a B for music and was accepted for the Bachelor of Music degree course at two universities.

As for my progress at university, it is difficult for me to assess, but at the end of my first year I was accepted for the Honours Degree course. There are about 150 music students in the university and I have been chosen to play in the orchestra on several occasions. This year, one of the professors asked myself and three other students to form a string quartet, and he tutors us in his own home. I have also been chosen to play in a concert for — when he comes to officially open the new music centre at the university.

In my first year I was recommended to do the performer's degree, but have since changed this to the writing of a thesis, which I think will be of more value to me.

This year it has been suggested that I do research – assuming that I obtain a First at the end of my third year.

Looking back, it seems that I had an interest in music from an early age, but for some reason, probably lack of opportunity, I was unable to communicate this enthusiasm to others (even learning to play the violin was someone else's suggestion) or to transform it into any sort of conventional music making. My interest was probably not nurtured in the right way from an early age – for instance, I did not see a concert or professionally produced opera until I was fourteen – the age at which I also began violin lessons.

My main instrument now is, of course, the violin, with piano lessons as an integral part of the degree course, plus three modern foreign languages.

If my life seems to have revolved around music then I have given a wrong impression, for I had little contact with it for many years. Before I was sixteen, I never considered myself primarily as a musician. I had other ambitions and was extremely interested in English literature, and had practically decided to go in for teaching. Nevertheless, some of the earliest things I can remember are connected with music, and for as long as I can recall I have had particularly strong feelings of affection and fascination for music.

REFERENCES

Barker-Lunn, J.L. (1970), *Streaming in the Primary School*, N.F.E.R.

Bereday, G.Z.F. and Lauwerys, J.A. (eds.) (1961), *Concepts of Excellence in Education. The Year Book of Education*, Evans Bros.

Bloom, B.S. (ed.) (1956), *Taxonomy of Educational Objectives. Handbook I: The Cognitive Domain*, Longman.

Boyton, P.L. (1941), 'The relationship between children's tested intelligence and their hobby participations', *J. Genetic Psychol.*, 58, 353–362.

Branch, M. and Cash, A. (1966), *Gifted Children*, Souvenir Press.

Bridges, S.A. (ed.) (1969), *Gifted Children and the Brentwood Experiment*, Pitman.

Bridges, S.A. (1973), *IQ–150*, Priory Press.

Bridges, S.A. (1975), *Gifted Children and the Millfield Experiment*, Pitman.

Bruner, J. (1966), *Toward a Theory of Instruction*, Harvard University Press.

Burt, Sir C. (1975), *The Gifted Child*, Hodder & Stoughton.

Butcher, H.J. (1968), *Human Intelligence: its nature and assessment*, Methuen.

Ciha, T.E., Harris, R., Hoffman, C. and Potter, M.W. (1974), 'Parents as Identifiers of Giftedness, Ignored but Accurate', *Gifted Child Quarterly*, 18, 191–195.

Combs, C.F. (1964), 'Perception of self and scholastic under-achievement in the academically capable', *Personnel & Guidance Journal*, 43, 47–57.

Davie, R., Butler, N. and Goldstein, H. (1972), *From Birth to Seven*, Longman.

DeHaan, R.F. and Havighurst, R.J. (Revised edition) (1960), *Educating Gifted Children*, University of Chicago Press.

D.E.S. (1977), *Gifted Children in Middle and Comprehensive Secondary Schools*, (H.M.I. Series: Matters for Discussion 4), H.M.S.O.

D.E.S. (1978a), *Mixed-Ability Work in Comprehensive Schools*, H.M.S.O.

D.E.S. (1978b), *Primary Education in England. A Survey by H.M. Inspectors of Schools*, H.M.S.O.

Devon County Council (1977), *Find the Gifted Child*, Devon Education Department, County Hall, Exeter.

Douglas, J.W.B. (1964), *The Home and the School*, MacGibbon & Kee (also in Panther Books).

Evans, K.M. (1962), *Sociometry and Education*, Routledge & Kegan Paul.

Freeman, J. (1977), 'Social Factors in Aesthetic Talent', *Research in Education*, 17, 63–76.

Gallagher, J.J. (1964), *Teaching the Gifted Child*, Boston, Allyn & Bacon.

Gear, G.H. (1976), 'Accuracy of Teacher Judgement in Identifying Intellectually Gifted Children: A Review of the Literature', *Gifted Child Quarterly*, XX, No. 4.

Gear, G.H. (1978), 'Effects of Training on Teachers Accuracy in the Identification of Gifted Children', *Gifted Child Quarterly*, XXII, No. 1, 90–97.

Getzels, J.W. and Dillon, J.T. (1973), 'The nature of giftedness and the education of the gifted' Ch. 2 in Travers, R.M.W. (ed.) *Second handbook of research on teaching*, Rand McNally & Co.

Getzels, J.W. and Jackson, P.W. (1968), *Creativity and Intelligence* New York: Wiley

Gibson, J. and Chennells, P. (1976), *Gifted Children: Looking to Their Future*, Latimer New Dimensions. Also available from NAGC, 1 South Audley Street, London WIY 5DQ.

Guilford, J.P. (1950), 'Creativity', *American Psy.*, 5, 444–454.

Guilford, J.P. (1967), *The Nature of Human Intelligence*, McGraw-Hill.

Gulbenkian Foundation (1978), *Training Musicians*, London, Gulbenkian.

Hargreaves, D.H. (1967), *Social Relations in A Secondary School*, Routledge & Kegan Paul.

Hargreaves, D.H., Hester, S.K. and Mellor, F.J. (1975), *Deviance in*

Classrooms, Routledge & Kegan Paul.

Havighurst, R.J., Hersey, J., Meister, M., Cornog, W.H. and Terman, L.M. (1958), 'The importance of education for the gifted', Ch. 1 in *57th Year Book of the National Society for the Study of Education Part II*, The University of Chicago Press.

Heim, A.W. (1970), *Intelligence and Personality*, Penguin.

Hildreth, G.M. (1966), *Introduction to the Gifted*, McGraw-Hill.

Hitchfield, E.M. (1973), *In Search of Promise*, Longman.

Hollingsworth. L.S. (1942), *Children who test above 180 IQ Stanford-Binet: Origin and Development*, World Book Co.

Hopkinson, D. (1978), *The Education of Gifted Children*, The Woburn Press.

Hoyle, E. and Wilks, J. (1974), *Gifted Children and their Education*, D.E.S.

Hudson. L.(1966), *Contrary Imaginations*, Methuen.

Hudson, L. (1968), *Frames of Mind*, Methuen.

Illingworth, R.S. and Illingworth, C.M. (1966), *Lessons from Childhood*, E. & S. Livingstone.

Jackson, S. (2nd ed.) (1971), *A Teacher's Guide to Tests and Testing*, Longman.

Jacobs, J.C. (1970), 'Are we being misled by fifty years of research on our gifted Children?' *Gifted Child Quarterly*, 14, 120–123.

Jensen, A.R. (1973), *Educational Differences*, Methuen.

Keating, D.P. (ed) (1976), *Intellectual Talent: Research and Development*, Johns Hopkins University Press.

Kellmer-Pringle, M.L. (1970), *Able Misfits*, Longman.

Kellmer-Pringle, M.L. and Varma, V.P. (eds.) (1974), *Advances in Educational Psychology 2*, Hodder & Stoughton.

Kellmer-Pringle, M.L., Butler, N.R. and Davie, R. (1966), *11,000 Seven-Year-Olds*, Longman.

Kerry, T. (1978), 'Bright Pupils in Mixed Ability Classes,' Br. Educ. Res. J., 4, No. 2, 103–111.

Lawrence, D. (1978), 'Remedial help: attitudes matter most', *The Times Ed. Supp.* (Correspondence) 21 July, No. 3289.

Lawton, D. (1975), *Class, Culture and the Curriculum*, Routledge & Kegan Paul.

Laycock, S.R. (1957), *Gifted Children*, Copp Clark, Toronto.

Lovell, K. and Lawson, K.S. (1970), *Understanding Research in Education*, Hodder & Stoughton.

Lytton, H. (1971), *Creativity and Education*, Routledge & Kegan Paul.

Malone, C.E. and Moonan, W.J. (1975), 'Behavioural Identification of Gifted Children', *Gifted Child Quarterly*, XIX, No. 4, pp.301–306.

Nash, R. (1973), *Classrooms Observed*, Routledge & Kegan Paul.

Nash, R. (1976), *Teacher Expectations and Pupil Learning*, Routledge & Kegan Paul.

Newland, T.E. (1976), *The Gifted in Socioeducational Perspective*, Prentice-Hall, New Jersey.

Newson, J. and Newson, E. (1977), *Perspectives on School at Seven Years Old*, George Allen and Unwin.

O'Connor, M. (1977a), Your Child's Primary School, Severn House.

O'Connor, M. (1977b), Your Child's Comprehensive School, Severn House.

Ogilvie, E. (1973), *Gifted Children in Primary Schools*, Schools Council Research Studies, Macmillan Education.

Painter, F. (1976), 'Research into attainment levels of gifted British primary school children' in Gibson, J. and Chennells, P. (eds.) *Gifted Children: Looking to their future*, Latimer New Dimensions.

Painter, F. (1977), *Gifted Children: Their Relative Levels of Scholastic Achievement and Interests: Teachers' Views on Their Educational Needs*, SSRC Project, pub., Pullen Publications, Knebworth, Herts.

Parkyn, G.W. (1948), *Children of High Intelligence: a New Zealand Study*, New Zealand Council for Educational Research, Oxford Univ. Press.

Pegnato, C.C. (1958), *An evaluation of various initial methods of selecting intellectually gifted children at Junior High School level*, Unpublished Doctoral Thesis, Pennsylvania State University.

Pegnato, C.C. and Birch, J.W. (1959), 'Locating gifted children in junior high schools: A comparison of methods', *Exceptional Children*, 25, 300–304.

Pickard, P.M. (1976), *If You Think Your Child Is Gifted*, Allen and Unwin.

Povey, R.M. (1972a), *Intellectual Abilities*, Hodder & Stoughton.

Povey, R.M. (1972b), *Exceptional Children*, Hodder & Stoughton.

Povey, R.M. (1975), 'Educating the gifted', *Ass. Ed. Psychologists Journal*, Summer, Vol. 3, No. 9.

Rapoport, R. and Rapoport, R. (1971), *Dual Career Families*, Penguin.

Rapoport, R., Rapoport, R. and Strelitz, Z., (1977), *Fathers, Mothers and Others*, Routledge & Kegan Paul.

Raven, J.C. (1965), *Guide to Using the Coloured Progressive Matrices*, H.K. Lewis.

Robb, G. (1974), 'The education of gifted children' in Kellmer-Pringle,

M.L. and Varma, V.P. (eds.) *Advances in Educational Psychology 2*, Hodder & Stoughton.

Rowlands, P. (1974), *Gifted Children and Their Problems*, Dent.

Schools Council (1972), *Working Paper 42: Education in the Middle Years*, Schools Council.

Sears, R.R. (1977), 'Sources of Life Satisfications of the Terman Gifted Men', *Am. Psych.*, Feb, 119–128.

Sears, P.S. and Barbee, A.H. (1977), 'Career and life satisfaction among Terman's gifted women.' In Stanley *et al*. *The Gifted and the Creative: A fifty year perspective*, Johns Hopkins University Press.

Shields, J.B. (1968), *The Gifted Child*, N.F.E.R.

Spooncer, F.A. (1972), *Group Reading Assessment*, Hodder & Stoughton.

Spooncer, F.A. (1976), *The Assessment of Reading*, Hodder & Stoughton.

Stanley, J.C., George, W.C. and Solano, C.H. (eds.) (1977), *The Gifted and the Creative: A fifty year perspective*, John Hopkins University Press.

Stones, E. (ed.) (1970), *Readings in Educational Psychology*, Methuen.

Stott, D.H. (1976), *The Social Adjustment of Children*, Hodder & Stoughton.

Taylor, B. (1978), *Parents' Guide to Education*, David and Charles.

Tempest, N.R. (1974), *Teaching Clever Children 7–11*, Routledge & Kegan Paul.

Terman, L.M. (ed.) (1925), *Genetic Studies of Genius*, Vol. I: *Mental and Physical Traits of a Thousand Gifted Children*, Stanford University Press, California.

Terman, L.M. and Merrill, M.A. (1960), *Stanford-Binet Intelligence Scale*, Third Revision Form L–M N.F.E.R., Harrap.

Terman, L.M. and Oden, M. (1959), *Genetic Studies of Genius*, Vol. V: *The Gifted Group at Mid-Life*, Stanford University Press, California.

Torrance, E.P., Bruch, C.B. and Goolsby, J.M. (1976), 'Gifted children study the future'. In Gibson, J. and Chennells, P. (eds.) *Gifted Children: Looking to their Future*, Latimer New Dimensions.

Vernon, P.E., Adamson, G. and Vernon, D.F. (1977), *The Psychology and Education of Gifted Children*, Methuen.

Wall, W.D. (1960a), 'Highly intelligent children: Part 1', *Educ. Research 2*, 101–110.

Wall, W.D. (1960b), 'Highly intelligent children: Part 2', *Educ. Research*, 2, 207–217.

Ward, V.S. (1961), *Educating the Gifted*, Charles E. Merrill Books, Columbus, Ohio.

Warnock, H.M. (1978), *Special Educational Needs*, Report of the Committee of Enquiry into the Education of Handicapped Children and Young People, H.M.S.O.

West Sussex County Education Committee: Psychological Service (1974), *Gifted Children*, West Sussex County Council, County Hall, Chichester.

White, J. (1970), 'The Bloafed and Gifted', The *Times Ed. Supp.*, 20 Nov., No. 2896.

Worcester, D.A. (1956), *The Education of Children of Above Average Mentality*, Nebraska University Press, Lincoln.

Young, D. (1964), *Non-Readers Intelligence Test*, Hodder & Stoughton.

Young, D. (1973), *Oral Verbal Intelligence Test*, Hodder & Stoughton.

Subject Index

international year of, 70
classroom organization, 18ff, 30, 116,
    128ff, 141, 173ff, 187
class size, 43, 141, 149
collecting, 36, 116, 153, 198, 212, 217,
    221
communism, 106
community service, 63
convergent/divergent thinking, 10,
    11, 131, 225
counselling, 3, 49, 68, 73ff, 127, 145
counsellor, 2, 69, 75, 76ff
craft, 33, 34, 60, 66, 121, 218, 221
creativity, 7, 11, 124, 136, 188, 207
creative
    activities, 136, 160
    writing, 33, 37, 45, 137
culture générale, 94, 100
curriculum, 4, 21ff, 30ff, 58, 60, 62,
    66, 77, 95, 99ff, 109, 115ff, 123ff,
    159, 164ff, 172ff, 206
    tropopause, 131, 175

dance, 26, 48, 94
Daily Telegraph, 169
day release, 22
debating, 36, 40
Denmark, 104
Democracy, 94, 95, 96, 99, 105, 106
DES, 1, 16, 22, 23, 26, 27, 41, 42, 46,
    48, 54, 57, 66, 69, 80, 103, 118,
    138, 140, 175
Devon County Council, 115
DHSS, 66, 68, 73
doctors, 64, 65, 74, 109, 145, 154, 220
drama, 48, 66, 136, 216

education
    act, 48
    classical, 101, 104
    comparative, 92ff

comprehensive, 53, 55, 98, 100,
    102
democratization, 95, 98
elementary, 100
further, 98
general, 60, 62
liberal, 94
modern, 101
musical, 55ff
officers, 122, 141
secondary, 95, 101, 137
technical, 101, 104, 178
tertiary, 137
theory of, 97
vocational, 101, 104
educationist, 3, 22, 45, 54, 56, 121
EEG, 201
egalitarian, 53, 54, 94, 95, 98
electronics, 66, 137, 216, 217
elitism, 4, 18, 50, 54, 66, 92, 95, 99,
    101, 105
England, 101ff
English, 33, 34, 47, 162, 163, 170,
    177, 178
enrichment, 4, 21ff, 42, 47, 68, 96,
    114, 116, 131, 132ff, 156, 159,
    172ff, 194, 206
encyclopaedia, 152, 165, 198, 224
environment, 13, 90, 125, 133, 148
environmental sciences, 60, 176, 177,
    180, 183
erasmian ideal, 94, 101, 106
ESN, 2, 18, 62, 193, 201, 220, 228
equality, 53, 110
    of opportunity, 53, 94, 95
Essex
    education authority, 121
    working party, 123ff
Europe, 3, 93, 97ff
excellence, 54, 56, 80, 93, 94, 100,
    102, 103
    centres of, 58, 59

Index of Names

The Harper Education Series has been designed to meet the needs of students following initial courses in teacher education at colleges and in University departments of education, as well as the interests of practising teachers.

All volumes in the series are based firmly in the practice of education and deal, in a multidisciplinary way, with practical classroom issues, school organisation and aspects of the curriculum.

Topics in the series are wide ranging, as the list of current titles indicates. In all cases the authors have set out to discuss current educational developments and show how practice is changing in the light of recent research and educational thinking. Theoretical discussions, supported by an examination of recent research and literature in the relevant fields, arise out of a consideration of classroom practice.

Care is taken to present specialist topics to the non-specialist reader in a style that is lucid and approachable. Extensive bibliographies are supplied to enable readers to pursue any given topic further.

Meriel Downey, General Editor

New titles in the Harper Education Series

Mathematics Teaching: Theory in Practice by T.H.F. Brissenden, University College of Swansea

Approaches to School Management edited by T. Bush, J. Goodey and C. Riches, Faculty of Educational Studies, The Open University

Linking Home and School: A New Review 3/ed edited by M. Craft, J. Raynor, The Open University, and Louis Cohen, Loughborough University of Technology

Control and Discipline in Schools: Perspectives and Approaches by J.W. Docking, Roehampton Institute of Higher Education

Children Learn to Measure: A Handbook for Teachers edited by J.A. Glenn, The Mathematics Education Trust

Curriculum Context edited by A.V. Kelly, Goldsmiths' College

The Curriculum of the Primary School by A.V. Kelly and G. Blenkin, Goldsmiths' College

The Practice of Teaching by K. Martin and W. Bennett, Goldsmiths' College.

Helping the Troubled Child: Interprofessional Case Studies by Stephen Murgatroyd, The Open University

Children in their Primary Schools by Henry Pluckrose, Prior Weston School

Educating the Gifted Child edited by Robert Povey, Christ Church College, Canterbury

Educational Technology in Curriculum Development 2/e by Derek Rowntree, The Open University

The Harper International Dictionary of Education by Derek Rowntree, The Open University

Education and Equality edited by David Rubinstein, Hull University

Clever Children in Comprehensive Schools by Auriol Stevens, Education Correspondent, The Observer

Values and Evaluation in Education edited by R. Straughan and J. Wrigley, University of Reading

Middle Schools: Origins, Ideology and Practice edited by L. Tickle and A. Hargreaves, Middle Schools Research Group